Bobbi,
Mae West said,
"One life is enough if
live it well."
To living life at its
best.
Greg

SAMSARA

Between Two Worlds

[signature]

Greg Murphy

FriesenPress

Suite 300 - 990 Fort St
Victoria, BC, V8V 3K2
Canada

www.friesenpress.com

Copyright © 2020 by Greg Murphy
First Edition — 2020

All rights reserved.

Edited by Kent Baker and Syr Ruus.

No part of this publication may be reproduced in any form, or by any means, electronic or mechanical, including photocopying, recording, or any information browsing, storage, or retrieval system, without permission in writing from FriesenPress.

ISBN
978-1-5255-6616-5 (Hardcover)
978-1-5255-6617-2 (Paperback)
978-1-5255-6618-9 (eBook)

1. BIOGRAPHY & AUTOBIOGRAPHY, PERSONAL MEMOIRS

Distributed to the trade by The Ingram Book Company

Dedication

This book is dedicated to my dear friend Eddie, who died much too soon and to all the "Jack's" of the world who wish only to peer into the "Rabbit Hole" but who end up getting swallowed alive.

> *"Each and every life, it seems, is bounded by a world of dreams"*
>
> The Moody Blues

Disclaimer

This story follows a certain pattern of my life as I journeyed through these worlds photographing and documenting various aspects of life as I attempted to understand the zeitgeist of the times and where we were heading. During these times I was exposed to, educated and influenced in esoteric ways not otherwise possible. I saw firsthand how the pursuit of money and the development of ego can corrupt the strongest people and destroy the best of relationships.

I met scores of interesting people and had many adventures that have inspired this story.

While there are real people and real events in it, this account contains characters who are composites of the many interesting people I met or heard about on my travels. Some of the adventures are also condensed, embellished or recast to tell the story that I want to tell. Also much of it took place years ago and memories are seldom perfect.

In some ways this is a timeless tale...the prodigal son...high stakes adventure...sinners and saints...heroes and villains...intrigue, trust, love, betrayal, life and death...the timeless dance of life—Samsara.

While this story is attempting to convey the essence of my experiences, any similarity between people depicted in it and anyone living or dead is purely coincidental.

Foreword

When Greg asked me to write a foreword to his novel, it occurred to me that his novel might actually be considered a foreword to my life.

For as long as I can remember, Greg was the Uncle, my father's best friend, who gave me the greatest gift of all: a sense of adventure and courage to follow my dreams. While some children were regaled with fairy tales, I was told real life stories of lands far away, airplane rides across oceans, van treks on one way switch backs, celebrations in the desert, languages I never knew existed, crazy characters seemingly pulled from the stuff of dreams.

I may have lived in tract-home suburbia, but because of Greg, it never occurred to me that this is where I would stay. His visits gave my childhood color, excitement and the confidence to follow my own north star -- becoming a TV writer, creating my own stories of adventure and living an extraordinary life in Los Angeles and beyond.

When Greg started writing this story — it's really tough to pin a date down, as I believe he's been writing this in his head for decades — there was a bit of skepticism. Writing a novel is tough enough, but writing a novel that would encapsulate the spirit and eccentric principles by which Greg has tried to live his life by might be damn near impossible. How to wrangle such spark and chaos into an ordered stack of pages? And yet here we are.

This book not only represents an enormous accomplishment and a wonderful read, it's a stunning ode to the man who wrote it: endlessly positive, generous to a fault, open, curious, hilarious and kind. It's a tale of misadventure, but at its heart, it's an epic love story to a life well-spent. I could not be more proud of my mentor. I love you dearly. To many more adventures!

Sheri Elwood
Los Angeles, Ca
04.01.20

Samsara: Sanskrit... To wander.. continuously, between life, death and rebirth

Introduction

This is the mostly true story of a young lad from a well-to-do middle class family who came of age during the turbulent sixties.

Disillusioned with the state of world affairs, he was driven by a burning desire to see the world before it was possibly destroyed by catastrophic nuclear events or irreversibly altered by out of control industrial pollution, political corruption and proxy wars.

Deeply affected by the death of his best friend, he set out on an adventure-quest to see the world and find some meaning in the madness.

Jack O'Brians journey will take you on a wild ride through the drug-fueled counter culture of the sixties, seventies and eighties...from the rugged coast of Nova Scotia to the hippie enclaves of Bombay and Goa, India...to the wilds of Afghanistan and the hidden hash farms of Morocco as he is swept along with a group of international hash smugglers over a span of fifteen years.

Samsara is a revealing zeitgeist of the era and Jack's inner struggle to recognize his core values and find his path toward them.

Table of Contents

Part One

Chapter 1: Intrigue in Kashmir 1

Chapter 2: The Takeover of America: November 22/1963 7

Chapter 3: The Late Sixties: Major Shift in Social Values 15

Chapter 4: Learning the Ropes 21

Chapter 5: Death of My Friend 25

Chapter 6: The Times, They Are A-Changing 29

Chapter 7: Friends and Lovers 39

Chapter 8: Heading to Kashmir, March 1972 41

Chapter 9: Srinagar, India 51

Chapter 10: Heading Home via Athens 65

Chapter 11: Chance Encounters of the Most Amazing Kind 69

Chapter 12: Cosmic Connections 75

Chapter 13: Greece to Turkey: Test of Friendship and the Kindness of Others 83

Chapter 14: Turkey and Iran: Danger and Foreboding 93

Chapter 15: Bombay and Goa: Land of the Freaks 101

Chapter 16: Heading to Kashmir January 1973 119

Chapter 17: No Man's Land 129

Chapter 18: Kathmandu February 1973 133

Chapter 19: Goa after Nepal, February 1973 139

Chapter 20: Visions in the Sky. 145

Chapter 21: Hitch-Hiking Through the Desert 153

Chapter 22: Conflict and Connections. 161

Chapter 23: Afghanistan 167

Chapter 24: Dangerous Circumstances. 177

Chapter 25: Amritsar. 191

Chapter 26: Delhi 201

Part Two 209

Chapter 27: Back to Canada. 211

Chapter 28: European Re-Connect 215

Chapter 29: Spring '74 227

Chapter 30: Adventures in Ketama. 249

Chapter 31: Morocco-Holland Connection Summer & Fall '74 . . . 257

Chapter 32: Enjoying the Life 74-75 265

Chapter 33 : The Big Time 269

Chapter 34: Bad Times. 277

Chapter 35: Heading East From Amsterdam 289

Chapter 36: PADI 1977 293

Chapter 37: Feet in Both Worlds 309

Chapter 38: Near the End. 323

Chapter 39: Closing In 335

Epilogue 339

Afterword. 343

Acknowledgements 347

Chapter 1

Intrigue in Kashmir

I was wrenched from my sleep by a ferocious racket next to my head. Someone or something was violently pummeling the window beside my bed. Was some wild creature about to tear through the wall and rip me apart?

It was in the wee hours of the morning sometime in mid-March, 1972 and I was sound asleep on a tourist houseboat on Dal Lake, Kashmir, in the remote Indian Himalayan Mountains.

Instinctively, I flung off the heavy weight of blankets pressing me into the bed and sprang to the window, yanking back the heavy drapes. There, directly in front of me, just inches away, separated only by a thin pane of glass and some wire mesh was a most hideous, nightmarish creature, insanely pulsating on the outer screen. It was a giant bat with at least a twenty-four inch wingspan screeching like an insane banshee. I reeled in shock flinging the drapes closed as I stumbled backwards tripping over my own feet and fell, crashing to the floor, my heart pounding like a jackhammer.

The reality of my situation struck me full force like a whack in the forehead with a frozen boot. Fuck! I did it this time! Was I totally insane? Maybe I should have thought this through a little better... I was just a regular guy from Halifax, Nova Scotia, Canada, a sea-swept-backwater at that time, relatively speaking; a whole other world. I'd just turned twenty-three and had made my way via Amsterdam, Athens, Istanbul, Tehran and Delhi, finally arriving here in Srinagar, Kashmir.

I'd come on a whim with a vague plan to ship back ten kilos of hashish to Canada hidden in furniture, but I never really thought about big, sinister looking bearded men wrapped in heavy woolen, hooded capes called *phirans--w*ild looking characters who could easily cut my throat and dispose of my body in the lake, weighted down with rocks, or just leave my corpse somewhere for the feral beasts to devour... never to be found. These thoughts mushroomed in my head in a kaleidoscope of panic. I could just become another foreigner...disappeared...

I'd already played my hand so they knew I had cash with me. A few hundred dollars was considered a vast amount in this remote region of the world and I had three thousand dollars with me...

Just a few hours earlier I'd met with a couple of these intimidating looking characters through Iqbal, the owner of my houseboat. He had arranged a meeting with them after I had confided in him "the purpose of my mission", as he termed it.

As the afternoon merged with approaching darkness, a heavy fog descended over the lake imparting an isolated, eerie feeling on an already lonely place. As I sat in the parlor contemplating my fate, a *shikara,* a small gondola type boat, ubiquitous to the region, emerged from the gloomy fog. Silent and foreboding, the specter drew nearer appearing like a phantom gliding over the inky gunmetal surface with barely a ripple.

With a bump that shook me from my reverie, Iqbal and his two henchmen arrived. Stealthy climbing the three steps to the ornately carved veranda, leaning for ward and clutching their *phirans* close, first one then the other, stepped through the doorway of my houseboat, where, before my eyes, they morphed into fierce looking giants, well over six feet tall. I don't know what I was expecting but surely not these wild, murderous looking characters!

After exchanging our *Salaams, (greetings)* we moved to a big, round walnut table in the back dining area. Washed by the faint yellowish light of a dimly lit oil lantern, which added a ghost-like quality making it feel more like a séance, we spoke in hushed tones in a most clandestine manner, with Iqbal acting as interpreter. Weird shadows danced on the wall making it feel all the more macabre.

Summonsing forth my most *macho* bravado, I made my pitch to these dangerous looking cohorts about wanting to buy a few kilos of hash, have it concealed inside furniture and shipped to Canada.

"No problem", they responded in unison. No problem at all.

"Everything is possible" they emphasized while placing their hands over their hearts, down-cast eyes and bowed heads accented by that quirky little head bobble that is so typical of Indians. "No Problem" was their mantra. I was assured of the very best quality of hash, for there was, to quote Iqbal, "none better in the whole valley."

I could feel these descendants of old donkey traders from countless generations past sizing me up with their piercing black eyes shaded by the thickest, bushy, black eyebrows I'd ever seen, all the while assuring me with these most solemn gestures of their sincerity.

Yet I was still somewhat naive, trusting in the basic goodness of people every where, but, finding myself here in this far away place, I figured I'd better tread lightly, play their game, be a businessman and show no sign of weakness.

I told them I only had five hundred dollars for a small trial run and this would have cover the costs to buy the hash and the furniture and whatever other expenses were involved… like paying off one of their "brothers" in customs or a relative that worked in shipping…whatever the case may be, and, if it worked out I'd be back with thousands of dollars for much bigger shipments. This was "Just the beginning," I explained, hoping to insure my safe passage out of Kashmir and possibly establish an on-going relationship.

With everything finely "hashed out," they said they'd be back for me tomorrow night and we would go to another "brother's" factory, just across the lake in Srinagar town where we would make final arrangements for the furniture according to my instructions.

After bidding me their best goodbye, (Salaams) they slipped away in their shikara, gliding silently away upon the black water, absorbed by the somber shroud of darkness that isolated me from the rest of the world.

The servants turned up the oil lamps while I moved to a big, overstuffed chair in the comfortable living room area, where I flopped in front of the glowing red embers of a small wood stove, the only source of heat.

I was feeling quite elated, perhaps even a bit cocky. I had completed the first step in accomplishing my "mission" and who knows, I might actually pull this off. As I sat there pondering my situation while eyeing my "servants"; three young Kashmiri boys and their father, Mohammed, I thought "this was the kind of adventurous life I could get used to"…

The boys squatted on the floor close by, like frogs ready to pounce, eager to attend to my every need-- a cup of tea, offer of a more comfortable chair, more cushions, perhaps some food. Springing into action to light my cigarette, if I reached for my pack or if I looked like I might stand up, they would scramble to move a table or anything that might be in my way.

This service, "totally duty," as they referred to it, continued even to the point of trying to tuck me into bed, in the most innocent way, when the time came. Hilarious! ...and so to sleep...perhaps...to dream....

And never did I dream that a year and a half later I'd find myself wasted away in a rat-infested hotel in Old Delhi after a life-altering odyssey through Afghanistan, Pakistan and India....

Chapter 2

The Takeover of America: November 22/1963

Halifax, where I was born and grew up, was the epicenter of the world's mightiest man-made explosion prior to the detonation of the first atomic bomb invented by Robert Oppenheimer and his team of scientists. (They learned much from the Great Halifax Explosion).

In 1917, during the first world war, a French ammunition ship, The Mont Blanc, laden with TNT and other explosives bound for Europe, collided with a Belgian relief ship in thick fog in Halifax harbor and exploded, destroying a large part of the city, killing two thousand people instantly and injuring another nine thousand.

My neighbors and dear friends, the Earls, were a family that had experienced first hand the effects of the horrific Halifax Explosion. Blinded by flying glass and blown through walls, several members of that family would recall over the years, during casual kitchen chats, the events of that terrible day. Those stories, along with our school drills on how to react to a nuclear attack very much impressed on me the fragility and uncertainty of life...how you can be here one moment and gone the next--just like That!

I considered myself very fortunate to be part of this extended family of survivors...

In our schools, during the fifties era of the cold war, we had drills on how to react to a nuclear attack as well as educational talks and film footage about the catastrophic, annihilative force of nuclear attack and fallout. I remember feeling anxious and threatened, especially about the horrific effects of radiation on your body. I removed my ring because I didn't want some doctor to have to chop off my finger as my body swelled from grotesque, radiation poisoning.

The world had changed. It had become a ticking time-bomb, a truly dangerous place where no one would ever *really* be safe again. The possibility of nuclear annihilation had become our new reality-- Robert Oppenheimer's quote from the *Bhagavad Gita* that fateful day, July 16, 1945 at the Trinity nuclear test site in New Mexico when they exploded the first atomic bomb, said it all. "I am become death, the destroyer of worlds."

≈

The old neighborhood I grew up in was one of *those places* where life happened in the streets. This was the era before television when neighbors were much more social and everyone knew everyone. The women, mostly housewives, talked over their fences while hanging laundry out to dry; the kids ran amok through the streets and backyards playing hide and seek. Neighbors congregated on each other's doorsteps and chatted long into the warm summer evenings...Life was simple...life was sweet...or so it seemed to me as a young boy...and then things changed...

I was fourteen when I arrived home from school that afternoon of November 22, 1963, to find my mother sitting in front of the television with tears streaming down her cheeks. President John F. Kennedy, the hope of the free world, had been assassinated and the world would never be the same. Along with her and millions of others around the world, I felt the loss as an enormous personal tragedy.

What now?

This seemed too big, too significant; it felt like something major had shifted in America and, indeed, the world. As a young boy I didn't quite comprehend the ramifications or the magnitude of this world-altering event, but upon reflection, a few years later, I felt that the forces of evil, a powerful criminal element, had suddenly gained the upper hand in a world struggling for its humanity; A new reality born of bloodshed was spawned in that moment, destined to reshape America and the world.

I felt a sense of anxiety even at that young age. I'm quite certain that JFK's assassination along with a few other defining moments in history, and a few personal near death experiences, had a profound effect on my psyche, influencing my *Samsara*-- my journey toward understanding.

≈

Frank Earl, the father of the afore-mentioned Earl family and I became the best of friends over time, even though Frank was my father's age. He was a major influence in my life. He showed me what "Real" was.

After returning from France where he was badly wounded in action during the World War II invasion of Normandy, Frank started a carpet installation business and I worked for him part-time while in high school. Most of his work took place around Lunenburg, an historic town on the South shore of Nova Scotia, an area steeped in legend and folklore, including ghost ships, pirates and rum-runners. It was the home of the famous fishing and world champion racing schooner "Bluenose," captained by Angus Walters. Walters and such men were of a culture and a time described as an era of "Wooden ships and Iron men."

The rum-runners of the twenties and thirties probation era intrigued me most and some of those mansions Frank and I worked in were the homes of now respectable rum smugglers cum businessmen--politicians, a police chief and many other of these men who had made their fortunes smuggling rum in small fishing boats from the French islands of St. Pierre and Miquelon, off the Newfoundland coast, and delivering it down along the Eastern US seaboard to the likes of Al Capone and other notorious gangsters.

Some of these "old salts" made a great impression on me. I admired them for their courage, bravado and lack of bullshit. What made the greatest impression on me however, was the fact that nobody cared about how these old outlaws had amassed their fortunes. Many were now considered pillars of society, the financial backbone of the area. The fact that they had made their fortunes illegally was of little concern to anyone. If anything, they had become folklore heroes.

Often, after we finished our work, out would come the traditional drink of the south shore, a bottle of black rum, and more than once we got a good buzz on with these old guys. I was the wheelman on the long drive home, as Frank was usually a bit more corked than me. It was on these occasions that Frank and I truly deepened our connection. We discussed many things, from life in the trenches to what was really important--the honest approach to life versus the bullshit approach and the importance of integrity and living a life you believed in.

~

My first "Near death experience" (NDE) occurred in my backyard in 1963 when I was fourteen. We all had bows and arrows in those days--Very powerful fiberglass bows with deadly, steel-tipped, wooden arrows.

I was struck on that exact pinpoint of my chin by an arrow shot by one of Frank's sons. It ricocheted off a cardboard box we had hanging from a tree and that steel point arrow miraculously bounced off my chin bone, leaving only a tiny scar, instead of glancing upward and in through my teeth and throat or downward and through my neck, either of which scenario quite likely would have been fatal.

Another NDE occurred while swimming at a local yacht club. I sprang up onto a floating dock where my fingers found an electrical outlet for the boats. Caught in the grip of an indescribable violent force that throttled me about like a rag doll as the electric current ravaged me for what seemed a long time before I was hurled back into the water, dazed and disoriented but alive...just another day.

Had I fallen forward instead of back, it would have been my last day.

I was often a target of the saintly Sisters of Charity who commanded the Catholic public school I attended from kindergarten to grade nine. Because of my rebellious Irish spirit, revolutionary heart and refusal to comply with their dictatorial demands, intended to turn us malleable Innocents into obedient, unquestioning robots, I suffered their wrath through many "strappings", and other forms of psychological punishment, which only strengthened my resolve to rebel against their tyranny.

Around the age of fifteen, as my interests expanded into the realms of girls, booze, old cars, music, and all those good things, I began to hang out with a group of wilder kids who lived just a few blocks away and had a funky old clubhouse in their backyard they called "The Shack". This is where I met Mort. He was a short, solidly built, bull of a guy with a sparkle in his eye, a quick intelligence and a mischievous laugh. We would become lifelong friends and allies.

I had my first toke (marijuana high) in 1967. I was eighteen. I couldn't believe it! I had always been conditioned that *drugs were drugs*; there was no distinction between them. They would all dull your mind and drag you down into a soul-decaying spiral of madness.

But this marijuana high I experienced was so light, not anything like I had been led to believe. If anything, things were clearer and more real, not all dopey and confused. It was not the "Reefer Madness" nonsense that had been foisted on American and Canadian public since the 1930's.

The first thing I thought was that I had been lied to. The second thing was; I could do business with this in good conscience. Being a natural born entrepreneur, I reasoned if government could sell alcohol and tobacco, I would have no problem selling cannabis, that is, if I ever had any to sell... it was just a passing thought...

This was the late sixties....The cultural revolution was exploding. The attitudes of youth towards "established" social behavior were being ripped apart: sexuality, music, fashion! All over North America there were ongoing protests against unjust wars and the wanton destruction of our environment...

for profit of the few. I was very much influenced by all of this and like so many of my generation, I feared for our future.

Many of us were striking out against the establishment as never before. We weren't buying into the "Work for the corporation" philosophy, where you were expected to conform to society's projected mandate without question. Whether you like it or not was immaterial: Just sign on, do as you're told, shut your mouth, be a good robot, let others decide your fate... work for forty years, get your gold watch and retire to your place in the sun.

Important Future Warning from the sixties: You'll need sunscreen because we will knowingly destroy the ozone but that's OK, you'll adapt, that's what we do. And those that don't will die of cancer.

Chapter 3

The Late Sixties: Major Shift in Social Values

We were crossing the threshold of a new era. Social values were rapidly changing.

Previously taboo subjects were being discussed openly. I thought that since I had been lied to about marijuana, perhaps many of the other street drugs were not half as bad as they were made out to be either.

Compared to some of the crazy experiences my friends and I previously had with alcohol, which included getting violently ill, car accidents, fighting, and a list of other stupid shenanigans... cannabis was a joke. The down side of cannabis was nothing compared to the proven ill effects and dangers of alcohol.

School was a drag, something I perceived as a necessary evil. I did what I needed to do in order to pass, exerting the bare minimum of effort. What an unfortunate attitude I think now, looking back... I really thought I knew everything I needed to make my way in the world. Oh, the brashness and ego of youth!

I became a scuba diver and found that visiting the underwater world was more amazing than any drug or adventure

I could imagine. I considered a career in commercial diving, but upon investigation it didn't sound like a fun career; diving often to extreme depths, in the dark, breathing mixed gases, with lots of danger and debilitating effects on the body. The life expectancy of a commercial North Sea diver at that time was ninety days! Underwater welders died at a rate of one every five days.

The last of our teen years passed with my friends and I engaged in the usual teenage stuff; Hanging out, wilderness camping, Friday and Saturday night dances, trolling certain areas of the city for girls in someone's father's car, making out in the back seat, meeting new people, expanding our horizons, exploring the possibilities...

Alcohol was our drug of choice based on availability and it was a chief factor in a number of deadly car crashes involving some of our high school friends...

In the spring of 1968 Jerry, one of my closest neighborhood friends was relocated to Toronto by his mother when she decided she needed to save him from the degenerative influences of the neighborhood riffraff...that would be us.

~

I failed my final provincial school exams that year which counted for a hundred percent and thus failed the year.

I was not in a good place. I was suffering from rebellious teenager syndrome; on- going conflict with my father at home; fed up with school. Desperately needing to step out of this scene, I decided to go to Toronto for the winter, hang out with Jerry and earn some money working in the factories.

Returning to Halifax in the spring I found a number of my "Shack" buddies and other friends getting married. It seemed like an epidemic...I started feeling like I was being abandoned... What about all those dreams and adventures we'd discussed over the years? Was that only talk? I needed re-affirmation that there was something other to life than getting married and getting a job right out of school.. Couldn't that come later, after we got to "see the world" or do whatever it was that really cranked us up? We were only going to be young and carefree once.

I convinced one of my more adventurous friends, Curly, to ride the freight trains up to Quebec and back, in the same vein as Woody Guthrie and the depression era vagabonds.

Following that adventure, Gut, my best drinking-and girl-chasing-buddy and I hitch-hiked across Canada and back. I had twenty dollars in my pocket when I left Halifax.

How's that for optimism?

Shortly after our cross country odyssey, Gut also succumbed to the epidemic. I went back to school in September and finished high school.

Eddie, another close friend since childhood and I were spending a lot more time together over the winter of '69-70. That's how it went with a big group of friends; you wove in and out of closer relationships over periods of time because of common interests and changing circumstances. Most of us had done LSD a few times over the past year or so and Eddie and I really connected through the heightened experiences we shared. Neither of us would take "acid" without the other being present in case of a "freak out." We ran the "buddy system" like in scuba diving... one always aware of the other... non-verbal communication... Connected. We had each other's backs. Eddie and I shared some pretty far out all-nighters and the intensity of those experiences brought us ever closer together, deepening our relationship and elevating our sense of connectedness...kindred spirits you might say.

Hallucinogenics like LSD, and others, like peyote, ayahuasca and such have been used by shamans of various cultures for centuries to connect with nature or the spiritual; the cosmic realm, if you will. Incredible things can happen when you are under the influence, including amazing insights and perceptions. Doors to other realms are opened but there is a real danger in entering the *rabbit hole*, including the possibility that you might get lost and never find your way back...as happened to another of our group, our good friend Jules whose family owned the "Shack" property.

The words of the English poet, William Blake, sum up the LSD experience pretty well for me:

> *"To see a world in a grain of sand*
> *and Heaven in a wild flower*
> *to hold infinity in the palm of your hand*
> *and eternity in an hour"*

Eddie and I developed a very deep, intimate connection which endured outside the actual "trip" itself. Perhaps it was somewhat comparable to the phenomenon experienced by twins where one will finish the other's sentences or know what the other is going to say before he says it.

Eddie, Shag (one of Frank's sons) and my brother, Hammer, went off to Sudbury Ontario to work in the nickel mines over the winter and earn some big green. I enrolled in St. Mary's University in September of 1970 and was content to be there. Grass and hash had become ever more available over the past couple of years and a lot of people I knew, especially university friends, were getting high and dabbling in the business side of it. We were enrolled in commerce, after all!

Because I was smoking hash on a more regular basis now, I had become part of a network of sorts with expanding connections. Before I knew it, I was getting quarter ounces and ounces for friends and basically smoking my hash for free. It was a way of life at university and several students I knew, across all of the social strata, were doing the same thing. It wasn't long before my little endeavor started becoming profitable.

Quality was my thing and people knew they could depend on me.

Chapter 4
Learning the Ropes

The Canadian Government LeDain Commission study of the non-medical use of drugs was underway and through my university connections I was invited to partake in the program.

The research involved going to the home of a Psychology professor from Dalhousie University and getting blown away on the finest hashish available, provided by the governments of India, Nepal, Afghanistan, and Lebanon, and passed along, compliments of the Canadian government. Mike, my "jailbird" friend, who I met in the Halifax Police lock-up one night when we were both seventeen, joined me along with a mixed gender group of about twelve students.

The "research" involved smoking superior quality hashish at these gatherings. We would get stoned, listen to great music and have a high old time. I loved this research program and was a willing participant. This hash was far superior to anything that was available on the street.

Sometimes we got so stoned we could barely function. "Rose of Lebanon," case in point. Getting this stoned was really *overdoing it* for research purposes, and not something most people would normally do in a social environment. The program would have been better described as the "study of the non-medical *abuse* of drugs."

Although consumption could be quite excessive at times no one that I knew experienced any long term or psychotic effects. I hate to think of the consequences had we been abusing alcohol, cocaine or even prescription drugs to this excess. Fatalities would have been a strong possibility. As the research continued over years, it was concluded that cannabis was far less harmful than tobacco, alcohol and quite a few other pharmaceuticals that were "legal" and the final recommendation of the LeDain Commission was that cannabis should be legalized.

As it happened, one of the guys facilitating the program would, on occasion, provide me with a pound or so of the various hash, which resulted in me becoming somewhat legendary among my small-but-expanding circle of friends who appreciated a good toke.

By the time my brother and friends Shag and Eddie arrived back from Sudbury in the spring of "71, I was well involved in dealing hash. Thanks to the LeDain connection, my circle of contacts expanded substantially to include one at Rochdale Free College (as it was known), in the heart of downtown Toronto.

Rochdale was an experimental, student-run, alternative-education and cooperative centre where students and teachers lived together in a high rise apartment complex, that had become an infamous place known as "Canada's Drug Superstore" where anything and everything was available. Security for the building was handled by the Satan's Choice Motorcycle Gang and you had to have a password to get in. Our password was "Hangnail", the name of our contact's dog.

Once connections were established, the rest was easy. Mort and I became partners and would take turns going up to Toronto to bring back a few pounds of either hash or hash oil. We would pay a female resident friend of Jake's, our contact at Rochdale, to carry our purchase out of the building in a guitar case or a baby stroller or some such thing, and deliver it to us a few blocks away, as the building was under constant surveillance by the local police and RCMP.

The atmosphere in the building was bizarre to say the least. Different drugs were sold on different floors. Cannabis was spread over a couple of floors, cocaine and amphetamines on another. LSD and other psychedelics on another, all distinct from one another.

Cocaine, speed and related drug floors were very heavy, tense and paranoid and not a comfortable place to be. The LSD floor was all strangely painted psychedelia with tripped out characters floating around the hallways searching for their minds. The cannabis floors were peaceful and also painted psychedelic but generally with a laid back hippie vibe and lots of friendly, pretty girls hanging out...

~

Getting the hash back to Halifax was fairly easy. Once away from Rochdale we just wrapped it so it wouldn't smell, threw it in a suitcase and put it in checked or carry-on baggage, as there was virtually no airport security in those days. The one and only time I missed a plane, because of a traffic snarl, turned out to be very fortunate for me because there was a bomb scare and that plane I was to board had all the baggage removed and searched. Was it luck that I was spared? Or was it my fate to continue?

I wonder sometimes if getting busted then could have changed my whole life trajectory, but I'll never know. So many things like this happened over the course of my "career." So many schools of thought to ponder.... Who really knows, for certain? I find it hard to explain. I've had many discussions about this over the years and the question always remains...Is it fate, destiny, luck, karma...or some interwoven cosmic smorgasbord of all these that defines a purpose?

Perhaps I had a Guardian Angel watching over me... Eddie?

If there is any purpose to all of these experiences I sum up as my journey, my Samsara, I would be happy if it was indeed to travel this path and write this book which I dare to hope will serve a higher purpose than just being another adventure story.

My wildest dream is that *Samsara* will sell millions of copies and I will use the money I earn to support the causes I believe in; the things I have learned from this odyssey that I believe are of true and lasting value.

Love is the answer, and *believing* is the key to creating a better world for all.

Chapter 5

Death of My Friend

Eddie and the boys returned from Sudbury in the spring of '71. Mort had split up (again) with his wife and childhood sweetheart, Sandy, and Mort and I rented an apartment together, in the neighborhood, just around the corner from Eddie's house.

This was to become "party central." We even had an electric pipe, a fish bowl size globe that sat inverted over a heat element upon which a piece of hash would be placed and, Oh my....

The globe would bellow with ever more dense smoke until someone took a draw on the inhalation hose that protruded from the bottom. There was absolutely no sensation of inhaling anything but air, but upon exhalation you would cough your head off and be instantly stoned. What an instrument! One for the museum of drug history for sure.

Eddie had developed a lump in his armpit, about the size of a golf ball, shortly before he returned from Sudbury. Before long it was twice the size and continuing to grow. Tests revealed the dreaded diagnosis: Cancer.

He was handed a death sentence...three months. The doctor said to Eddie, "Enjoy your summer." He and *we* surely did that...

Almost immediately we met a group of girls who had just moved to the area and the six of us paired up. Mort, Eddie and I were inseparable along with my brother Hammer, Shag, and a few other close friends. Eddie's father bought him a motorcycle which Eddie referred to as his "going away present."

We had one hell of a summer with lots of parties with good friends, great music...lots of love and good vibes. By early August the lump in Eddie's armpit grew to the size of a tennis ball.

He started to fade around late August, loosing weight and energy. On Labour Day Weekend we had a big party for him at my family home. He called it his going away party, although no one wanted to or could believe or accept the reality that he was actually going to die..and soon.

The following week as he sunk further into the abyss, Eddie was admitted to the hospital. Hammer, Mort, Shag and I went every day to visit him. Sometimes we took him a joint. The nurses never said a word. They were very cool. Whatever Eddie wanted was OK with them.

One morning as we entered the room his curtain was pulled around his bed. Thinking he was asleep, I pulled the curtain back to have a peek and what I saw will remain with me forever. He was all doubled up on his bed, clutching his pillow into his chest with this intense, wild-eyed look of horror, like an animal in agony caught in a steel trap.

The vision sent me reeling. All I could think of was his internal organs must have been rotting away and dripping like melting wax.

I ran for the nurse and the first one said "it wasn't time." I freaked out and another nurse came rushing over and, quickly realizing what was happening, fixed another shot of morphine and hit him up. There was no more "waiting" after that.

The next day Eddie was really wasted. He lay there on his bed, emaciated, breathing with the aid of an oxygen mask, but, as always, the joker; he made what must have been a huge effort to pull his mask aside and say "one -Adam 12," a line from a corny, weekly T.V. cop show popular at the time.

We all had a chuckle and stood around for awhile, not knowing what to say or how to deal with the situation. It was obvious that he was too weak to really be there for us. We hung around for awhile in some sort of "twilight zone," until we realized it was probably better to let him rest. It was day seven. As we we were heading to the door saying "See you later Ned," (our nickname for him) he made another huge effort, and, with what must have been one of his last acts, leaned up and called out my name before slumping back onto his pillow.

I walked back over to his bedside as he held out his hand. While smiling up at me he gripped my hand. Without a word being spoken, a wellspring of deepest feelings passed between us as we gazed into each other's eyes until finally, Eddie closed his and released his grip on my hand. It was 'goodbye' but I couldn't quite fathom it at that moment.

Feeling numb and dazed, I walked out of his room and joined the others in our expanding cloak of misery. We left the hospital. Nobody spoke for a long time.

Eddie slipped his earthly tether in the early hours of the following day...his final trip.

I was living back at my parents house as I was enrolled in University for another year. My mother gently opened my bedroom door around nine that morning and broke the news.

She had known Eddie since childhood and it rocked her world just like the rest of us.

Eddie had a massive funeral. The church was packed. His parents were blown away. They had no idea he was so loved by so many. Six of us, his closest friends, carried him to his gravesite and laid him to rest... the first one of the neighborhood gang to go...

I returned to University but was unable to focus. Something seemed to have shifted within me. I was adrift. I felt undone... angry and confused.

Chapter 6
The Times, They Are A-Changing

The early seventies was a major transitional time in the world and I felt it full on--not just in my intimate sphere of being but in the world in general. Technology had changed the sixties. Television brought war, poverty, environmental disasters and so much more into our very homes. We became witnesses as opposed to viewers. Social values had been turned upside down. Many were confused by the shifting status quo.

There were a lot of people who believed, like myself, that the world was doomed from either nuclear war or pollution. Many of us believed that if we made it to the year 2000, we'd be doing well, but what kind of world would it be? Certainly not the peace and love kind of place we wished for; not a world of compassion, caring and sharing, but more likely a world of war, fear, poverty and extreme social injustice.

Where I lived, lakes and rivers were being acidified and species like the Atlantic Salmon were already in danger. Jacques Cousteau, the famous French oceanographer and inventor of the "Aqua Lung", was warning us about the destruction of many of the ocean's reefs due to accelerated chemical, Industrial and nuclear pollution that he personally witnessed as he and his team of ocean scientists dove, researched and documented the underwater world.

The Vietnam War had been raging throughout the sixties and that whole unwanted mess of American intervention in other parts of the world was becoming more and more prevalent. New weapons of mass destruction were being invented and used. So many innocent people were dying worldwide largely because of American imperialism.

Robert Kennedy and Martin Luther King Jr. had both been assassinated along with JFK.

These were the leaders so many of us had been pinning our hopes on...

American political leaders were being exposed as corrupt and unscrupulous. The CIA was conducting "Black Ops", their term for clandestine interference including anything from mayhem to murder. With their help political leaders in foreign countries were overthrown if America's ruling elite thought it could help them expand their power around the globe. To this day, many people around the globe, like myself, still believe the CIA was involved with both of the Kennedys' assassinations and possibly King's as well. JFK's for sure.

Life, liberty and the pursuit of happiness seemed more uncertain, more fragile... more threatened than ever.

～

By mid-October all the leaves had disappeared from the trees and my world was bleak, cold and dismal. Life itself felt bleak and dismal. Prior to Eddie's death I had never known anything like this kind of depression. Despite my concern over the deteriorating global situation, and relatively minor adolescent *growing pains,* life had been sweet. I was blessed with an abundance of friends, love, comfort, health, security... all of the good things life has to offer. I was a "golden boy" from a good, well respected, middle class family, surrounded by friends and opportunity; contentment mostly filled my days. I was generally happy.

These days nothing seemed to matter. My world was grey, colorless... empty.

I went through the motions of attending classes until one particularly shitty day in October with freezing temperatures and wet snow falling, I made my way over to what had become Mort's flat, books in hand, on my way to classes.

I stopped by, as much to commiserate with Mort, as to check if Mike and his rather dubious friend Ken had dropped off the money they owed us for a pound of grass. They hadn't, and as Mort and I sat there pissed off and glum, stewing in our misery, feeling our deep sense of loss over Eddie, the phone rang. It was Mike calling to let us know he and Ken were on their way over. They arrived without the money, most of the grass, some lame excuse, and a bottle of whiskey.

It was ten o'clock on a Tuesday morning... Screw it all.

We proceeded to drink the whiskey and smoke the grass and at some point Ken mentioned that he had a credit card and suggested that he rent a car and we all drive to Florida.

Ken was a lunatic and not one to be trusted, but when you were with him there was sure to be never dull moment. He was the adopted child of a very well-to-do, well respected Halifax family and as he got into his teens he began doing all kinds of crazy things, like using his adopted father's well known and well respected name to finagle airline tickets to anywhere, on a whim, or renting a car or hotel room, or any such notion that might pop into his maladjusted mind. He was a real con in the classic sense. Clean cut, well mannered, Ivy league appearance... Very believable. A true sociopath. Mike was the opposite, rough-cut and very hippyish-looking with long black hair and a thick mustache, appearing better suited to be a lead-singer in a rock band.

On this cold, depressing, wet, miserable morning Ken called a taxi and disappeared. We never knew if he would return because he was so full of shit, you couldn't believe a word he said. But sure enough he came back an hour later with a brand new Oldsmobile Cutlass and another bottle of whiskey.

The next thing we knew, we were heading south in the middle of a major snowstorm with only the clothes on our backs, a small bag of weed, one suitcase (Mort's) and a few hundred dollars in cash between us.

As it turned out the stolen credit card Ken had was Mort's (we didn't find this out until we were in Florida and I thought Mort was going to kill him on the spot.) Ken had snagged it out of the mailbox on the way into Mort's apartment that morning. It was a Gulf Oil card, good for rental cars, gasoline, Holiday Inn Hotels and restaurants...all that we needed!

We had an insane trip to Florida, stopping first at a Holiday Inn in Maine and several others along the way, drinking in their bars and eating our fill of the best the restaurants had to offer and ordering whiskey by the bottle to our room.

Our demented Ken had conjured up the cover story that we were a Canadian rock band taking a break after touring the country, so he told the manager at one hotel along the way and that became our story. We were just lucky no one asked us to perform. That would have been funny.... Or not!

After five days we ended up in Fort Lauderdale and hung out there for most of the week soaking in that lovely Florida sunshine. The hotel we chose was a charming, vintage hotel/motel near the beach with a fabulous sunken poolside bar that miraculously (Hydraulic) rose up out of the ground each day about the same time we stumbled, all bleary eyed down to the pool, usually around noon. We were treated like royalty and the weather was so great we were content to just hang out and relax... after the tour and all...

We spent some time in Miami and one thing really struck me. There were a lot of older, retired people there who appeared well-off, but many seemed to have a sad, confused air about them, as if they were lost. Was this not the Shangii-La lifestyle they had been promised after a lifetime spent chasing the dollar? I felt a deep sense of sympathy for them.

Mike, who was always fidgety and had a hard time sitting still for more than ten minutes started getting antsy as the days went by and got Ken to scam him a plane ticket home so he could see some "new Love" he had recently met. So, he quit the band and was gone, just like that.

Mort, Ken and I thought we should check out Jamaica since we were so close, only to arrive on that beautiful Caribbean island with a credit card that was only honored on mainland North America. Shit! Montego Bay and no money...

We still had a bit of cash so we hired a cab from the airport. The driver "Cascade" was totally insane. I still have his card on which is printed "for safety, reliability and dependability call Cascade"... Not! ... Although...two out of three ain't bad., considering...

The car was a total wreck with no brakes, therefore his favored method of stopping was to grind off half a fender against a wall. A maniac behind the wheel, he said "You didn't need brakes if you had a good horn!" We flew around blind corners with the horn blaring, sending people scrambling for their lives...literally! Anxious and breathless, we were constantly craning our necks to see if we had hit anyone, so close were some of the near misses.

We told Cascade of our financial predicament and that we wanted some weed and a place to crash for the night. He knew the local magistrate and arranged for a fairly decent room, actually; a self-contained apartment with a big patio on the upper level of the man's home.

Next on the agenda was the weed. Cascade drove us into Montego Bay and dropped us off in the centre town, and said "I'll be right back." Suddenly we found ourselves standing on a street corner in the middle of this foreign land surrounded by very black people who started jeering at us and making daunting cat calls. We began to feel very uncomfortable. The sun was just going down and as it became increasingly darker some of the gathering crowd started moving ever closer to us which made it all the more freaky. We were thinking if Cascade doesn't get back here quickly we are dead meat.

The situation was becoming increasingly tense with ever bolder and more aggressive shouting. I was thinking we needed a way to escape when suddenly it dawned on me what it must be like to be a black person in some hateful place like the southern U.S.A. There's no place you can hide. You can't run away and "blend in" with the crowd. You are totally exposed and vulnerable, at the mercy of the mob. Not a good place to be.

I started feeling whiter by the second. I'm sure I was glowing a radiant, fluorescent white by the time Cascade arrived a few minutes later bouncing up the street and over the curbs in an attempt to stop. I can tell you, we were some happy to see his pearly whites and that wreck of a car!

Rescued, perhaps just in the nick of time, we dove into the wreck, grateful to be extricated from that situation. Ravenous now, we headed to a restaurant of Cascade's recommendation for some authentic fried chicken. The chicken was indeed delicious. What was not so delicious was the group of heavy looking Jamaican guys around our age who kept staring at us from the moment we walked in. It was obvious that they were talking about us and not in a good way.

None of us had ever experienced any degree of racial tension before and this kind of hostility was really unsettling. A couple of these guys had big machetes with them, not an uncommon sight there in those days.

We had just about finished our chicken and were anxious to leave when one of these guys got up and, with an air of belligerence, sauntered over to our table, slid up a stool, sat down staring directly at Ken from three feet away and said "I'm getting bad vibes from you."

Major Fuck! All I could envision was being hacked to death by these guys.

This was classic Ken shit. He was a magnet for trouble. I think it was his look— that straight, clean cut Ivy league appearance that enabled him to operate with such aplomb as he did, but which also got him into trouble, especially in rough places like this.

Mort and I kept trying to keep the guy calm telling him we were from Canada... first time here and not looking for trouble. We offered to buy him and his friends a drink, doing our best to diffuse the situation, while Cascade just sat there crunching away on his chicken, bones and all!

Somehow we managed to keep things calm while putting forth our best bravado. We paid the bill and moved slowly toward the door while Cascade shucked and jived with "the brothers," convincing them we were cool Canadians. It was all very tense and I think we were lucky to get out of there intact. Definitely the wrong place at the wrong time. Perhaps another NDE? Who knows!

Needless to say we were totally wired after that so we rolled up a big honking joint in brown paper (no cigarette papers here) and leaned into a good buzz while Cascade chauffeured us around Mo-Bay. Along the tour, as he bounced around in his seat, hyper excited, he casually asked "You boys like some black pussy?" Before we could even answer, he pulled up beside a girl walking along the road and asked her if she'd like to "fuck these nice white boys!" Honestly ... by now there was nothing sane about this whole trip.

The girl leaned her head in the window scrutinizing us and said "you boys want to fuck?" and again, before any of us could say a word in our stoned state of disbelief, she jumped in the car and off we went, back to our apartment where Cascade had a great time flirting around, entertaining her, while Mort, Ken and I continued on with the weed and a bottle of Jamaican rum we had purchased at the airport.

We carried on smoking and drinking and laughing our asses off at the absurdity of it all, while Cascade enjoyed a fabulous time, bouncing off the walls enjoying our rum, our weed and his new-found girlfriend until the wee hours when they finally left and we crashed...comatose at this point.

He did come back later in the morning as he promised, to drive us to the airport. Dependable...just like his card says! All smiles, stoned out, thrilled to be alive, and still blown away by this crazy adventure with Cascade, we bade him farewell at the airport, knowing that we'd never forget him and wondering if we'd ever see him again.

Of course we smoked as much *ganga* as we could on the way to the airport so when we arrived back in the U.S. an hour or so later, all bleary eyed, you knew that the U.S. customs officers would pounce on us, sure that three young, red-eyed hippie types, returning from a twenty-four hour trip, with one suitcase between them, were making a suicide run from the land of ganja.

Ken and I walked through the customs inspection area first, followed by Mort with our one suitcase. Being a nervous type to begin with, and sweating profusely, Mort was certain to attract attention and sure enough...

The uniforms came at him from all sides, six of them, like a tsunami, ushering him into a little room where they made him take off his platform shoes which they took and beat the heels against a table. Next they strip-searched him and finally they tore his suitcase apart. Poor Mort, he was a wreck while Ken and I, also ushered into the search room, just enjoyed the whole process, having light-hearted banter with the customs agents, knowing we were safe.

We had smoked as much as we could and left the rest behind...or so we thought...you could never be sure with Ken. He's the kind of guy that would stash it in your suitcase when you weren't looking...letting you unknowingly take the risk so that he might have a toke if and when you made it through the gauntlet. A real charmer that Ken! But somehow he had redeeming qualities....he made good on most of his scams and, after all...we were willing participants.

On parting company, one of the customs officers gave us a nod and commented snidely "The grass grows tall in Jamaica, eh boys." Oh Mort, my brother...The times we had!

Safely ensconced back at our Holiday Inn poolside bar, we leveled off from our Jamaican adventure with the aid of several whiskeys. All was well. Later that night, Mort, all liquored up, just had to call his wife and make amends for his crazy ways. After an hour on a payphone with Sandy as he was lamenting his misery, expressing his undying love and begging for forgiveness and another chance to make it all up to her, we decided it was time to head back home.

The next day we pointed our chariot due north and began the long journey home to the frozen zone. The drive was uneventful, It was just a drag heading back to the shitty, cold weather now that the adventure was over.

Home again, I resumed classes but in essence I just drifted through a gray world semi-present, struggling to be there. I walked by Eddie's house everyday on my way to university and the emptiness I felt was compounded by the barren bleakness of the colorless winter landscape.

When the credit card bill arrived, I think it was for more than the car was worth. Mort, of course claimed no knowledge of anything, never having received said card...and that was the end of it. He was never contacted again. Well...that was easy!

Meanwhile, he, who had so earnestly repented his maligned, twisted ways and sincerely expressed his undying love for Sandy from that pay phone on the Fort Lauderdale beach, was no sooner back home when he re-emerged as ignorant and nasty as he could be to her, and left again. Schizoid! Go Figure! That was Mort.

Chapter 7

Friends and Lovers

Mort was pissed. He had a Jekyll and Hyde personality; a real Gemini. He hooked up with a little tart, who appeared to me like she was just out for a good time at his expense.

I couldn't stand the sight of this little Jezebel and what made it even worse was that we had stood on the beach together, drunk, holding each other and crying about Eddie and Sandy while sharing this intense, raw, emotional tangle with her. I had come to know Sandy quite well over the years and she was a real solid, loving, good woman who put up with a lot of his shit and she certainly didn't deserve this kind of treatment from him. Over the next few months he got right down and dirty, shooting speed and heroin while hanging out with the local motorcycle gang who were soon to become a chapter of the Hell's Angels. He was hard on the head at times, my dear friend Mort. He did however, have redeeming qualities and we remained good friends throughout our lives, right until the end. He passed away in 2004.

Mort, Sandy, Eddie and I had been close friends for several years, Eddie and I since childhood and Mort and Sandy since about the age of fourteen. While Mort and I had a parting of ways, becoming estranged from each other, Sandy and I became closer, commiserating and comforting each other over the loss of both Eddie and Mort. Before long our intimacy grew and we eventually started sleeping together.

Mort, who couldn't give a shit, continued on his merry way getting all fucked-up again and by the end of February he got the boot from his not-so-lovely new girlfriend and did another turnabout, adamant this time that he was going to straighten out his life.

In March he moved back into his parents house, which was attached to Sandy's place, and started repenting. Some people you just can't understand. They possess a certain kind of madness they can't seem to control, but mostly, their heart is in the right place. To know them is to love them... in spite of their periodic bouts of madness. Who are we to judge?

I could see that Mort truly was trying to make amends for his insanity and I felt his sincerity and anguish, as always. I began to feel like an intruder. I had to leave.

Chapter 8
Heading to Kashmir, March 1972

After gaining his university degree, my older brother had recently returned from two years of travel through Europe and the Far East to such places as India, Nepal, Pakistan and Afghanistan to name a few, with stories of the wildly exotic. Based on his accounts, I was fired up to see some of these places, especially Kashmir. Just the name alone...Kash-mir, sounded so intriguing...Kathmandu was another....visions of Genghis Khan danced in my head...

The thought of a wild adventure in these far away places reignited the smoldering embers of my soul. The thought of scoring some of that top quality hash, that LeDain had introduced me to, made my blood boil.

Still feeling out of sync from my surroundings, the feeling was intensified by the estrangement I felt with Mort. I felt out of place, as if I didn't belong anywhere.

Having only a small bankroll, I approached a friend to see if he would be interested in investing in my trip to India to send back a few kilos of hash. He was, and just like that, I was on my way to India, via Amsterdam.

I have no idea what I was telling my parents about all of this craziness, surely not that I was off to India, but looking back, especially as a parent myself, I know I must have been a terrible worry to them...

Early one morning I arrived in the damp, Dutch city of Amsterdam with only a vague idea where I was going and really no idea what this expanded world was all about. I always felt safe, that is, I never felt threatened by the unknown. Having a pragmatic approach to life, the anticipation of the unknown excited me. I always felt confident that I could deal with any situation that might arise and if it was my fate to die then I'd die and wouldn't be around to worry about it. Insha Allah. A rather selfish outlook in hindsight...

Hitch-hiking in my teens, I did have some freaky moments but I was able to handle them and based on my upbringing and emerging life experiences, it seemed to me that most people were basically decent. Thus I didn't have any preconceived fears, other than of pick-pockets and the obvious "back alley" bandits.

Amsterdam was intriguing, especially the Red Light District, where I stayed, with all of the wonderfully wild and zany characters flitting about. I spent a couple of days there in a student hotel getting my bearings but the dampness and chill that seemed to go right through me, suggested a cheap flight to the Greek Island of Rhodes would be a better place to acclimatize. And so, off I went.

The small coastal village of Lindos was enchanting and I hung out there for five days enjoying the warmer weather and the Greek hospitality, after which I made my way by boat to Athens from where I got a not-so-cheap flight to Istanbul, Turkey.

Istanbul ... again, the name alone intrigued me and I thought it would interesting to experience some overland travel from there.

Istanbul was Intriguing indeed! I stumbled around the old city for a couple of days, hooking up with some Westerners I met at the Grand Bazaar market. They informed me about the train to Tehran they were booked on and, that I had to have a receipt from the bank where I changed my money in order to purchase a ticket. The money changer who had ripped me off at the airport had also failed to give me a receipt. I was quickly learning the ways of the world!

At the train station the next day I was only able to purchase a ticket as far as the frontier. "Fine" I said, figuring I'd buy another ticket at the border, no big deal, thus consigning myself to the train trip from hell.

We didn't even get out of the train station before trouble started. I was sitting in the waiting area with my new-found friends, a tall lanky Swiss guy and his petite Chinese girlfriend, watching them play chess. The cavernous hall was packed with travelers including a group of about twenty young Turkish soldiers. They kept glancing in our direction, some of them looking a bit cocky and perhaps a bit resentful of us young, free, Western travelers, anomalous in that time and place.

It was obvious they were talking about us when one of them finally swaggered over to join us, abruptly planting his ass down beside me without a word. It was also clear he spoke not a word of English.

No problem. We just smiled, acknowledging his "stone face" while we continued on as before, when all of a sudden he boldly reached over and started messing with the board, jumping men like you would in checkers. Taken by surprise, we all reacted at once. Annoyed with his rude behavior, we emphatically gestured, scolding him to stop what he was doing, which he did, but not for a few moments, and not until he was ready. Then he just sat there staring blankly at each of us in turn as if deciding his next move.

For his next move--he whipped his bayonet from its scabbard, gripping it tight in his hand immediately before me, for a very long moment, before flipping It over, holding it by the blade, handle facing me and gesturing for me to take it. I was thinking "Fuck you, I'm not touching that."

The situation was tense and becoming more so by the second. I really wasn't sure what to make of it, so I just shrugged my shoulders with that universal open hand gesture that means *I don't understand what you want.* He continued staring at me with this kind of cold, unfocused look, again, for an overlong period of time. I really had no idea what his problem was and I couldn't get a read on him; his eyes were expressionless. Eventually he flipped the bayonet over again and very slowly replaced it in its scabbard, all the while scrutinizing us with his cold, dead-eye stare until, obviously disgusted, he stood up, and swaggered back to rejoin and commiserate with his comrades.

We avoided making eye contact with them but we would catch their disparaging stares and feel their hostile vibes. You never know what may happen in these situations but I knew one thing for certain; I would never have laid my hand on that bayonet!

When the train left Istanbul, there were about ten of us Westerners on it, young traveling, hippie-types, including myself. Unfortunately, we were split up all over the train. I was in a compartment with five Turkish men, wherein I slept on the top fold-up shelf, more like a luggage rack than a bed, but I took it by choice.

My coach buddies consisted of a very nice, well-groomed, educated, thirty something engineer who spoke excellent English, and a very amicable, refined looking, elderly gentleman with a nicely trimmed grey-white handlebar mustache, who didn't. The elder wore an English tweed sport jacket with leather elbow patches and sported a beautifully engraved, double barrel shotgun. The three of us sat on one side of our compartment.

Across from and facing us, about four feet away, sat a fat, disgusting, slimy looking middle aged pervert who would have been well cast as the stereotypical "greasy Mexican bandito" we used to see in those old western movies. He had a cardboard box full of the foulest smelling goat cheese you can imagine and occasionally when he caught my eye, he would assault my senses with the most lewd gestures. Lastly, but certainly not least, were two young, twentyish, homosexuals who groped each other constantly as they giggled and tried to entice me to join in their gaiety. We were to be bound together like castaways in this confined rolling box for the next five days. Oh Boy!

The engineer and the elderly gentleman were both embarrassed for me and extremely apologetic for the behavior of their debauched countrymen. It didn't bother me other than the odd goose I got from the "twins," as I came to think of them. They were harmless and even entertaining at times. I enjoyed the company of the engineer and the old man, with whom I was able to communicate through the engineer. The pervert was another matter...he was just disgustingly vulgar and I did my best to ignore him and avoid any eye contact with him.

All of us Westerners joined up in the restaurant car to swap information and stories mostly about the waiters and porters who were truly rude and obnoxious to us. They considered the girls among us as something akin to prostitutes because they traveled alone. These assholes considered it OK to grope them, which they did when the opportunity presented itself.

On one occasion I actually had to pull a big, fat, middle aged man off the tiny Chinese girl when this obnoxious asshole followed her into her car and wrapped his arms around her like a big bear! I was just happening by on the way back from the dining car to my compartment when I saw this attack take place. I grabbed the guy from behind to his surprise and pulled him off her. Between me yelling at him and her screaming he skulked away disgruntled all the while hurling curses at us.

The full five days continued like that with snide remarks directed at us in the dining car mostly from the wait staff but from porters as well. We always had shitty service, always the very last ones to be served. I had that awful feeling that they spit in our food before giving it to us. Yuk! I could never understand why those people on that train had such loathing for us.

We, as a group or individuals did nothing, to my knowledge to offend them, other than just by our mere presence. I just put it down to fear and gross ignorance.

When it came time to sleep the seat-back lifted up to form a middle bunk, the actual seat became the lower bed and I climbed onto the uppermost ledge on our side, fully clothed with my passport and valuables stuffed down the front of my shirt, curled up safely away from the pervert and the "giggling twins."

I had gotten used to the "twins." They were kind of funny. They were always pleasant, happy, almost childlike in ways, snuggling together on their lower bunk, blowing me kisses and gesturing for me to join them. I didn't mind them, they were harmless enough.

The jostling of the train put me to sleep quickly and no one disturbed me. And so it went, "us" and "them" all the way. Overall, It wasn't so bad. Despite the surly train staff I had a fascinating trip sharing many interesting conversations and stories with my more refined coach-mates and the other Western travelers as we passed through what seemed like a hole in time to another age.

It was the pervert who stole the show. Even now when I think of him...my skin crawls and I can feel my facial expression change to one of disgust.

Our time bubble passed through tiny, far-flung villages... we saw colorful gypsies, ragged and rough looking goat herders, camel drivers and traders with horse-drawn carts full of various wares. The train seemed to stop for any and every person who appeared along the way..

We arrived at the frontier, which was nothing more than a mud-brick shack in the middle of nowhere, and I mean The Mother of all "NO WHERES!" My ticket was only good to the frontier which I assumed was the border where there would be border guards and buildings of some description, but I was seriously mistaken.

It was the middle of the night when two big louts came into my car and I was forcefully told to get off...GET OFF !

The conductor and the ticket collector forced me to take my belongings and leave my compartment. The engineer and the old man had both gotten off the day before so there was no-one to intervene on my behalf. The pervert was also gone and only the gigglers remained. Although I could see their concern, there was nothing they could do for me. I was rudely escorted to the end of the car and ordered to get off, despite my pleas.

There was absolutely nothing friendly here, just the vastness of the steppes... just darkness, ...danger...and...death...

As I was desperately arguing and pleading with these nasty ignoramuses who seemed to be enjoying some perverse satisfaction in tossing me out into the black, foreboding night, they coupled on several more Iranian cars which were joining on for the rest of the trip to Tehran.

A benevolent Iranian policeman traveling on this new group of cars and, luckily for me, spoke some English, saw what was happening and intervened on my behalf, informing the sadistic Turkish conductor that I was coming with him and, that he would take care of my travel documents and money situation. That was the end of it. The nasty prick of a conductor, slumped away, beaten, his lust for power crushed.

I eagerly joined my rescuer in a beautiful sleeping car of elegant wood panelling, heavy, rich, brown velvet drapes and separate, built-in bunk style beds with comfortable mattresses and fresh, crisp white sheets! Heaven! What a treat!...and a dining car with white linen service, great food and a truly superior class of people! The rest of the trip was first class!

The policeman was well educated, married with two small children and just a decent guy. I have no idea what my fate might have been had I been hurled out into the blackness of night by those other nasty ill-breds. In this wild and lawless place I might have been murdered by bandits, my body never to be found...just another young traveler... disappeared. Such is life... here one day, gone the next... Inshallah!

Was I just "lucky" again? I had to wonder...fate, destiny, karma, luck...the question remains.

I thought about those people on the Turkish train and tried hard to make sense of it. Why were the staff, to a person, and many of the passengers, but not all, so nasty and hateful to us? I would meet many Turkish people later on during my travels who were lovely, kind people, just like most people I have encountered from many cultures over my lifetime. It really bothers me that the heart can be so cold. I think it depends largely on whether you are raised in a fear-based or love-based situation...

Eventually we arrived at a huge lake and the Iranian section of the train was loaded aboard a rail ferry at a place called Van from where we were ferried across the water of Lake Van to to a place called Tatvan. From Tatvan we rolled out on to the awaiting tracks and continued our trip onward to Tehran.

When we got to Tabriz, the first major Iranian city en route, I was able to change money and repay the policeman for my ticket. We parted company here, and I wondered at this seemingly incidental encounter; this person who appeared out of nowhere for a short but crucial period of time, influencing this moment that may have changed everything for me.

≈

It was the era of the Shah and the scene in Tehran was very westernized.

Alone now, without the company of any Westerners I ambled about the streets of Tehran where I encountered the most attractive women I had ever seen in my life; Stunningly beautiful silky-skinned creatures and olive complexions dressed to the "nines" in the latest Paris fashions strolled about in groups, laughing and carrying on. They would whistle at me and flirt from a distance. I was totally awestruck.

At first I thought there must be someone else near me who they were signaling but upon checking I realized there was only me and indeed, *it was me* they were flirting with. Well, when I got over the shock of disbelief I was delighted. My fantasies soared! But alas ...it was short lived. These girls were brave as a collective of six, eight or ten but whenever I approached them, all smiles and welcoming, they shriveled before my eyes, abashedly avoiding eye contact while shyly turning away in extreme embarrassment. What a pity!

I noticed that the men were all in groups as well. You never saw men and women together. Quite often the men were holding hands but not in a gay way, it's just how they are, it's part of their culture. I didn't run into any Westerners in two days and it was obvious I wasn't going to have much fun here, so I made flight arrangements and two days later I boarded a plane bound for New Delhi, India.

Chapter 9

Srinagar, India

I arrived in Delhi airport mid-morning intending to continue right on the Kashmir but was told I'd have to wait several hours while repairs were made to the plane that would carry me to my final destination…Srinagar, Kashmir!

This was not reassuring, but what to do?

It was very hot, crowded and noisy inside the terminal building and people kept approaching me with questions like "where are you from?" and "what is the purpose of your mission in India?" or they would want to look at my watch. They were all friendly enough, just innocently curious, but I needed some space.

I went outside to search out a comfortable place under a tree where I could sit quietly and read my book. The first thing that struck me was a distinct smell in the warm spring air. Kind of a spicy, aromatic scent that I would come to recognize as distinctly and quintessentially India.

I spotted a large tree nearby with big leafy branches that cast a perfect shade over the grassy area beneath it, creating the ideal spot for me to sit in peace and quiet and read my book. It wasn't long before I started to attract a crowd of "admirers."

First a couple of young guys casually sauntered up and sat down cross legged directly opposite me, just a few feet away. It didn't feel intrusive--more casual, matter of fact. They nodded and smiled and I returned their greeting/acknowledgement. Not long after they arrived, they were joined by three more young men who sat down cross-legged beside them. A few more drifted over, taking up positions on the opposite side of my initial audience of two. They continued to arrive, casually sauntering over and squatting down on their haunches or sitting in that typical, crossed legged, yogic Indian way. I carried on reading and tried to ignore them but the swarm soon grew to about fifteen or so gathered around me in a semi-circle as if I was going to give a lecture. Occasionally, one of them would reach out and gently touch me or touch my watch. I was to learn later on that they were especially fascinated by watches and it was not uncommon for a stranger to approach you and grab your wrist (gently) to have a closer look. It could be funny or disconcerting, depending on how you were with It.

This group I had attracted were friendly enough. They were obviously discussing this alien amongst them, like I was on exhibit; perhaps it was my strange attire, perhaps my white skin, or the color of my eyes or hair, who knows what they were thinking.

I found it amusing at first, then a tad annoying and finally downright disconcerting, so I finally went back into the terminal building to try and find some undisturbed space. After a few more hours of sitting inside I was able to board my two hour Indian Airlines flight to Srinagar.

At the Srinagar airport, I was met by a diminutive, middle-aged Muslim man who introduced himself as Mohammed, addressed me as Sahib and acted like he was expecting me. I had made no reservations but Mohammed was a very likeable, disarming little fellow who spoke excellent English and told me he had been "expecting me."

I told him I wanted to stay on a houseboat but he knew that already and the New Rajan houseboat was awaiting my arrival. So, off I went with him across Dal Lake by *shikara*, a gondola-like craft outfitted with a huge overstuffed cushion-bed-couch, overhead canopy and tied back velvet drapes that could be closed for complete privacy. Our shikara pulled up to the front veranda of the "New Rajan" with its three steps leading down to the water. You stepped out of the boat onto the bottom step.

The houseboat was owned by Iqbal Khan and Mohammed was his chief servant. The houseboat was beautiful. All wood, about ten meters long and five meters wide, ornately hand carved, inside and out and well-appointed with local handmade carpets and exquisite walnut furniture. I was treated royally by Mohammed and his family of servants at my every beck and call.

Before long the word was out that a foreigner had arrived and I was besieged by *"hawkers"*— local craftsmen who sold their wares from shikaras began to collect outside, hovering nearby like birds of prey, patiently waiting for a chance to show me their beautiful treasures. Not to buy, of course, "just looking" was the term they used, as they explained that it was their "duty" to show me what they had aboard. No need to buy anything, they assured me...*just looking*. It was their duty, how could I resist?

These treasure laden shikaras were heaped with everything from carpets to furs of lynx and wildcat, precious and semi-precious stones, carved wooden items, the legendary pashmina shawls and all kinds of amazing things. It was incredible really, I felt like Vasco da Gama or one of those early explorers. Of course I had only to *"just looking"* and, of course, I ended up *just buying* a couple of beautiful silk carpets, some semi-precious stones and a beautifully carved walnut jewelry box. One could easily blow a bankroll in one session of "just looking."

And so my next two days were spent sitting comfortably in the houseboat sipping tea and eating delicious treats of all sorts served by my servants while "Just Looking" at all of the hawkers wonderful wares.

The first morning, when they realized I was awake, two of Mohammed's young sons tried to drag me from my bed into the bathroom to give me a bath. But I was having none of that, finally convincing them to just chill and let me take care of my bath room needs myself. There was nothing weird or sexual about it, they were just so excited to have a Western guest that they tried to do everything possible to pamper me, unsure what I might or might not like but ready to try anything that might garner favor.

After my hard-won solitary bath, I was ushered into the dining area of the houseboat to a large, round, beautifully hand-carved walnut table and offered eggs and rolls with jam and tea. The servants hovered nearby anxious to refill my cup and attend to any other need I might have.

On the second day Mohammed and I mentally jostled trying to feel each other out, until finally I felt comfortable enough to reveal the true purpose of my mission to Kashmir and pop the big question. Could I purchase a few kilos of Hashish and have it concealed in furniture to be shipped back to Canada? "Of course Mr. Jack, whatever you like, anything is possible."

This was to be the mantra I would hear time and time again during my travels in India.

Iqbal was subsequently informed of my mission and came to visit me later in the day assuring me in his most sincere manner that he would be only too happy to help me acquire "the best hash in the entire valley."

"How much money did I have to spend?" was the next question.

Feeling somewhat apprehensive now that the reality of my situation was beginning to sink in, I thought I'd better not reveal how much cash I really had with me (around three thousand dollars, a veritable fortune in that part of the world, and a sum that some people would kill for) so I told him I had five hundred dollars, and that he would need to arrange everything within that price range. I explained how I wanted to have the hash concealed in the furniture and then have that furniture shipped to Canada. I explained that this was a trial run and if successful I would return to do much more business.

After several cups of tea Iqbal headed off via the shikara he had arrived in, manned by one of his personal attendants. As time went by I was to find that Kashmiris were fabulous "fibbers."

That evening I sat around the houseboat with Mohammed as he told me stories of his life in the Indian army and about life in Kashmir, while his three young male offspring squatted nearby on bare feet waiting patiently for any sign or slight movement on my part that would trigger an eruption as they leapt into action to move a table or offer me more tea or whatever. I tried to dismiss them, but they would have no part of that. They were programmed to serve...that was their sole purpose...to be at my every beck and call. Finally I just gave in and tried my best to abide by their customs.

As I listened to and got to know Mohammed, our connection grew and I felt a sense of safety and protection in his company. Iqbal was another matter. He was a bit odd and often stared at me with an unsettling quizzical look from under thick bushy eyebrows. He seemed to be cold all the time and was constantly clutching a blanket tight around his shoulders, as if he'd never felt warmth in his life.

Iqbal always wore a lambswool cap called a *karakul* perched on his closely shaven head. He was hard of hearing, especially when it came to money matters. He would seem really stunned as if he could not quite grasp the idea of a lesser sum of money than he had proposed and I would have to practically yell at him and repeat it two or three times before he got it. A pained expression would appear on his face when things weren't in his favor. It was really quite comical.

Bedtime was a hoot. Again, Mohamed's kids would try their hardest to persuade me to let them give me a bath, which wasn't going to happen under any circumstances. They had to settle for tucking me into bed. They were so good-natured and innocent I couldn't help but laugh at the absurdity of it all.

Another fine day dawned and the bath thing was getting easier now that they were getting the message. I enjoyed another great breakfast and spent the day with Mohammed & Co. cruising around the snowy, mountain-peak encircled Dal Lake and the edges of the centuries-old town of Srinagar. I reclined in a very comfortable shikara as Mohammed filled me in on the amazing history, beginning with the Kushans--tribal people from Afghanistan and Pakistan who ruled until the 14th century when the area came under Mughal rule.

Such notables as Akbar The Great and other Mughal emperors who followed the Kushans reigned until the early 18th century when Kashmir came under the rule of the Durrani Empire for a short period. Next came the Sikhs, who were the dominant power until the British forced their way in during the mid-nineteenth century. The British ruled India until their withdrawal in 1947 culminating in the partitioning of the Indian subcontinent and the creation of East and West Pakistan.

Kashmir has remained a disputed region between India and Pakistan ever since. It was all incredibly fascinating listening to Mohammed as I was *shikaraed* around totally enthralled by the magnificence of the Kashmir valley.

The evening brought with it a heavy fog making an already enchanted place seem kind of eerie, and when Iqbal and his companions silently emerged from the gloomy mist, I watched, transfixed, imagining Charon, the boatman on the River Styx coming for me.

After they entered my houseboat offering me their traditional greeting "As-Salum-Alakum" (peace be with you) we conducted our business, making our arrangements for the following evening.

I wondered what these big, heavy looking characters must be thinking of me:

Some kid from another planet who must have a lot of balls or be out of his mind. I myself was thinking the latter. "What have I gotten myself into now?" was my main thought. Nevertheless, I was as cool as I could be and we ironed out a deal. It almost became a gong show as Iqbal would constantly say "How Much" every tine I said a figure. He couldn't seem to hear any figure below one hundred dollars a kilo for the hash. I knew it was five times the price, but landed in Canada it would be worth ten thousand dollars a kilo. One hundred times the price!

After an hour or so of this back and forth haggling with Iqbal constantly saying "What?" and me shouting in his ear some low offer, to which he would repeatedly say "Just a little bit more." and then "What?" again to my repeatedly unacceptable offer, followed yet again by "just a little bit more." Iqbal was acting with such earnestness and I knew he was fleecing me, which made it all the more comical. I had a hard time not to burst right out laughing which nearly happened a couple of times with the "whats", but I knew that would not be a good thing as he had to present a certain decorum. We finally settled on a price of around forty dollars a kilo and agreed to consummate the deal the next night. They would come for me after dark.

I had kept it together while Iqbal and his henchmen were here but now in the early morning light after a nerve-racking night I was really freaked out! I was sure they were going to murder me in this far away place and dispose of my body, and that would be it. I'd just disappear, never to be heard from again.

Immediately I wrote a letter to Sandy telling her what I was up to and the names of Iqbal and the houseboat with instructions that if she didn't hear from me by such and such a date, she should go to the police and explain what had happened.

After breakfast I got Mohammed to take me into Srinagar where I mailed my letter, feeling better that at least I had some kind of "insurance."

That evening spawned the same ominous, creepy fog that shrouded the area in mystery and intrigue as Iqbal and the *killers* arrived. We lost no time with idle chit-chat. After their brief greetings and checking that I had the cash with me, I climbed into the shikara with them and we silently slipped into the foggy blackness of night.

I had debated calling the whole thing off but since I had already committed to the deal, I decided that was too late. They knew I had money with me, so they could murder me anytime, it really didn't make a difference… perhaps I was just being paranoid.

The silent glide across Dal Lake was nerve-racking to put it mildly. No one spoke a word and I was stressed the whole way, thinking…is it going to happen on the lake? How would they attack me? Would they wrestle the cash from me and try and drown me? Would I have a chance to tell them about the letter? All of these thoughts ricocheted around my brain like pinballs flying wildly around a pinball machine as we glided across the still, black surface of the lake in tense and total silence.

Arriving at the old wooden boat dock at the edge of town, we were met by another tall man standing beside a black car with doors open and motor running. It was all beyond strange, it felt a bit macabre like a scene right out of an old wartime spy movie as I was quickly whisked into the back seat between Iqbal and one of his co-conspiritors, while the other murderer jumped in the front with the driver and we immediately sped off as if we were being chased.

We tore through the ancient town of mud-brick and rough wood, speeding through centuries-old, narrow, twisting, dimly lit passageways, more like narrow donkey-cart paths, certainly not streets designed for speeding cars.

Because of the speed we were traveling and the road being so narrow I don't know how we managed to avoid hitting the few people walking about. I kept turning to look out the back window to see if they were ok. I'm sure the door handles must have grazed at least some of them.

After about ten minutes of this high anxiety mad dash, we came to an abrupt halt at the beginning of a foreboding dark alley and I was told to get out. "Oh Shit," I thought. *"The proverbial Back Alley."* This was IT if ever there was one: There was one dim light bulb attached to a wall about ten meters in; beyond that, there was only darkness.

My mind was racing, not to mention my heart, and I'm sure my adrenalin and cortisol and whatever other chemicals my stress levels were producing were at record highs! Should I just bolt, run for my life... But where? Iqbal motioned for me to fall in with him while the other two fell in behind us, much too close for my comfort!

Every nerve in my body was on HIGH ALERT, especially my back nerves. The feeling was almost electric, like they were burning, as if the nerve endings were reaching out through my skin like tentacles sensing the air, as we descended ever deeper into this abysmal, black passageway. It was all I could do to keep it together, thinking that at any moment I was going to feel the cold steel blade plunging into my back, separating my ribs, skewering my internal organs.

Deeper into the darkness we walked. My mind was racing: Was this to be my fate? Murdered at the age of twenty-three in a back alley in this far away Himalayan town of Srinigar?

With every nerve in my body firing, we arrived at a doorway in the side of one of the buildings. Iqbal knocked three times and the door opened. We were invited to enter by a young man cloaked in a long white kaftan. What a relief, if only momentarily. There were no women anywhere, I was realizing more and more. Strange, I thought.

A steep flight of narrow, dusty, well-worn wooden stairs took us up to the top floor of a furniture factory with several rooms full of the most amazing walnut furniture; Tables, chairs, cabinets, lamps…everything you could want and more, most of it ornately carved along with some more classic pieces. And the prices! By Canadian standards, they were giving it away.

I was introduced to yet another swarthy, thick-eyebrowed *hombre* who was the factory owner. His name was Hajj Kiran, something or other, "Hajj" being a term of respect, meaning one who has made the Hijj pilgrimage to Mecca.

Hajj Kiran, a most gracious man, probably in his late fifties, with a decent command of the English language, invited me, Iqbal and the "killers" to join him for tea around another table in a dimly lit room where we spoke again in hushed tones, (always hushed tones).

Hajj Kiran assured me that he had been in the hash business for a very long time and that he regularly shipped hash-filled furniture all over the world. Not just any hash, mind you, but "the best in the entire valley!" So I could set my mind at ease. All I had to do was choose the furniture I wanted and he would send it along with the hash hidden inside. What more could I ask for?

I chose a dozen pieces but *Hajj* insisted that I take more. Money was no problem. He would trust me to send him the money when I got home and after everything arrived. Wow! I had to like that deal!

That was all I needed. I "bought" practically everything in the place. As I pointed out pieces that I liked, one of three servants present would scurry off with it to another room. This continued for an hour or so until the showrooms were practically empty and I had chosen enough to fill a small container.

So, I brought out my money and gave Hijj my five hundred dollar downpayment while his manager made up my bill of sale. With our transaction completed, we sat down to a celebration feast of pigeon, goat, (including their esophaguses) I was told, (horrible) along with other unrecognizable "delicacies."

Everything was so incredibly spicy I thought my lips were bleeding at one point. There was nothing to drink, "no alcohol, Muslims being abstainers", only a glass pitcher of water that looked like it had been scooped from the lake, complete with algae and slime. I knew enough to know that I couldn't insult these people by not partaking in the special dinner they had arranged for me, so I hoed in and at a certain point I just had to drink the water to extinguish the flames in my mouth.

Big mistake! About three hours later I was struck violently with a severe case of the "flying axe handles" an old army expression from the trenches, my dear friend Frank called the "shits." This condition would stay with me until I got to Greece three days later.

With our business concluded, I was escorted back up the alley, by Iqbal et al, not nearly so terrifying now. The spy car was waiting and I was whisked back to the waiting shikara where I parted company, quite comfortably with Iqbal and his two buddies.

With a huge sigh I stretched back on the grand cushion of my shikara, shaking off the intensity of the last few hours as the ferryman ferried me across my imaginary River Styx to the safety of my waiting houseboat.

I figured I'd probably never see the furniture or hash again, but so what. It was one hell of an experience and I was still alive to tell the tale! Plus, there was always the chance that they might send it, and it might arrive….

I spent the next two days hovering close to the toilet with something akin to dysentery… Not to be too gross, but I'm sure, as the saying goes… "I could have shit through the eye of a needle to the end of the white line!" If you have never been so afflicted, please indulge me as I explain.

It begins with terrible rumblings in your gut followed by a sudden painful and uncontrollable urge to "go." You have *mere* seconds to get on a toilet. The pain in your bowels is excruciating and even if you make it to a toilet you have to be able to drop your pants and get your ass into position within a millisecond, because, at that critical moment when you release your bum and leg muscles to allow your pants to drop, the floodgate opens.

The third day, feeling a bit better and somewhat confident that I could control my bowels sufficiently, I bid Mohammed, his family and Iqbal farewell, anxious to board a plane and get the hell out of there. Next stop New Delhi. From Delhi I would hop on the first available flight to Athens. I just wanted to get my ass back to "civilization" ASAP. I was still a bit freaked out by the whole Kashmiri experience, and, truly, thankful to still be alive…

Chapter 10

Heading Home via Athens

By the time I landed in Athens, I still had diarrhea but at least I could manage it now. That Dal Lake water was a great weight-loss elixir although I wouldn't recommend it!

I was about to have another incredible experience, but it seemed I was having a lot of incredible experiences....

As I was walking down a street in central Athens, a city of about two million at that time, searching out a youth hostel, I stopped a well-dressed middle-aged lady who looked like she might speak English. Upon inquiring she replied that she did indeed speak English, and then asked me where I was from.

I replied that I was from Canada but from a little known place she probably never heard of: Nova Scotia. She was shocked and then told me she had a brother living in Halifax who owned a small restaurant. Then she was doubly shocked to learn that not only did I know the restaurant but it was in my neighborhood, three blocks from my home and that I had been going there as long as I could remember and, in fact, it was our teenage hangout. I saw her brother Jack practically every day and knew his daughters as well. Too much! What are the chances?

What is it about these serendipitous or perhaps synchronistic events? I would have many more over time and they always made me wonder: What's it all about?

Can it really just be coincidence or random occurrences? I think the jury will always be out on this one...

Jack's sister directed me to the hostel where I hooked up with five other young travelers like myself and the next day we all set off together for Amsterdam in a VW bus owned by one of them.

For me, experiences like these are the essence of freedom and the *joie de vivre* that so expand our sense of connection to the world. I think they are important especially when one is young, carefree, less biased and open to other perspectives.

We made it as far as Thessaloniki in the north of Greece the first evening. It was dark when we pulled off the road into a farmer's field. The Greeks were such nice, hospitable people, we didn't think there would be a problem just sleeping by the side of the road sprawled out inside and outside of the van in our sleeping bags and blankets.

In the early morning as we started to stir and move about, an old lady dressed in traditional black Greek attire appeared and beckoned us to follow her toward a farmhouse across the road, a short distance away.

We had no idea what she wanted but we gathered ourselves up and followed her in a sort of bewildered procession that could have been a modernized version of Hansel and Gretel.

She led us through a small doorway into an ancient abode made of fieldstone and hand-hewn wooden beams where we were graciously welcomed into a big old kitchen with whitewashed walls and a fieldstone floor. There was a fire burning in a walk-in stone fireplace across from a huge harvest table set with plates and cups and loaves of freshly baked bread. On the ancient black-iron stove sat a big old, battered, black metal pot of warm goat's milk. This visual cornucopia, the bursting aroma of freshly baked bread and, best of all, the old lady's beaming ear-to-ear grin flooded us with a sense of gratitude. It was amazing! We were all totally blown away.

We feasted on a bounty of bread, milk, cheese and eggs and reveled in this genuine, heartfelt Greek hospitality, more of which I would experience the following year when I would make another overland journey through this same region on my way back to India.

None of us could speak a word of Greek and the old lady spoke not a word of anything else but she made us feel so welcome. Although we had well transcended the need for any spoken words, we thanked her profusely in several languages. Our amazement, smiles and gestures said it all. As we left, she stood in her doorway like a loving mother waving goodbye to her children. It felt like that. *It was like that.*

~

We continued on our journey through Greece and Yugoslavia and within a couple of days were cruising through the fairytale land of Austria. I can't speak for the rest of my companions, but I was blown away by the spectacular scenery. Having just returned directly from India, I might have been experiencing a bit of culture shock but whatever it was, this ride was a magical experience for me as we meandered along a narrow ribbon of twisting roads through pristine mountains and the lush, verdant valleys bursting with the kaleidoscopic colors of the new spring growth.

The little pastel-colored storybook houses brought to mind Snow White and the seven dwarfs and along with the spellbinding, awesome experience I was having, I wouldn't have been surprised to see Snow White and the boys step out from one of the pretty little cottages.

It took us almost a week to get to Amsterdam. There I bid my latest travel companions farewell and hopped on the big silver bird, making my way back to Halifax to continue on with my life as part of the sixties-seventies counter-culture.

Chapter 11

Chance Encounters of the Most Amazing Kind

Hooking up again with Mike, we began a partnership and spent the rest of the spring and most of the summer traveling between Halifax, Toronto, Ottawa and Montreal in a classic old hippie van. We knew people all over and we had a grand time moving along from one party to another, selling grass to finance our exploits.

Sometimes we would score our "dope" in Ottawa from Tom, a high school friend from Halifax who had moved there a few years earlier. Sometimes we would go to Rochdale, in Toronto, where on one of these visits, I met Jade, a lovely "hippie chick" who would carry my purchases out of the building. Being a regular at Rochdale, she was ignored by the constant police surveillance.

With the summer of '72 drawing to a close and all the partying winding down, Mike and I were pumped up for a grand adventure. I asked Jade if she would be interested in coming to Amsterdam with me and Mike in the fall to carry some hash back and she was…

My Kashmiri furniture never did arrive. All I received was a request from Hijj to send more money. I knew I had been scammed, but I didn't care. It had been one hell of a journey and a most enriching life experience, and at least I knew my way around some other cultures and what to expect. Since we now had a contact, of sorts, we figured we'd make our way back to Kashmir and this time we would be much better prepared to make a small fortune smuggling hash back to Canada. We made one last visit to Rochdale to arrange with Jade for the trip in mid September. When the time arrived Mike and I flew to Toronto to collect her and the three of us boarded a flight to Amsterdam.

We arrived early that sunny morning and checked into a small tourist hotel on the Damrak, one of the main streets in the centrum near the central station. I shared a room with Jade as we had been attracted to each other during those visits to Rochdale. This didn't go over well with Mike, but that's the way it rolled out.

We got the hash, about five kilos, from Noah, the contact Mort had made previously, and built it into some wooden souvenir type things that we repainted and made ready to go.

The next item on the agenda was to buy a VW camper. We found a really neat old VW window van with a sliding roof that someone was selling in front of the American Express office on the Damrak. This AMEX location had turned into an impromptu travelers market for vehicles and assorted other paraphernalia that people were dumping after their travels. We outfitted the van with sleeping bags, camping and camera equipment and most important of all, an eight-track stereo system with great speakers for our overland trip to India.

Then, with our contraband innocently placed in the back we headed to Hoek Van Holland on the Dutch coast and boarded a ferry to Harwich England, from where we would drive to

London. London, Heathrow, was low on the international "Drug Suspect" list, which is why we chose it over Amsterdam. Flying from Amsterdam was like carrying a sign that said "Have drugs, search me." The plan was for Mike and Jade to fly back to Halifax with Jade carrying the "package." Mike would take possession of it and pay Jade once she cleared customs in Halifax, and then she would return to Toronto.

There was absolutely no problem getting into England, although the customs officer who processed us seemed a bit uncertain whether or not to have us searched. We certainly didn't look like the straight tourist types, Mike with long hair halfway down his back and mine not as bad but still hippie looking and Jade, well she was a sweet young thing who probably saved our asses.

Perhaps that knife edge moment of uncertainty by the border guard was one of those defining moments of my life. A different decision by the customs officer might have changed everything and set me on a completely different path, altering my life forever. I'll never know. He waved us on....

The drive to London's, Heathrow airport was without incident. These were the days before global terrorism and airport security was almost non-existent. Mike and Jade left on their flight and I drove back into London to await the money that Mike would transfer to me through American Express after he sold some of the hash.

I left Heathrow airport with our last ten English pounds and a nearly empty gas tank and managed to get on the wrong motorway, heading away from London. By the time I was able to correct my mistake, I was miles away and had to put five of my ten pounds in the gas tank. I wasn't very happy about that.

Hungry and tired, I eventually made it to the Knightsbridge area of London, where I planted the van on a quiet residential street beside a little park. I covered the windows with newspapers and became a sidewalk gypsy for the next several days. As the weather was still very nice, I didn't mind it at all, sleeping in the van, walking in the nearby parks and strolling around the commercial area of quaint little shops just taking in the sights. Knightsbridge was a nicely manicured village within the big city.

I bought a stick bread and some cheese and water and hung out in a nearby laundromat that provided some tables, chairs and magazines for the patrons. It was here that I met a lovely lady about twenty years my senior, a Mrs. Cowie. During the course of our conversation, I told her of my situation, excluding the smuggling part, of course. She was sympathetic to my plight of waiting for money to be transferred, and quite interested to hear of my plan to drive to India.

We met again a couple of days later, this being my fourth day since Mike and Jade had left and I'm sure I was looking pretty bedraggled by now. Nice lady that Mrs. Cowie was: she invited me to her home to get cleaned up and have a bite to eat. Dear Mrs. Cowie, how considerate indeed. Her apartment was huge, with high ceilings, expensively appointed with precious hand-made Persian carpets and fine furnishings. I was treated to a hot bath in a huge porcelain bathtub after which I was further treated to a fine home-cooked meal.

It turned out she had a son about my age, Andrew, who showed up later that evening. He was friendly and gracious like his mom and invited me to join him and his friends at a nearby pub. We had a great night and returned to the apartment in the wee hours, where I crashed on the couch that Mrs. Cowie had prepared for me with nice fresh sheets and blankets.

After a fabulous, full English breakfast, I sauntered down to the American Express office to find that my money had finally arrived.

I returned to the Cowie flat to inform them and bid them farewell, and especially to thank them both for their amazing hospitality. Before I left Mrs. Cowie gave me a personal hand-written letter of introduction to her friend, the British Ambassador to Bhutan, residing in New Delhi.

Wow! Another chance/ serendipitous meeting that blossomed into a remarkable experience that would remain with me my whole life. Oh, the wonder of travel and those fulfilling life experiences that only happen when you are spontaneous... open and aware. I wonder about the cosmic connection / spirituality of such encounters...

I was actually kind of sad that my money had arrived. I could have handled another day or so of this hospitality, but with money in hand I was anxious to get back to Amsterdam and hook up again with Noah, the mad Israeli and his French Canadian friend and roommate, Zac.

Chapter 12

Cosmic Connections

Zac was on the run from Canadian authorities on charges of kidnapping and extortion resulting from an incident involving the junkie son of a prominent Montreal businessman with huge political ambitions.

The heroin-addicted son had ripped Zac and his buddies off for a kilo of hash resulting in a bizarre tangle of events back in Montreal. Zac foolishly agreed to a crazy kidnapping / ransom scheme conjured up by the son that went off the rails and ended up with Zac and his friends being charged with kidnapping and attempted murder. (Another story).

And thus, Zac's life was suddenly and extremely altered.

How your life can change in an instant...especially when you walk on the wild side....

Zac and Noah invited me to move in with them in a room they occupied a couple of floors above the Egg Cream Restaurant, a famous hippie/ traveler hangout on St. Jacobstraat, one of the many narrow meandering alleys in the rabbit warren area of Amsterdam Centrum.

The Egg Cream was a gathering place in the sixties and seventies that attracted free-spirited, vagabond youth from all over the world. It was also the departure place for the "Magic

Bus," an old, English double-decker converted into a psychedelic freak tour-bus that weaved its way from Amsterdam to Bombay and all the cool places in between, truly "A Magical Mystery Tour."

Our room above the Egg Cream consisted of just that: one room, with a couple of sticks of furniture along with a kitchen area and a shared WC (bathroom) located down the hall.

We slept in sleeping bags on foam mattresses on the floor and always started our days around noon by hauling on a huge hash joint rolled by Noah as soon as his eyelids became unglued and peeled back from his eyes, and always before we got out of our sleeping bags.

I can still see Noah dangling a string down three floors to the entrance of the Egg Cream and beckoning some patron to tie a cigarette to it for the tobacco to roll a joint if we were out. We had lots of adventures and fun times during this period of seeking out contacts in the hash business ...One adventure in particular stands out...

It was approaching midnight on a drizzly, wet, cold and dark night, with a thick cloying fog shrouding the Nieuwezijds Verburgwall, one of the main, meandering streets weaving through this seedy core of Amsterdam we inhabited. The atmosphere of this location on this particular night was sinister indeed and would have made a great setting for an assassination scene in a John Le Carre spy thriller...

I had made arrangements with some Italian guy I had met earlier in a student bar in the Red Light district. This particular hangout was kind of "shady" but always interesting and a popular place to meet and make contacts for lots of things or to just meet other young travelers from all over the world.

The mood was eerie and desolate as I stood silently waiting, enveloped in heavy fog, and bathed in the misty yellow glow of a nearby streetlamp. I was shivering, wet and miserable, not having a good time fighting off the icy tentacles that kept creeping up inside of my coat while I waited for this guy to show up for our eleven-thirty rendezvous.

After twenty minutes of standing there I felt as gloomy and desolate as my surroundings.

My new Italian "friend" was to bring me a kilo of "very good Moroccan hash", as he described it. He was supposed to go get it and meet me here at the entrance to this ominous looking back alley, St Jacobstraat, where I lived.

I waited, wondering if the guy would even show. I'd give him ten more minutes, that's it. At five minutes to midnight this very thin, wiry, nervous little guy finally arrived.

So here we were, standing in the shadows at the entrance to this dark, mist shrouded back alley about to do a drug deal, when up pulls a swarthy, middle-aged, rough looking Arabic character on a bicycle. He quickly dismounted right in front of us and said, point blank to my *Italian*, "Come with me I want to fuck you!" I couldn't fucking believe it!

Ahheeee! screamed my little *Italian* and bolted off up Neiuwezzijds like the proverbial "Bat outtta Hell."

In total disbelief, I yelled "Asshole" at the equally stunned bike man, as I tore off after my guy, or more importantly, my hash, yelling "wait, stop...it's just some freak."

Half laughing and half pissed off I finally caught up with this would-be Olympic runner about half a kilometer away and got him to calm down, convincing him that it was just some crazy nut who happened by and we should just finish our deal and split...just fade into the anonymity of Amsterdam. And so we did....

Back in our tiny room I recounted the story of my unexpected encounter which elicited paroxysms of hysterical laughter from both Noah and Zac. Noah couldn't straighten out for an hour and Zac wasn't much better.

I called Noah "the madman"...he was such a crazy character with an incredible sense of humor and, actually, a contagious laugh. He could walk into a room full of strangers and within minutes have everyone in stitches, not because of jokes or anything like that but just because his deep, raucous uncontrollable laughter was infectious. He was a handsome guy with black hair and a thin, chisled face, set off by a salt and pepper goatee, and the wildest, piercing, black eyes you can imagine. He brought to mind Rasputin. You couldn't help yourself if Noah "got into one." I've never seen anything like it to this day. One in a million, as they say.

We shared many great times and lots of laughs, dare I say ... and, most importantly, as time would reveal, he introduced me to the I Ching, the ancient Chinese book of wisdom which would become a great influence on my life ...

It was here while living with Noah and Zac that I met English Dave and several other interesting people from various parts of the world who were also in the "business/lifestyle" and on a similar quest as myself...experiencing life, searching for something, not exactly sure what *IT* was but we were searching for it. We were w*ild cards*... mavericks, rebels and renegades....searching out ourselves and our place in a rapidly changing world.

Noah had a friend, Abe, from his childhood back in Israel, who lived nearby.

We would often go there on Sunday afternoons to hang out, listen to music, have great chats, smoke hash and enjoy delicious home-cooked meals prepared by Abe's wife, Sarah.

They were part of a group of Israeli friends, most of them ex-commandos, who would sometimes drop by for a visit and some of Sarah's great cooking. They were a wild bunch, a couple of them were criminally inclined types but all of them were really fun, interesting and engaging people who liked to socialize, smoke hash and have a good time. We often had deep and meaningful conversations about life and I enjoyed their friendship and considering their philosophy.

Living above the Egg Cream was another fun experience. We smoked hash almost constantly and partied every night at the infamous Oxhoofd, a late night, all-night International dance bar with the most varied and eclectic patrons, where anyone from Keith Richards of the Rolling Stones to famous movie stars might and did show up.

We spent most of our nights here and usually never saw our beds until the sun came up... lived like vampires, we did. Breakfast was usually downstairs at the Egg Cream around two p.m. or so, after several large joints and gales of gut-splitting laughter due mostly to Noah and his zany sense of humor.

Life continued on like this for the next two months while I periodically packaged and shipped hash back to Halifax for Mike to sell.

By now it was mid October and we needed to be on our way before winter set in. I was to send one last shipment before Mike came and we set off for India.

Noah met some *Amsterdamse* girl by the name of Elise at the Oxhoofd who had a friend, she said, a local *Amsterdamer* who had some really good Moroccan hash for sale. We asked her to set up a meeting, which she did a few days later and a rendezvous was arranged on one of the *Herengracht* canal bridges. Noah and I arrived at the appointed hour, met Elise, parked our van on the bridge and waited for her friend to arrive. It wasn't long before Johan, a tall, lanky, long blond haired Dutchman with a big German Shepherd appeared.

We met and shook hands and each felt an immediate bond with the other...

Kindred spirits. Johan and I were destined to become life-long friends and travel the world together sharing many adventures...

Intuition was always my guide and it served me well during these years, and throughout my life.

I walked with Johan down one of the near-by side streets to a shop that was owned by his friends to pick up the hash, while Noah remained in the van chatting with Elise, arranging some later rendezvous, no doubt. Noah was a real ladies man. They loved him...and he loved them ...all.

After doing our deal Johan walked back to the van with me and joined us as Noah rolled a joint with Johan's hash. It was "top drawer." The four of us got a good buzz on, shared a great laugh and all became friends from that moment on. I got Johan's phone number and told him I'd look him up when I returned from India....sometime.

Another "chance meeting" perhaps... Perhaps something to do with the Chaos Theory...perhaps destiny, fate, karma... Pick one.

I sent the hash off to Mike which he quickly sold and then made arrangements to fly over so we could begin our overland journey to India in our most cool Volkswagen hippie bus.

Mike had been getting a bit weird lately on the phone. I don't know if he was still pissed off about Jade or what, but shortly after he arrived in Amsterdam he made some negative comments about me hanging out in Amsterdam having all the fun while he did the "dirty work." I'm not sure exactly what it was really all about but for sure there was bad blood between us before we hit the road.

I was still feeling pretty raw from the loss of my dear friend Eddie even though a year had passed. It was important for me to maintain my friendship with Mike.

As I mentioned previously, I met Mike some years earlier when we were about seventeen. We went to different high schools in Halifax, but I had seen him around. One night we were all arrested and thrown in the city jail together--Me, my brother and one of Frank's sons, for "loitering" in front of a local coffee shop / hangout and Mike for being intoxicated in a public place. We were teenagers...17-18 years old.

Mike was right out of it when the police tossed him in the same big cell that we were in. He started to get the spins and the next thing he was throwing up his guts all over the place. I grabbed him and got him to the toilet and held on to him until he upchucked all he could and then I helped him to a bunk where he passed out. Our fathers were called and we were released to them around midnight but we didn't know what happened to Mike. He was still passed out in the cell when we left. I met him several months later at a party and that is where our friendship began. Crazy Ken, who I mentioned earlier on, was his friend...

I was shocked to learn that Mike didn't have much more cash than we had before I sent all those packages back to him but I was determined not to lose another friend especially over money, so I let it go, anxious as I was to get on the road and begin this great overland adventure with a good friend.

It was the late October and the weather was turning as we set out. I can still see that day clearly in my mind--cold and overcast. Zac and his cute little Dutch girlfriend, Mad Noah, Mike and me standing by the van laughing and horsing around *almost* as usual, the difference being the level of feeling as you look into the eyes of your friend; that unspoken acknowledgment, that deep sense of kinship you've developed and share, and you wonder if you will ever see them again... and then the farewell hugs.

As Mike and I drove away they stood in the road, arms around each other, waving until we faded into the distance. One door closing, another opening... I wondered what lay ahead for us.

We made it as far as Berchtesgaden in the German Alps, the infamous place where Hitler had his notorious command post known as "The Eagle's Nest."

Chapter 13

Greece to Turkey: Test of Friendship and the Kindness of Others

Our clutch blew out just as we approached this charming Alpine hamlet. The first thing we did was find a repair shop and then get a room as it was much too cold to sleep in the van. The next order of the day was to find a pub and sample some of that fine German brew. It wasn't long before we hooked up with some local hippie types like ourselves, two guys and three frauliens who were also at the pub enjoying the local grog. We spent much of the next three days with them while we waited for the clutch assembly to arrive. The Dutch custom was to drink beer from small glasses. Here they drank beer from huge, liter glasses. It was all good! And the hangover was the same.

The clutch was repaired and we set off again through the picturesque winding mountain roads experiencing that special kind of sweet sadness that leaving friends, whether old or new, elicits.

Our next moment of truth came as we were crossing a snowy mountain pass in the Swiss Alps and encountered a blizzard. It was extremely tricky driving but fortunately I had lots of winter driving experience back in Canada during my early days behind the wheel with Frank, and I was able to maneuver us safely through the most treacherous moments. We eventually made it out of the mountains and continued on toward Yugoslavia.

After western Europe, Yugoslavia seemed really depressing. Being an Iron Curtain country it was relatively poor and "gray." Everything seemed colorless, bleak...maybe it was the time of year. It seemed to lack the sense of freedom or optimism that was prevalent in the rest of Europe that we had seen thus far and I found it particularly depressing to watch sad looking people dressed in drab clothing lining up in front of bland shops waiting patiently to get their meagre rations from mostly, empty shelves.

As the weather wasn't so terribly cold now that we were out of the mountains, we slept in the van at nights in fields just off the road or in isolated parking areas.

We picked up a young German hitch-hiker along the way. We were anxious now to get to Greece and the warmer weather.

Arriving at the Greek border one evening around dusk, we were informed, almost apologetically, by the Greek Customs Border Officers that they were obliged to inspect our vehicle before we could enter their country. Very politely we were asked if we would mind them doing a thorough search of our van as they were training some new border guards. Yea, right....three very hippie looking young guys driving east from Amsterdam...I'm sure they would have searched our camper very thoroughly whether we consented or not...but how gracious of them to present it in such a nice way. I just love the Greek mentality.

They did their thing very professionally for half an hour or so digging under seats and poking around in every nook and cranny. When they were finished the commandant and his two aides invited us to join them at a little cantina for a shot of Ouzo or two..or three...These border guards were genuinely welcoming and extremely hospitable and very interested in our intended adventure, life in Canada and our world view. What a great welcome to Greece. Again!

We were quite comfortable with these guys and could easily have stayed and gotten shit-faced with them, but we excused ourselves explaining that we were anxious to get to the islands. They understood and wishing us a safe journey, they graciously bid us farewell.

Heading off into the gathering darkness of the Greek night with a lightly falling rain wetting everything, all was cozy in the van and the road was decent. We had driven about an hour or so with the rain steadily increasing, making the road a bit slick. About forty kilometers from the town of Thessaloniki, rounding a turn on an upward grade the front tires just suddenly slid sideways on a very slippery railway crossing when, just like that we were airborne, the van coming down head-on into the top of a nearby cement foundation.

My head slammed through the windshield, as I drove the steering column and the steering wheel forward with my chest while smashing my knee upwards into the dash. I just remember a deafening crash along with a severe whack to my head. It all happened so fast.

Mike, who was beside me in the front, whacked his ankle and the hitch hiker (Karl) in the back, came catapulting forward and smashed into the back of the front seat slicing the bridge of his nose. All in all we were pretty lucky that other than minor cuts and bruises, no one was seriously hurt.

Dazed and perhaps in shock to some degree, I was befuddled... trying to make sense of what had just happened and trying to understand if everyone was ok... trying to get my orientation. I heard this muffled voice in the distance yelling "Where's the money, where's the money?"

I couldn't quite comprehend what Mike was going on about when a crack to my jaw snapped me back to reality.

He was freaking out about the money. I couldn't really grasp what he was on about. Astounded, I sat on the ground and pulled off my boot and gave him all the money I had stashed and then I just sat there by the van in a kind of stupor...like a dream...shattered...

It didn't seem very long before the police happened by on their regular patrol. They were concerned about me and helped me into their car and drove me to the hospital in Thessaloniki. As I was later informed by Mike, they then returned to the accident site with a bottle of Ouzo which they shared with Mike and Karl.

It seemed that in Greece any event calls for Ouzo !

I woke up in the morning between crisp white sheets with an outstanding headache and was told I had a concussion along with a badly bruised knee, bruised ribs and other assorted bumps, lumps, and contusions. The attending doctor and nurse wanted me to stay in the hospital but I was more concerned with getting back to the van to see how bad everything was and insisted that I had to go. They reluctantly consented to but only after I agreed to return for further examination after I dealt with the van.

With their help translating I hired a tow truck and drove back with the driver to the scene of the accident, where Mike and Karl were hanging out waiting for me. Mike was pissed off that I had wrecked the van, as if I did it on purpose. He just wanted to get the fuck out of there. I took a deep breath and said I'd take care of everything and he could just fuck off... wherever.

The van was towed to the local VW dealer/service centre in Thessaloniki. We all rode along in the tow truck, where upon arriving, Karl thanked us for the ride and split. I took half the money and Mike took off to Athens leaving me to deal with the van. I really didn't care much for him and his fucked up attitude at this point.

I went back to the hospital where they did some further tests and examined me a bit more and then directed me to a nearby doctor's office in order to get a prescription. As I sat in the crowded waiting room feeling kinda bummed out about Mike's reaction more than anything, the doctor came out to call another patient and spotted me sitting there. He came straight over to me and took me into the examining room. I was a bit embarrassed and gestured that there were several people ahead of me, but the doctor insisted and without speaking the language it was difficult to explain my reluctance so I just conceded.

The doctor spoke very limited English, but made me understand that I needed to get some medicine and tried to explain to me where I had to go... to a pharmacy to get this prescription filled but "it was all Greek to me." He realized I had no idea where to go, so he grabbed his jacket off the wall hook motioning for me to follow him as he barked something to his secretary on the way out; I presume, that he'd be right back.

We hopped in his car and drove to a pharmacy but they didn't have what he wanted so, off to another we went. This time he found what he was looking for. As I began to dig out my drachmas, the good doctor pulled cash from his pocket, slapped it down on the counter and insisted on paying for my prescription. I was, of course, gobsmacked.

We then jumped back in his car and he dropped me at a near-by hotel leaving me with his limited English words "You are a guest in our country, have a safe journey."

I was blown away by the hospitality and kindness of these Greeks I had met so far...There's something very special about Thessalonikians ... they must have a highly developed kindness gene or something!

These are the experiences that warm your heart and continue to do so when you look back.

The next day I went to the VW service centre, expecting to find a typical little "garage" but what I found was a most amazing, modern diagnostic centre, more advanced than anything I'd ever seen in Canada.

The place was huge, easily accommodating twenty vehicles at a time. It was spotless and the technicians/ mechanics all wore white smocks, like lab workers.

The manager was gracious and spoke very good English. After I explained my situation he made some phone calls and then wrote notes along with directions, explaining that the notes were parts descriptions for the junk dealers and addresses to junkyards and parts places for me to give to taxi drivers. Over the next two days, I was able to locate and pick up most of the parts I needed at a fraction of the new part cost.

The van had come down hard into the foundation. The front wheels were splayed sideways; the whole front was smashed in, including the windshield from where the steering wheel now protruded. The passenger side was severely mangled and the double side doors were crumpled, with one actually hanging off. It was a mess and it would take several hundred dollars, at least, just for used parts to make it driveable, not to mention labour costs...

On the fifth day I went to collect the revamped van and was surprised to see how good it looked considering the bashing it had been through.

There was a brand new windshield. The front was pretty well hammered out with a few wrinkles here and there. The steering mechanism and under-gear had been replaced with the used parts. The passenger side was straightened out do some degree (if you didn't focus on the wrinkles), and the side doors worked just fine again. There were a few gaps where a small animal or the wind could get in, but without having the bodywork completed to make it look new, It was vastly improved and very drivable. I felt my energy renewed, excited that I could continue my adventure of driving East.

Now for the bill... I figured it was going to be several hundred dollars at least, maybe over a thousand, so you can imagine my astonishment when the manager handed me a bill for the equivalent of about twenty-five dollars!

"Impossible." I said.

The manager just smiled and replied "That's what it is. You're a guest in our country, we wish you well, have a safe trip."

Again, I was gobsmacked!

I paid him the token amount and thanked him profusely and drove away thinking just how utterly wonderful and benevolent these people were to a total stranger.

As I continued in the direction of Athens I wondered how things were going to play out with Mike. I met him in the central Athens square near the American Express office. He was in a much better frame of mind, though I should have realized then he wasn't the kind of friend I needed, but I was more interested in putting the past behind us and continuing on with the adventure. So I just blew it off as Mike just being temporarily rattled, choosing to believe that he would come around to his old self. We had been good friends for several years now and after loosing Eddie I wasn't eager to lose another close friend.

Everyone has their moments.... N'est ce pas?

We spent the next few days wandering around the ancient streets of Athens, checking out the Parthenon, the Acropolis and other fascinating sites, drinking copious amounts of retsina, the local red wine (yuk) in the many cozy little bars and cafes scattered throughout the meandering narrow alleyways surrounding the ruins.

Mike seemed to be his old self and we were having a fine time as usual.

Proceeding ever eastward, we took a car ferry over to the island of Rhodes, famous for the "Colossus of Rhodes," the gigantic statue of the Sun God Helios, over a hundred feet high and considered to be one of the Seven Wonders of the Ancient World. Unfortunately, it was destroyed in an earthquake back in the day, but its grandeur lives on in the imagination.

We found a small *pension* (guest house) and hung out in the main town of Lindos for several more days exploring the countryside on rented motorcycles and walking with the ghosts as we time-traveled through the ancient ruins with Socrates, Plato and Aristotle here in the "Cradle of Western Civilization."

You might say the next leg of our journey was perilous; To get to Turkey our battered van had to be hoisted onto the back of a small fishing boat. With a thick rope netting wrapped around it, the van was hoisted up by a crane operator on shore who slung it out over the water and dropped it onto the back of the boat with little room for error. It was a precision maneuver. *Ker-plunk* !

Rolling and pitching on the sea, with no life jackets for crew or passengers and the van looking like it might fly off the back at any point, we headed toward the coast of Turkey, about three hours away where we arrived at a little port called Marmaras where the water is the bluest blue I have ever seen.

Our boat was tied to the side of the wharf but the variance was about five feet or so from the boat deck to the top of the wharf and the boat rose and sank continuously about three or four feet with the waves, pitching this way and that.

I was wondering how they were going to unload the van as I didn't see a crane anywhere in sight. It soon became evident that I was going to be the one to unload it by simply driving across the gap over two planks, each about a foot wide.

"Is this even possible with the boat being jostled around by the rough three to four foot swells" I wondered. There didn't seem to be any other choice and we had to get the van onto dry land and be on our way.

By now a small crowd of thirty or so had gathered around to watch this event unfold and see if I would actually make a mad dash up the uncertain planks to the safety of the wharf or plunge over the side into the churning sea and drown.

"Precarious" would be a huge understatement to describe the scene. Absurd, dangerous, you've got to be kidding...are other terms that come to mind. What to do? There were no other options.

I got in position with the front wheels on the edge of the planks. This was a one shot deal with no room for error. I timed it so that just as I felt the upsurge I gunned the motor and somehow, with the heave of the sea I managed to shoot up the planks and onto the wharf amid handclaps and cheers! That was hairy and I think it was as much luck as skill that I made it. What a rush!

There was a middle aged American lady among the crowd of spectators who walked over to me and Mike and asked us where we were heading in such a beat up old wreck. When we told her "India" she didn't laugh outright but her expression said it all. She wished us "Good Luck."

Good luck indeed! We'd need some of that.

Chapter 14

Turkey and Iran: Danger and Foreboding

Marmaris Turkey:

At this time Marmaris was a newly developing tourist town offering few amenities like restaurants, hotels, small shops and such. We were tempted to try and find a few grams of that legendary Turkish hash but the penalties were extremely severe. There were stories circulating all over Europe about the informers who would offer to sell you hash or other drugs and once you bought them would turn you into the police for a reward, so we weren't about to take any chances with that.

After purchasing a few supplies at a local shop, we headed off into some of the most amazing countryside we'd seen thus far. As we left the coast heading inland, the lush green landscape of a spectacular, verdant river valley, bounded on either side by gently sloping hills, welcomed us with disarming coziness. We passed small farms with rustic log cabins appearing as if they came right out of early American folklore.

Seriously, we wouldn't have been surprised to see Daniel Boone step out from one as we passed by.

We drove for two days through sparsely populated countryside before entering the foothills and began our ascent into the higher regions of the Taurus Mountain range ...The Bull ... aptly named. These mountains would live up to their reputation. Rugged and dangerous.

As we moved through time and space we saw many interesting places, similar to the region known as Cappadocia where the sides of the mountains were honeycombed with caves. Some of these caves had been chiseled out to form entire subterranean cities where the ancient inhabitants hid from the Mongols and other invading Barbarian hordes. Most of this area was extremely rough and dry and it appeared as though life would have been a struggle at the best of times.

Whenever we stopped in a small village along the way we were immediately swarmed by local villagers, mainly younger boys who would surround our van sometimes five and six deep, besieging us for anything we might have to give away. Talk about rock star status! Or aliens from another planet, more likely, as I'm sure these people knew nothing of rock stars, having zero contact with the outside world in those days--no phones, televisions or anything of that nature. Word of mouth was it.

Sometimes we would crank up our great-sounding stereo system and treat our curious neck-craners to the strains of Elton John belting out "Country Comfort" or the Rolling Stones, "Dead Flowers" or some other rock and roller banging out the tunes.

On a couple of occasions it got really freaky when we were inundated by large mobs of a hundred or more. Some of the more aggressive boys would start rocking the van and trying to open the doors. Fearing that these less friendly types would either tip us over or just pick us up and carry us away, we would begin moving slowly along, picking up speed as they continued pounding on the van ever more aggressively, threatening us with their distorted, ugly faces until we could break away and leave them yelling in our dust. What a scene--these strange, demented-looking people, several with facial deformities and/or crossed eyes, pressing their faces against the windows, looking like characters from "Village of the Damned."

When we got hungry, we would look for a restaurant. These were not "restaurants" in the sense that we were familiar with, but rather of the rough, mud-brick, hut variety, that we would stumble across every so often.

If possible we chose those on the outskirts of villages where there would be less chance of being mobbed. These shacks were usually dark little places that we entered through a small doorway to find ourselves standing on a dirt or mud-brick floor. Always there would be several pots of the most delicious, aromatic, mouth-watering food simmering over open wood fire--dishes like lamb stew, stuffed peppers, roasted and stewed vegetables, and soups served with delicious home-made bread.

We would barge in like a couple of cowboys from an old Western movie all bundled up in our foreign attire (big winter parkas), and point at various pots. There would usually be a rough wooden table or two where we would sit and wolf down the amazing fare like Barbarians, tearing off large chunks from the thick round bread and soaking up all of the delicious gravy and juice ....mmmm SoGood !

And all for pennies!

As always, we were curiosities to anyone (men only) who might be present. This was 1972 and not many foreigners were passing that way. There was never an issue with the people we chanced upon in these restaurants or in the countryside. We ate extremely well and continued pushing on ever deeper into the remote mountainous region of southern Turkey. The only problems we chanced upon were with the bored, aggressive younger men and teenage boys we encountered in some villages.

As we climbed higher into the Taurus Mountains and ever closer to Iran, things got hairier. At one desolate place we pulled into a gas station, the only structure around for a good many miles. The area was arid and inhospitable, offering nothing but dirt, rock and dust.

While I was standing by the gas pump waiting for the attendant, two young local guys around our age approached me and indicated that they needed a ride in the direction we were heading. I immediately felt a sense of danger and said to Mike that I thought these guys were bad news, so we just let on that we would give them a ride after we got our gas.

Meanwhile, the young boy who had begun pumping our gas crouched down beside the pumps where he couldn't be seen by them and caught my eye, warning me with the universal death sign--fingers drawn across the throat. The two would-be riders, were getting antcy, gesturing that they wanted in the van but we continued stalling them indicating that they should just take it easy as we needed to check things over before we were ready to leave. When the kid finished filling the tank and I paid him....(I hope I gave him a good tip) I jumped in the drivers seat and with a wink and a nod to the kid, Mike and I drove off leaving the would-be robbers in our dust.

I wonder sometimes what might have happened if we'd given those guys a lift. Robbery, perhaps. Murder? Who knows what may have happened out there in no man's land...perhaps they would have cut Mike's throat as we drove along and then forced me to drive to some even more isolated place where they would murder me as well and dispose of our bodies.... We could have ended up just two more "disappeared" young travelers, never to be heard from again. End of story.

~

It wasn't long before the temperature dropped significantly and we started seeing snow on the ground. We had to pile blankets and sleeping bags around our legs as the icy cold wind blew in through the cracks and crevices, resulting from our crash. Soon we were into deep snow territory with hard-packed snow and ice covering the entire road surface and snow banks piled high on the roadside as we gradually edged higher into the mountains.

One night as we crept along in the extreme, threatening, bitter-cold and darkness, feeling somber and exposed, isolated from everything we knew or had ever experienced, we pondered what we were going to do if the motor quit. We were in dangerous territory and hadn't seen any signs of life for a long time.

The temperature had plummeted to around minus forty at least, and stranded without heat for any length of time would most likely mean death. Still we continued on, fearful of letting the engine rev to slow or stall. And then, like magic, an unlikely intervention occurred again. A life-saving place of lodging that looked warm and inviting appeared like a mirage. It looked like a western style hotel/motel complex, completely anomalous to the region. "Hotel California" by the Eagles hadn't been written yet but if it had I might have thought this could be it.

Beyond relieved, we stopped and got a room. After getting settled, we went to the dining room to find a group of five

English travelers, four men and one woman who were making their way along the same route as us to India. They were all at least ten years older than us and traveling together in an older Land Rover and, like us, they had the good fortune to find this place and avoid the risk of continuing on in the plummeting temperature that promised nothing but peril.

This was our first brush with Westerners since we left Marmaras, and as usually happens at these impromptu encounters, we enjoyed a fun evening getting to know each other, sharing our histories and trading travel stories.

In the morning as we were preparing to leave, I found that the van was frozen solid. It wouldn't come close to starting. The English folks helped us by towing us behind their Land Rover for quite some distance before our engine finally fired up and we were able to continue along under our own steam. With such extremely cold temperatures we had to be very careful about shutting the engine off again.

Our new-found friends made sure we were all right and hoping that we might run into each other again, they bid us safe journey and drove off. Would we ever cross paths with them again, I wondered? Who knows?

As we chugged along we would encounter areas where the ice melt run-off from above had frozen across the road surface creating a patch of slick ice slanting downward and outward over the edge. These run-offs were usually located around a bend that was shaded from the sun and could span twenty feet or more. The mountain roads were precarious at the best of times, unpaved and barely wide enough to accommodate two vehicles. Add to that no guardrails and a sheer drop-off of three thousand feet or so... not a place for the faint-of-heart.

Whenever I had to cross one of these slippery ice patches, I would slow down to barely a creeping crawl and just inch along as we jerked and sideslipped ever closer to the edge and certain death.

"Twitch", as we had nicknamed Mike because of his nervous fidgeting on our infamous trip to Florida, sat beside me twitching and jerking about in his seat, or both of us sat deadly still holding our breaths, peaking on adrenalin. I would have a death-grip on the steering wheel, hyper-vigilant with absolute awareness of the slightest movement. Each time we felt that awful side-slip, our hearts would jump with the realization that if we hit a patch that was just too slick we would slide sideways and plummet over the edge before we could even react. We had no choice; to go back was to go on.

It was the most intense, nerve-racking part of the whole journey and by the time we got to the next village, we were both exhausted from the stress. We had been flirting with death and we knew that we could not continue on without chains on our tires. It would be suicide to do so.

We were lucky enough to find some old tire chains in a service station that would suffice and had them modified and wrapped around our tires. Continuing on we felt a little safer but it was still nerve-racking as hell whenever we encountered those icy run-offs.

After a few days we crossed into Iran. We had made it through the worst of the Taurus Mountains and considered ourselves lucky to still be alive and relatively unscathed, but, by then, the chains were all broken apart and not much good anymore.

As we got closer to Tehran we discussed passing through the Hindu Kush Mountains of Afghanistan but decided against it.

We were lucky to be alive and we knew it. Trying to battle the "Killer of Hindus" as the name *Hindu Kush* translates, would be suicidal in winter time, especially in this vehicle.

In Tehran we were required to be interviewed by the police for some obscure reason that had been explained to us at the border crossing. The police commander was pleasant enough but asked questions like "Did we sleep together in the same bed?" We thought it was an odd question but as we slept in separate beds we told him so and that seemed to be the right answer. We weren't really up on the scene in Iran in those days, but it could have been *Bad News* if we were homosexual there in those days. We might have been stoned to death.

We explained that we thought it far too dangerous to drive through the Hindu Kush and he directed us to the Customs Compound in Tehran, where we filled out all the necessary paperwork and were given permission to leave our van in storage, fully intending to return someday and retrieve it. Insha Allah!

Taking everything that we could carry, like our sleeping bags, clothing, camera equipment and essentials we parked in the designated area of the compound. Everything else--our fabulous sound system, camping gear etc. we wrapped in blankets and stashed under the back seats. Based on the way the customs officer accompanying us was ogling everything, we were certain we would never see any of it again Tehran proved to be uneventful and with the lack of females and bars, we opted to get out of there. A couple of days later, we stepped onto an Air India flight bound for Bombay.

Chapter 15

Bombay and Goa: Land of the Freaks

Our flight arrived in Bombay, the "freak" capital of India (freaks meaning hippie types) on a bright, hot, sunny day; but then every day in Bombay was hot, bright and sunny unless it was monsoon season. We were glad to be out of Iran.

As we gathered our luggage and were making our way around the airport we were greeted by the "President of India," a senile, shriveled, little, old guy who said he was there to officially welcome us to India and offered us tiny fragments of broken mirror, at a price, of course. We gave him a few rupees and bought him a soda pop and he was quite pleased with everything.

After our auspicious welcoming we hopped a bus into the city. It passed through miles of the worst possible slums you could ever imagine. A real-life exhibition of extreme poverty, filth and squalor stretched for miles along the roadside in the form of shantytown shacks made from assorted refuse such as old cardboard, pieces of tin and plastic, old boards...whatever trash that could be found and used to form shelter.

Along side of the road was a river of foul drainage run-off-- slimy green and reeking of sewage. We watched in disbelief as one person squatted, having a shit or pee while a bit further along another would be washing up in the same fetid water.

Abject poverty in the extreme! There is no such thing as privacy for the destitute.

I never truly appreciated or realized just how fortunate and privileged I was, until I witnessed this state of human degradation first hand. Television and newspapers just can't do it. As horrible as it might appear on the screen, the intensity and impact don't just glance off, it strikes you with soul piercing intensity. The images are inscribed on you psyche, I think forever. Are you ever the same after... I'm not certain you can be...

We found our way to the Colaba area of Bombay near the famous Taj Mahal Hotel and the Gateway to India monument and wandered around until we located the *Rex and Stifles Hotel*, a well known hippie hotel/hangout.

This funky old wooden Victorian structure of fading charm, presented wide, decorative, covered verandas running the length of every floor--once genteel perhaps but now well-worn and approaching decrepitude. It just oozed character from a bygone era. There were seven floors, the first three being the Rex and the top four being the Stifles. Some walls separating the rooms were only wood up to about seven feet and the top foot or so up to the ceiling was wire mesh, but it was cheap, relatively clean and "the" place to be. For a few rupees, we got a room with two beds and morphed into the scene, just two more freaks in the land of purple haze.

Chillums (type of pipe) flowed freely among the guests scattered on the balconies in old wicker rockers and other well-worn furniture. It wasn't long before we were introduced to "Bombay Black"-- black, Kashmiri hash (charas) laced with a little opium. Needless to say the scene was pretty mellow around the Rex and Stifles.

A *"tola"*, (eleven grams), could be purchased on the street corner for a few rupees and that was all one needed. Food was an afterthought, but there were plenty of restaurants and food stalls everywhere...And then there were the real opium dens as well, with names like "The Lotus Social Club"...seriously!

Bombay was fascinating, but we were bound for Goa, the real Mecca of the world wide Freak scene. After a few days of orientation to our new environs and feeling somewhat assimilated into this exotic world, we made our way to the hustling, bustling docks of Bombay harbor which was indeed, another world, in-and-of-itself. Chaos was the order of the day.

Like other big overpopulated Indian cities, there was the inevitable crush of people from many cultures. Porters, "*Coolies*" as they were called, dressed mostly in *Lungis*, (a sarong wrapped around the waist), accompanied by an official-looking white cotton jacket, some with an official badge even, ran about in a frenzy, hustling everyone, especially foreigners with luggage, often trying to tear it from your grip. They worked for *baksheesh* (tips), this being their only source of income, and it was considered a prime vocation. If they did manage to wrestle your bag from you, you would have to chase after them because they could run off in any direction, not necessarily where you were headed.

It was total madness complete with a cacophony of noise and yelling. After an hour of fighting our way through the pandemonium and being misdirected twice to the wrong wickets, where each time we had to shove, push and pummel our way to the front of the line, it was obvious the term "orderly" meant nothing here. Finally, at the third wicket we lucked-out and with our hard-won tickets in hand, persistently beating off the coolies, we threaded our way to the designated dock and boarded a decrepit old scow for the overnight sail to Panjim, the capital city of Goa.

The boat was an ancient old steamer from the twenties or earlier and the only tickets we had been able to buy were for "deck passage." This was not ideal because deck passage was just that--claiming a spot on the deck and sleeping on that spot, which wouldn't have been so bad, the night being delightfully warm as we grooved along under a star filled sky with the other friendly peace-and-love transients.

The problem was bedbugs! Vicious, nasty, little bastards that infested the boat! They tortured us and there was no escaping them. If you've never had the experience, I'll explain:

All of a sudden, without any kind of warning, you'd jump up shouting with a burning-itch-pain as a line of six or seven red welts appeared somewhere on your body, compliments of one of these horrible little creatures, about the size of your baby fingernail, nowhere to be seen, having moved along after feasting on your blood repeatedly, as it trekked along your body. In a panic you'd tear at your clothing, searching all the folds and hidden places until you found the repulsive little prick and then, seething with disgust, you'd squish the life out of it along with your fresh blood. Revolting, hateful things that they are!

But that wouldn't be the end of it...the burning itch from the venom they injected would last for hours, driving you mad. There was no relief unless you were fortunate enough to have some astringent which helped a bit by relieving the worst of the itch. We were lucky enough to meet a Chinese lady in the sweltering cafeteria who, sympathetic to our suffering, shared her tiny bottle of wintergreen with us. Ah...such wonderful, sanity-saving relief!

The trip was enchanting, in spite of the bedbugs. We put into small ports along the way. Most of them were not large enough to accommodate our boat, so we would lay anchor offshore while cargo and passengers were offloaded onto little skiffs and large dugout canoes that came out to meet us. Local villagers would paddle out in smaller canoes and hover around, diving for trinkets and coins that passengers would toss overboard for them. It was a romantic scene from the past--something out of a Somerset Maugham novel...

We arrived at Panjim around noon the next day and disembarked with the rest of the passengers, jumping into the chaos of the Panjim docks, guided to the "group taxi" stand by some fellow travelers who were familiar with the scene. There was basically one make of car in those days; the Ambassador, a sturdy little car designed for six people, maximum. But most often the "group" taxis would be jam-packed with ten or more bodies woven tightly together with the driver squeezed halfway out his window.

When our time came, we were selected from the que and intertwined with the rest of the group for the last leg of our journey--about fifteen kilometers, having only a few mishaps along the way.

The first event was a flat tire which meant everyone had to disentangle and extricate themselves from the vehicle, which was a bit involved considering the Interwovenness of our bodies. Separated for the moment, we waited and watched while the driver's assistant replaced one completely worn-out tire with another almost as bad but still able to hold air.

Ready to roll, we all had to squish and mold ourselves back into the car again to continue along until, a few kilometers later, the engine quit, which wasn't quite as bad because for that event, only the assistant had to disgorge himself, fritter around and beat on the motor until the driver was able to fire it up again.

The drivers always have assistants, typically, skinny little guys who go along for the ride, soliciting passengers and helping out with such events that might occur and usually do. One important function of the assistant was to cram as many people as possible into the car. This was done by pushing on bums, hips, legs, shoulders, heads or whatever body part was preventing the doors from being closed.

There were two more engine "quits" before we finally arrived at Calangute Beach almost two hours after our departure. Ah, India! There's no place like it! --Just like the Air India ad states.

The road dead-ended at a small hotel where we untangled ourselves again, from the rest of the passengers, and with our packs, started walking between the palm trees toward the long, golden, sandy beach. There were several small houses scattered among the trees and the length of the seven-kilometer Calangute-Baga beach was strewn with beautiful, old, rustic, hand-hewn wooden dugout fishing boats The quintessential beach paradise.

Within minutes we were approached by a local *Goan*, a real character, by the name of Tommy DeSousa, who introduced himself as *James Bond Butterfly*, a self-described Sean Connery look alike, which he was ...sort of...if you can imagine a skinnier Indian/Arabic version.

"Butterfly" was a self-appointed welcoming committee and fountain of knowledge for the area. If you needed *ANYTHING*, he was the man to see!

We needed a place for the night so he guided us to Fernande's Guest House, a clean, charming, welcoming place nestled under the palms. And that's where we spent our first night in Goa.

The surrounding area was captivating, with lots of space between brightly colored houses scattered about the surrounding sand, grass and palm trees which made it conducive to walking barefoot just about everywhere--my favorite way to be in the world!

Dropping our stuff in our room, we sauntered over to a small central area with a couple of restaurants and *Chai* (tea) shops close to where the taxi had dropped us. The restaurants weren't exactly up to western standards but rather unsanitary little shacks that served food of some description.

One place didn't look too bad. They served roasted water buffalo with rice for the equivalent of twenty-five cents so we ordered that and chai--always chai. There was another place nearby which looked interesting, with an extensive menu painted on the wall. Perhaps we'd try that tomorrow. After our meal (which actually wasn't bad), we wandered around the area familiarizing ourselves with the lay of the land before we crashed early, exhausted from our sleepless boat cruise and aided by couple of pipefulls of Bombay's finest.

The next morning we ambled over to the restaurant with the big wall menu and ordered several dishes from the waiter who nodded and brought us chai, of course, to begin. There were a few other nomads like ourselves there who were also having chai and passing their *chillums* around. This was a common practice here. Everyone, that is all the freaks, smoked hash openly and the local police didn't care. No one cared... Calangute was a very mellow place.

There didn't seem to be much action around the kitchen and after awhile we asked the waiter about our order to which he responded with that unique Indian head bobble, like his head was loosely attached to his body, and brought us more chai. After an hour or so of chai and chillums we finally realized that this "restaurant" didn't serve food, at least not that day.

Ahh ...India ... There definitely is no place like it!

It was back over to the water buffalo restaurant where they did serve food and we did have breakfast of boiled eggs, toast and more chai.

With the help of Butterfly we rented a small house in the little community. It was pretty basic, just two rooms, one with a double bed and the other room with a bit of a kitchen. There was no running water or toilet but it had a great thatch-covered veranda and suited us fine as we didn't intend to spend much time inside.

Close to the water, surrounded by sand, shaded by palm trees and cooled by a gentle ocean breeze, it was Paradise!

The first thing I did was hit the local market and purchase a couple of big burlap sacks to fashion myself a hammock. I fastened one end to a corner post of the veranda and the other end to a big post I drove deep into the sand. I would sleep under the stars as long as I was here.

Sleeping under the immense, star-filled sky every night can best be described as an existential experience, awe inspiring, spiritual, even mystical. Night after night, I lay gazing into the cloudless heavens aglow with a million stars, feeling at peace, one with the universe, humbled--a mere speck of dust....insignificant...yet an integral part of it all.

Goa was that kind of place where the roaming youth of the world were drawn with the Intention to visit this "must see" version of Paradise for a short period but would , almost inevitably, end up staying for months. Life on Calangute-Baga beach was bliss, a haven for young travelers like ourselves doing more or less the same thing...expanding our universe ...searching for meaning, getting high, smuggling hash or other drugs, seeking adventure...looking for love...

Not long after we arrived in Calangute we met a couple of fellow Canadians, John and Peter, traveling with with a German guy named Marco. We all became friends and hung out together mostly everyday from then on.

Every day was spent swimming in the warm water of the Arabian Sea, sunbathing (clothes were optional), ambling barefoot around the beach and through the fishing community scattered among the palm trees. Food was incredibly cheap. Nine or ten freshly-caught, giant prawns could be bought at the local markets for the equivalent of about ten cents. A huge papaya cost about the same. There was jackfruit, a big weird looking growth but oh, so delicious... along with a cornucopia of other exotic fruits and vegetables available for pennies a pound. Quite often we would have the food we purchased cooked for us by our landlady, who lived nearby with her family.

Life was "but a dream." The weeks went by. We smoked hash and drank Kingfisher beer, (not too bad if it was ice cold) at the local hangouts. There was never any serious trouble, just the odd bit of minor thievery. Everyone was more or less lovey-dovey, just enjoying the freedom of youth and the tranquility of the time and place.

There was always a party somewhere nearby and every full moon, a huge three day event took place on near-by Anjuna Beach. To get to Anjuna one had to amble (lots of ambling) down to the end of Calangute/ Baga beach, wade across a river and continue over a hill following the well-worn path among the palm trees. Anytime you met another fellow wanderer tripping along was reason enough to stop and share a chillum... sometimes it took hours to complete the journey!

Once, (it must have been after several chillums), the most exotic-looking small banded snake crossed my path. Fascinated by its bright colors I gently held it under my sandal. As stoned as I was, kind of mesmerized actually, I watched it writhe around my foot and ankle, tongue flicking, until it dawned on me that it might be poisonous at which point I lifted my sandaled foot and it continued on its way. Oh My...

The full moon ritual on Anjuna had begun a short time before we arrived in Goa. Pete Townsend and The Who showed up with all their equipment and put on a free concert and then left all of their equipment behind for anyone to use. From then on monthly full moon parties became a tradition, with live music preformed by random musicians from all over the world who would just show up and play. I do believe I saw Jon & Vangelis there one time.

At any given full moon party there would be a few hundred people from every corner of the world, most of them stoned out of their heads on the free LSD that was handed out to anyone who wanted to partake, along with endless chillums that floated around. There was booze and various other drugs and people dancing naked or nearly naked in the sand, some making love in the bushes or right there on the beach. Huge bonfires lit up the sky and this place rocked for three days and nights every month. Wild and free ...this was the place to be... in 1973...

The author...first days in Goa.

Typical day on Calangute Beach

Calangute / Baga

Sometimes in the early evenings, we would gather on our veranda--our veranda being our kitchen and hangout area, as it was for most people. Various hawkers would wander by selling stuff-- honey or bread or fish or whatever. An old man would wander by sometimes hawking the most amazing, delicious fruit-cakes which we occasionally bought.

On one of his pass-bys we gave him a *tola* of hash and asked him to bake it into a cake for us, which he did.

He delivered it on Christmas Eve and the five of us ate it there on our veranda. We all got so stoned we couldn't move and just ended up passing out and greeting the dawn of Christmas Day right there, in the same configuration as the night before.

We thought we'd try again on New Years Eve but this time we only put in five grams of hash instead of eleven because we intended to go to a big bash that was happening down on the beach. New Years Eve 1973!

Shortly after eating the cake we started walking down the beach toward the party, a kilometer or so away. About halfway there we took a break and sat down in a circle on the sand. As the hash kept creeping up on us, each of us in turn, kind of fell back, one after the other, till we resembled spokes on a wheel all sprawled out in the sand.

As stoned as I was, I decided to try and make it back to my hammock because I didn't want to wake up in the hot sand all full of bites from the sand fleas, feeling dirty and itchy and hot and dehydrated... I'd done that before and it wasn't pleasant.

I did manage to make it back to our house and collapsed in my hammock, so zonked I couldn't move another inch. Then I heard something. It was a rustling sound coming from the thatched roof above me. Whatever it was, it sounded sizeable.

I wondered what kind of animals could be up there. Probably a big snake I thought, but I was too stoned to move. All I could do was listen as it moved along the dry thatch. Then it fell off the roof and landed right on top of my legs with a heavy thud and as quickly, fell over the side and onto the sand. From the feeling (no bones) and the weight, my best guess would be a big snake like a small Boa or a Python but I'll never know ...I couldn't even raise my head to look. Happy New Year !

Butterfly, who had moved into a room in a nearby house, started coming around, usually drunk and acting up, generally making a nuisance of himself. His usual thing was annoying the fishermen's wives with curses and insults.

They all put up with him because they had known him since he was a child. He was around forty or so and from a well-to-do local family. He had been educated in Saudi Arabia where he spent several years before returning to Goa a few years ago. He had taken up his position as local drunkard and oftentimes liaison between the freaks and locals, finding accommodations for wanderers like us and providing other such services as guide, finder of things and whatever else he could come up with.

He was harmless enough and it was funny and sad, at the same time, to watch him in action after he had a bit too much *Fenni* (the local drink). He could become increasingly obnoxious especially with the local women and anyone else who fell into his line of sight.

At other times, usually late at night after he had worn himself down by verbally abusing the neighborhood, you could hear him lamenting his life in the words of his song "Don't cry for Butterfly." It was usually in his room where he most often performed this woefully melancholy lament until the wee hours, interrupted occasionally by shouted curses from one or more of the locals if he persisted, driving them nuts, as he sometimes did. In the end, they just accepted him like you would a recurring rash.

One evening as we were hanging out on our veranda puffing away and grooving to the music from Marco's little music device, Butterfly, in his usual inebriated state, stumbled by, all strung out, moaning and groaning and getting in everyone's face, being a complete nuisance. None of us paid him much mind and after awhile he wormed himself directly under my hammock and started moaning his sad tune.

I noticed that his foot was all cut and bloody, so I got out of my hammock and managed to half-persuade and half drag him onto the veranda where I cleaned and bandaged his injury. He sobbed like a baby. He couldn't believe anyone would care enough about him to do this. I laughed. It was nothing for me but a simple act of caring from one human being to another, even if he was being a jerk. Who hasn't been a jerk at times? We all have our moments.

We continued our socializing and Butterfly eventually passed out. When I awoke in the morning he was asleep under my hammock like a faithful dog.

He was entertaining to say the least. Sometimes you could even have an intelligent, interesting conversation with him. He was well educated, spoke several languages and was just fucked-up, but certainly not a fool nor a nasty character by any means..

Bathing and toilet facilities were interesting. There were large wells scattered about as were toilets…both communal. A hammered copper vessel attached to a rope was thrown down the well to collect your water from which you could fill your own water container for home or pour the water over yourself and wash right there on the spot. The women wore lightweight saris and the men just a lungi for modesty. This whole procedure gave new meaning to the term "communal bath."

The toilet was another thing altogether. Some houses had their own outhouse, but most were communal, set off a bit in the distance. They resembled a typical outhouse made of thatched bamboo walls and roof set on top of a three sided cement foundation about two feet off the ground with a sloping and open lower back side.

Pigs and hens wandered about freely. The pigs, usually sleeping, sprawled about randomly. Anytime someone ventured toward the outhouses the pigs would stir and then follow in the direction of the soon-to-be-occupied outhouse. As you squatted over the precipice, for there was no seat, your bottom was exposed to the open back of the foundation for the benefit of the pigs that would stick their head in and devour your excrement. How gross is that!

Also, they could be pretty aggressive, especially if there was competition for the feast. You had to make a hissing sound like SSSSSTTT to keep them out of your ass. Just one of the rather odd experiences of life in Goa, but like anything else, you got used to it. I always wondered if they had taste buds because they also slurped up banana peels, papaya peels and other discarded food waste with the same vigor....

On occasion, our landlord would invite us to join the family for roast pig.

Suppressing gags we always declined.

Quite often we would go to the near-by town of Maupsa to pick up the things we couldn't get locally and to change money on the black market. It has long been the case in India that some of the wealthier shopkeepers pay about twenty percent above the bank rate for foreign currency, so most of the travelers changed with them.

To get around other parts of Goa we sometimes took a bus. This was always an experience! Mostly, they were dilapidated old wrecks jam-packed with people and animals...chickens or a goat, whatever the locals were transporting.

Unlike today, with so many people traveling everywhere, we were an unusual sight.

Quite often the locals would engage you in the most friendly, innocent, curious manner. *"What is the purpose of your mission here? Did your government sponsor your trip? Are you with the Hippies organization?"* It was lovely if you wanted to take the time to engage them. I enjoyed the interaction. And then there was their fascination with watches...

The other option was to grab a taxi and travel by yourself, but that was no fun and more expensive. Better were the group taxis, as I described earlier. At the taxi gathering-spots there would be several black and yellow Ambassador cars parked randomly with the drivers or their assistants yelling "Panji, Panji, Panji" or "Maupsa, Maupsa, Maupsa" or wherever, and for a few rupees (about twenty cents), you could join the "group" and travel as a local. It was always a laugh...if you didn't have to go too far. Eight people jammed into an Ambassador wasn't so bad.

My worst experience was being jammed into one with fourteen people that broke down a total of fifteen times between Maupsa and Calangute, a distance of about twelve kilometers. Each time I had to untangle myself from the driver and the assistant with whom I was entwined. Having rock-star status, I had the privileged seat next to the driver with three small Goans wedged in beside me, plus a young boy who was threaded among us, across our laps. I'm sure we could have won a Guinness world book record!

As they were mainly Catholic here in Goa, having been under Portuguese rule since it was conquered in 1510, until they were ousted in 1961, there wasn't that Muslim restriction on women mixing with men, as in other parts of India. The people considered themselves Goan...separate and distinct from Indians in general.

It was easy to get lost in time here and after about two months we decided that we should get on with our mission ....after all....we did have a mission.

Chapter 16

Heading to Kashmir January 1973

It was hard to tear ourselves away from the Goa beach scene but (sigh) one day we made our way to Panjim again by group taxi, this time with only a few passengers and without any breakdowns. It was another gorgeous, sun-soaked morning at the dock with all of the coolies frantically running about as usual, seeking "baksheesh."

I was destined to hear this term many times over as I traveled and encountered the beggars of India throughout in my journey.

The scene at the Panjim docks was always good-natured, intimidating only to the uninitiated.

We boarded the bedbug express to Bombay, again battling the horrible blood-sucking vermin. The only place of any refuge from the nasty little buggers was in the cafeteria, but that was at least forty degrees Celcius at the best of times.

Twenty-four hours later, we arrived back in the jostling madness of Bombay forcefully threading our way through the ultra-chaotic dock scene and back to the Stifles Hotel once again. After checking in, we set about making reservations to Srinagar via Indian Airlines... not the most reassuring airline in those days--their planes were always crashing! The train was out as was any overland travel because the mountain passes between Jammu and Kashmir were blocked with snow, so Indian Airlines was our only choice.

What a flight!

As we approached the Himalayas, it got really rough and we were bounced around like a cork on the ocean. The mountains were all around us and seemed close enough to touch, as we flew over a long, deep valley far below, between two ranges of mountain peaks. The plane would drop suddenly and jerk and twist like we were on a bucking bronco; then, abruptly, we were just a few hundred feet above ground as we careened in to land on an airstrip on top of a plateau about five thousand feet up. Scary shit!

At the airport we were mysteriously met by Mohammed, who was delighted to see me *again* and was "expecting us," or so he said. Don't ask me how he knew.

Either airport connections or he met every plane.

Mohammed ferreted us away from the other hustlers and soon we were back on the Rajan houseboat in the presence of dear old Iqbal. Mike was quite impressed by the scene and we hunkered down as the weather closed in upon us. There was a good deal of snow but the few roads were clear for the most part and we could move about.

We had Mohammed's entire family of servants at our every beck and call with Mohammed in charge. He was his usual entertaining self and since we didn't have any cigarette papers he would empty out cigarettes and refill them with hash and tobacco for us whenever we wanted a toke.

We told Iqbal that we were back for more hash but this time we would oversee the process of concealing it in furniture and take care of the shipping ourselves, with his help, of course. He agreed to begin making the necessary arrangements over the next few days--no problem. In the meantime we would enjoy the area and see the sights.

The houseboat was extremely comfortable--all hand-carved wood with intricate detail well-appointed with beautiful walnut furniture and hand woven carpets throughout along with a bevy of servants always at hand, that sometimes got to be too much...

And then there were the barefoot troops, all of Mohammed's six children constantly running around without socks or boots in the freezing cold and snow! Mike and I felt sorry for them and gave them most of our socks, but we never once saw even one of the children wearing them.

Every day Mohammed would ask us what we would like for dinner, then list off the choices--roast chicken, roast duck, what vegetables would we like... but every night when dinner arrived we were presented with mutton curry and rice.

On the third night, I asked Mohammed what was going on. "Every day you ask us what we want for dinner and we tell you chicken or duck, but every night you bring us the same thing--mutton curry." Mohammed's response was always the same. wiggling his head in the typical fashion, he would sheepishly reply, "Yes Sahib." "Yes Sahib, Yes What?" I'd say, and again he'd reply in the same downcast eyes, embarrassed way, "Yes Sahib."

Aaah India...There really is no place quite like it! You love it or you hate it, there is no in-between.

Some people find this aspect of the Indian culture a bit too frustrating to deal with, but I loved the foolishness and kind of innocence of it all.

Finally Mohammed suggested that if we *really* wanted to have something other than mutton curry, we could go hunting and shoot some ducks for him to cook. Great idea, we thought. We'd do it straight away and have duck for tomorrow's dinner!

Not so simple, it turned out. It took three days to make the necessary arrangements.

First we needed to procure a hunting permit and India, in those days, was the epitome of bureaucracy gone mad. To begin, we had to go to a small office in town and fill out forms in quintuple, without the aid of carbon paper, and this was just the beginning! Next we had to acquire permits for guides, then permits for the guns and finally, permits for the bullets! Each permit required a trample through the dirty, hardpacked snow and slushy puddles to visit some separate, dingy mud-brick office occupied by three or four thick-browed men in phirans sitting around a wood stove surrounded by walls piled high with old, discolored, dog-eared papers; forms in quintuple, no doubt, of previous years "permits" all piled up and archived for some future purpose yet to be determined.

All of this permit procurement took three days, because "interviews" were always conducted with each permit request. I guess the authorities wanted to satisfy themselves that Mike and I weren't about to start a revolution, or shoot ourselves or our guides, or all of the above.

On day four, we set out very early in the pre-dawn hours in three cars. It was bloody cold. After half an hour or so, we arrived at a rutted old road leading to a small lake. We would walk from here. We were a full contingent of a dozen bodies, including Mohammed, along with Iqbal, wrapped in his blanket over his phiran, looking cold and miserable as usual, one official guide, some other young men and several small children.

I couldn't believe my eyes. Even with two pair of heavy socks on inside of rubber boots my feet weren't all that warm, yet beside me was a small boy about five years old walking barefoot as if it were a warm summer day. And not just one, there were at least five small kids in our group all walking barefoot and seemingly not bothered by the cold at all! It was about a twenty-minute walk along a frozen old rutted, dirt road in sub-zero weather with ice and snow covering the ground.

Mind over matter? I have no idea, but that would be my best guess. How else was it possible that these little children's feet didn't freeze?

When we arrived at the lake, Mike and I were directed into a small open wooden boat along with the boat-handler who sat in the back, and another young guy who sat in front, all of us wrapped in phirans. In cold weather, Kashmiris carry wicker encased clay pots with wicker handles called *kangris* under their phirans that are filled with hot coals to keep warm. We each had one. They are quite effective, especially when you squat forming a tent with the kangri between your knees. These people even sleep with them. Tricky, I thought. Won't be trying that anytime soon!

As dawn broke and the first light appeared, a flock of ducks passed overhead. Mike and I each had double-barrel shotguns and let go our first volley only to hear a loud boom and watch the pellets shoot out with about the same velocity as throwing them by hand. The birds continued on, unfazed.

This was how our hunting expedition went. Sometimes as we shot straight up we would be showered by the pellets falling back on our heads. Sometimes there would be a good charge and we would actually take down a bird or two, tiny little quail-like things that they were, not much more than a mouthful. Other that that first flock we scared away, we didn't see any more ducks.

The first time we actually shot a bird we found out why the guy was sitting in the front of our boat. Without any warning he flipped off his phiran and sprang over the side into the frigid water like a Labrador Retriever wading out to retrieve our game! Then back he came, hopped into the boat and resumed his position under his phiran. We were flabbergasted and appalled!

This was too much for us and we strongly protested, but Iqbal and Mohammed and our guides reassured us emphatically that this was how it was done. It was fine with them and the "retriever." There was nothing we could do, but accept their ways though it sure felt weird being a party to this young guy jumping into the frigid water every time we shot a bird.

For a few hours more, we continued on with the hunt until we had a dozen of the tiny birds to sustain us over the next few days. As snow started to fall, we headed back to the houseboat. That evening we feasted on the little bird carcasses, roasted to perfection. We were done with mutton curry!

It was warm and cozy that evening on the houseboat nestled into its berth at the edge of Dal Lake, surrounded by the majestic snow-covered Himalayan peaks. Mohammed made us joints and entertained us with old Army tales as his sons squatted nearby, tending the fire and bringing us tea as the intensity of the storm continued to increase outside, dumping more snow over the valley. I really felt like some early explorer discovering this far away, exotic land.

The next day disaster struck!

When I awoke I couldn't lift my arm off the bed. Literally! I couldn't move! I didn't feel sick, yet somehow I knew immediately that I had hepatitis, the scourge of many a western traveler in India in those days. Shit! What to do now?

Mohammed was summoned. He took one look at me and ordered up hot, sugary tea...lots of it. He and his boys helped me into a sitting position and brought me teapot after teapot along with cold Limpca Cola, the horrible, sickly-sweet, Indian version of Coca Cola. Foul stuff indeed, but I was burning up and couldn't get enough liquids.

It was weird. I actually felt like I was melting. Feeling so wasted I was unable to stand until after having downed about six teapots full of the sugary tea and about a dozen cold Limcas. I made it to the living room with Mohammed's help--I was so weak...

I needed immediate medical attention but the storm was still raging. Going anywhere was impossible so I had to resign myself to the houseboat and Mohammed's care until such time as the weather cleared and we could get a flight out of there.

Just the sight of food made me want to vomit but I couldn't get enough liquids to drink. All this time my body was wasting away. Between the continuous sugar-tea, Limca and water I managed to stay hydrated while dropping about seven pounds each day. All I could do was sit there gazing out at the whirling snow and the surrounding landscape wondering where this "ride" would take me.

At the beginning, I weighed in at about a hundred and eighty pounds, and when this ordeal was over some ten days later, I was down to a hundred and ten pounds or less. I looked like a survivor from a concentration camp; especially so to others more so than myself.

Each morning when I woke up it was necessary to put another hole in the leather belt a friend in Halifax had made me before I left on this trip. Each hole was at least an inch in from the previous one. It was not a good feeling. By the third day I was turning a vulgar shade of yellow, not just my eyes, but my skin as well.

It was gross. My urine turned the color of old car oil and smelled most foul. Truly, it's the most disgusting disease, physically and psychologically, in part because people stare and shun you like a leper.

The author on the Rajan houseboat

Shikaras on Dal Lake

Many thousands at the Srinagar mosque

Slaughtering a goat for the feast

We cancelled our business with Iqbal who was most disappointed at losing the revenue, while doing his best to feign real concern for me as well. Love that guy!

He always struck me funny, trying so hard to be sincere. Mohammed, on the other hand was genuinely and extremely worried about me.

Three days later we lucked out. A break in the storm allowed us to get a flight out to Delhi. What a rush it was in that small plane screaming down the runway and right out over the edge of the plateau dropping and bouncing our way out of there through the turbulent air currents. It was the wildest plane ride of my life, worse I think than when we arrived! I was too ill to care.

Chapter 17

No Man's Land

Arriving in Delhi I immediately went to a doctor who confirmed what I already knew. He said there was nothing to be done for me. I should just rest and eat raw and boiled vegetables. No meat, fried foods or alcohol.

I was really wasted by now and not thinking clearly, if at all. It takes energy to think and I had zero energy. I was just "there."

Mike was starting to get strange again, blaming me for ruining his trip. He had wanted to go to Nepal and I was screwing everything up. I was so out of it, I really couldn't comprehend or care less what he was on about; I was doing everything in my power just to stay in the world. Mike wanted to go to Kathmandu. I didn't care about anything just as long as I could sleep.

Being a bit of a junkie at heart, Mike had a big bottle of seconal, (a type of hypnotic barbiturate pharmaceutical) that he had brought from home and liked to take now and then. He started giving them to me which further induced my stupor. He was soon leading me around like a catatonic zombie. We were on our way to Kathmandu…

I was there in body, but that was all. Mike dragged me on and off busses and trains all across India to the border of Nepal where the one and only road led up to Kathmandu.

The journey was all very vague as if in a dream. Sometimes I would find myself on an empty train; then I'd wake up to find it overflowing with people hanging out the doors and windows and on the roof; then I'd find myself propped up in a chair at some dusty train station in Jodhpur or Lucknow or some other parched desert place before being dragged on to another train.

After a few days of this trance-like journey, we eventually arrived at the Nepalese border. Between the combination of delirium from the hepatitis and the narcotic effect of the opioid seconal, I was so out of it I could have been on the moon.

At the Nepalese border, Mike arranged for our transportation to Kathmandu on the back of a truck carrying huge burlap bales of *beedies,* the poor man's cigarette (tiny rolled tobacco leaves tied with a thread). Mike and I, along with three other Nepalese "passengers" rode on top of these bales in the open back of this big truck. I was still much too out-of-it to really care what was happening...I was just being carried along. I had put another four holes in my belt by now... six or seven in total so far.

Our drive would take us about ninety miles up the narrow mountain road and, with luck, we would be in the fabled city of Kathmandu the following day.

Mostly I slept, as usual, but would occasionally be woken by the jostling of the truck as it made its way along the rough and rutted mountain road. Sometimes I would glance over the side into the abyss below. The mountain's of Nepal were the highest

I'd ever seen and the road wasn't very wide. Looking over the side of the truck, was like being in a plane.

When we met another vehicle there would be some serious jockeying for position. If we were on the outside, we would have to maneuver around the other guy as he hugged the mountainside in a spot wide enough for the two of us to pass. Sometimes we would be out over the edge in the truck's overhang with the wheels just barely on the very edge. I remember thinking that if we went over, it would take a full five minutes for us to hit the bottom!

When darkness fell like a curtain, the increased danger forced the driver to pull over and stop for the night.

At some point it started to rain. The driver and his assistant pulled a big tarp over the back to keep us and the cargo dry. The sides of the truck were open wooden slats up about a meter or so and above them was a skeletal metal frame. They tied the tarp down in a few places so it wouldn't blow off.

I was in my usual comatose state, when suddenly all hell broke loose! I awoke to sheer pandemonium with no idea of what was happening until I felt the truck lurching backwards and realized that Mike and the Nepalese were freaking out because we were trapped under the tarp. They were frantically yelling and tearing at the tarp, trying to escape before the truck plunged over the mountain side! Talk about a nightmare!

I jumped up in extreme panic, in spite of my stupor, and tried to claw my way out with the rest of them. It was a most horrible feeling--the truck lurching backwards with all of us, in total blackness, screaming, just waiting for that first back wheel to slip over the edge and then feel the truck tilt and roll over as it tumbled into the void and we plunged to our deaths.

All the commotion woke the driver in time to reach the brake and stop the truck on it's lethal trajectory.

It seemed that the emergency brake had let go during the night as the driver slept and the heavy rain dislodged the rock they had placed behind the wheel allowing the truck to roll backwards. It was only the compression from the engine that held us long enough for the driver to respond and save us all.

Well, That was a rush! But one I surely could have done without ! I bet I lost twenty pounds that night alone! You can be sure no one tied that tarp down the rest of the way!

Chapter 18
Kathmandu February 1973

We arrived in the ancient, exotic city of Kathmandu the following evening still shaken by the nightmare experience of going over the edge and feeling grateful to be alive, even if I was yellow all over.

There's nothing worse-looking than yellow bloodshot eyes! I was still dropping the obligatory seven pounds a day and along with the seconal, I was just coasting, more or less accustomed to my new semi-lobotomized state of being by now.

The things I remember most about Kathmandu were the narrow passageways between the mud-brick buildings, many with dark, carved wooden balconies and intricately carved doorways. I loved the mysteriousness of it all but was constantly banging my head on the low ceilings and doorways.

We stayed in a small hippie hotel on "Freak Street," the actual name given to the street because of all the hippies who were drawn there in the sixties for the legal hash sold in government-operated smoke shops with names like "Eden Hashish Centre," where every description of hash was available.

This was the final year for the legal hashish shops in Kathmandu. People had come from all over the world, mostly ardent hash smokers and connoisseurs. It was a very cool place to be. We ventured into the Eden Hashish Centre and bought an assortment of temple balls and various other delicacies. It reminded me of the corner candy shops at home with all the penny candies displayed in glass jars on the counter. You just helped yourself.

It was about this time that my fever broke. My weight, all hundred and ten pounds of it, or less, stabilized. I started to feel like I could eat again. The sight of food didn't make me feel like I want to vomit. That was the real turning point!

Walking down Freak Street, we were thrilled to run into the English people with the Land Rover who had helped us out in Turkey months before. They were shocked, of course, when they saw me...My clothes were hanging off me. I was "half the man I used to be." (The Beatles)

We went to a cafe where we reconnected and exchanged stories over coffee and snacks and then parted company again, wishing each other safe journeys. Perhaps we would all bump into each other again somewhere, sometime...

There were a couple small restaurants, one being "Aunt Jane's," that served authentic American apple pie, and a few other cozy hang-outs that played rock music and served coffee and food. They were great places for lounging around on big overstuffed cushions...grooving.. Cat Stevens music was *de riguer*... "Morning has broken," "Peace train".....pass the chillum.. It was, after all, the early seventies. Peace, love and a sense of adventure prevailed.

One day when I was feeling stronger and had been off of the Seconal for awhile, Mike and I rented motorcycles and, like time-travelers, glided our way through the mountains toward the border of Tibet, mostly on a newly-constructed Russian-built highway carved along the mountainside.

The scenery was breathtaking. Rope bridges were slung between cliffs miles high, with spectacular views of endless valleys far below. We photographed it all with our wide-angle and Zoom lenses on Kodak film we had purchased in Bombay before we left for Kashmir.

Along the way we picked up hitch-hikers. At one point, I had a *Gurkha* (renowned Nepalese warrior) complete with his *khukuri* (traditional curved knife) proudly seated behind me. Upon entering a small village, I spotted a group of kids playing and running around in the distance and was struck with that prescient sense of impending danger. *I just knew* one of those kids was going to run right out in front of me. I quickly geared down squeezing the brakes as much as I dare. Just as I come to a dead stop, one of the little girls, oblivious to any danger, found herself directly in front of me and, tripping over her own feet, stumbled and fell headfirst into my bike.

Immediately I was surrounded by what seemed to be the entire village appearing from nowhere. Angry men and women with emotionally charged voices and threatening gestures surrounded us in a most hostile and threatening way. Fortunately, my Gurka spoke up, calming the situation by explaining to them, obviously, that I had been fully stopped when the little girl fell into my bike and I wasn't at fault.

Gurkhas are extremely well-regarded in Nepal and, lucky for me, his words soothed the tension. Normally calm people, enraged at one of their own being struck by a passing vehicle, they had been known to toss an offending driver over the cliff. But for him I might have been flung into oblivion. This was typical reaction not only in Nepal but all throughout the region; India, Pakistan, Afghanistan etc. I even heard of one incident where the driver of a bus had to drive to the nearest police station with the body of a young boy stuck under his bus because the villagers would have killed him then and there had he stopped.

This premonition, prescience or whatever you choose to call it, prevented what could have been a serious accident. After a pretty tense few minutes things cooled off with just a few slight ripples from a couple of the disgruntled villagers. We continued on our way for several more miles, eventually dropping off my guardian-angel passenger somewhere along the way. As we parted company he offered me his hand and we peered into each others eyes with that unspoken acknowledgement that we had shared a significant life experience.

Several miles later the road ended at a small wooden bridge crossing a beautiful jade-green flowing river. We had reached TIBET!

On the other side hung a veil of mist shrouding a castle-like fortress mysteriously set into the mountain side, guarding the entrance into a forbidden land. It looked like a scene from that original Kung Fu movie popular in the seventies. I expected to see one of those famous Kung Fu fighters step out of nowhere. This mysterious aspect of the frontier just made it more intriguing!

Alas, there were two very unfriendly-looking armed Chinese-Communist soldiers standing guard at the far end of the bridge. We could tell just by looking at them there was no way we were going to walk over that bridge and approach them. They looked like they would shoot first--entering Tibet there and then was not to be.

We drove back a ways to an isolated area where we couldn't be seen by the guards and attempted to cross the river, but the water was ice-cold and moving much too fast which put an end to our plan, and that was as close to Tibet as we got.

Probably a good thing in hindsight.

Heading back to Kathmandu we realiized that we had dallied too long and soon would be draped in darkness making the high, winding, mountain road that much more dangerous. Oh Yea!

Mike's bike broke down and now we were stranded on the mountainside in the dark. There wasn't much traffic, but eventually we stopped a passing truck and offered to pay the driver to load Mike's bike onboard and take Mike along with the few other locals he already had huddled in the back. It was an open flatbed fitted with some wooden rails along the sides to prevent cargo from falling off. It was really dark and getting very cold as I followed the truck's tail-lights along this ribbon of asphalt as it wormed its way through the imposing mountains.

In Kathmandu later that night, after dealing with the bikes, we headed straight for one of the little hang-outs for some more Chai, chillums and company. We hung around for a few more days, while my yellow skin faded back to a more whitish tint and then booked a flight back to Bombay. No way were we going back down that death-defying road to the border of India.

The take-off from Kathmandu was exhilarating. After the cow-chasers cleared the landing / take-off field, we hurled down a short runway in a small prop plane, zooming past the wreck of an old plane that had crashed a few years before. Then we shot out over the edge of the mountain just like in Srinagar, where you suddenly found yourself five thousand feet or so above a deep valley...not for the faint of heart.

Chapter 19

Goa after Nepal, February 1973

Back in the sweltering heat of Bombay, we took a taxi from the airport passing again through miles of the most decrepit shacks looking very much like a refugee camp lining the road into the city.

Bombay was fascinating, especially in the Colaba area surrounding the Taj Mahal Hotel and the Gateway to India monument--a vibrant mishmash of streets and alleys that gushed with a smorgasbord of the exotic, ringed by a wide promenade along the seawall splashed by the Arabian Sea. The entire city pulsated with a thrilling sense of intrigue and excitement, along with an air of bejeweled splendor side by side with the worst poverty and deformity imaginable.

Hope and despair--Love and hate...every aspect of humanity swirled around in this cornucopia of life here in Colaba, Bombay. Vibrant and alive, swarming with colorful people from all over the world, of all ages, in all manner of dress, including a relatively small group of nomadic, hippie-vagabonds who traveled the world according to the seasons, smuggling drugs and dealing in assorted commodities, hawking them along the way whenever and wherever they could make a profit.

As time went on, several members of this hippie-gypsy tribe switched partners resulting in many mixed-blood children. It would be interesting to track them down today and see how their lives unfolded.

At night we shuffled along in the amber glow of streetlights through arch-covered sidewalks crowded with hawkers of everything, interspersed by areas where people lived right there on the sidewalk and slept on wooden-framed rope beds. I always felt a bit embarrassed, like I was walking through their homes. Indeed I was, for they lived their lives right there in the street--washing, shaving, breast feeding their babies, cooking their meals in battered pots over small gas stoves, seemingly oblivious to the hordes shuffling through their home.

As Lala, my rickshaw driver in Jaipur would describe life in that city years later...*"Life in full color*!" What an apt description.

Mike and I hung around the Rex and Stifles Hotel and occasionally made our way over to the Crawford Market which was another area infamous for Falkland Road, known as "the street of women in cages."

A large section of the street was lined with cement rooms with barred fronts exactly like prison cells. Prostitutes of all description inhabited these "cages." Young and old, pretty and repulsive, some with families... all wrapped in bright colored saris. Anything you could imagine or desire, and then some, was supposedly available here.

Drugs of course were another big draw to this area and we would jostle our way through the intensely crowded, narrow streets until we found the alleyway we sought that would take us to the old Palestinian who lived on the second floor of one of the crumbling wooden buildings.

Up one level of rickety, well-worn slanted wooden stairs brought us to a set of rooms with shuttered doors that opened to the balcony overhanging the alley and the bizarre outside world below. The old, bone-skinney Palistinian lay propped up on a kind of mattress layered in wrap-around white sheets with only his gnarly old feet and white haired vulture-like head uncovered. He was like a failed maharaja surrounded by his young attendant concubines. You could get whatever you wanted here: opium, heroin, cocaine, girls, boys, ... just about anything was available for a handful of rupies. We sometimes got a little coke just for a change-up from the Bombay Black hash.

One of our favorite haunts was the *Lotus Social club,* an opium den not too far from The Rex and Stifles. On our first visit, we actually asked a traffic policeman in the street for directions and he pointed to a funky old, two-story building with multiple wooden-shuttered windows just across the street. No clandestine operation here! The double-wide, battered front doors were wide open all the time. It could have been the entrance to an old time western saloon.

Climbing the worn-down staircase to the second floor, we entered a large room where several thin reed mats were scattered over the smooth, polished wood floor. At the end of each mat was a small block of wood, just big enough to accommodate the side of your head above the ear. We were ushered around some bodies lying in repose. It wasn't very comfortable lying on the thin reed mats on the hard floor with a hard block of wood for a pillow, but as you inhaled from the opium pipe, freshly prepared by your attendant, the wood "pillow" became like feathers and the floor, with it's rich patina, felt like a cloud...or just floating above it.....

Guests purchased "cups," little metal containers that held a gram of black tarry goo that your attendant collected onto the end of a long thin stick, twirling it around while heating it over a small flame until it turned the color and consistency of bubblegum. He then poked it into a small hole in the center of the enclosed pipe bowl and passed you the receiving end to hold while he guided the flame to the gum. You took a long slow draw and held it. It wasn't harsh at all and after a few draws you became extremely relaxed and mellow, indeed. After a couple more hits you were in La La Land where everything was just lovely and peaceful as you floated away on a dream.

You could still be present, if you wanted to be, but it was so pleasant to float away into a dream land where all was bliss and there was nothing to disturb you. At a certain point if someone wanted to saw your leg off you'd just smile and say "sure." If you've ever had a major operation...this is basically what they give you before they cut you open.

We only went here a few times. On one of our visits I I met a well-educated, well dressed, refined older Indian gentleman who was lying on the mat next to mine. He was wearing a freshly-pressed, clean white shirt and nice trousers and looked like someone's grandfather out for a Sunday stroll.

During one of those periods when I came back to awareness he caught my eye and in a kindly way spoke a few words, giving me what I later realized was a gentle warning. "Opium" he said, "is like the fountain of youth for the elderly but *death* for the young."

≈

It was during this time in Bombay that we heard about "een bane Willy", a young guy from Holland who got hit by a bus and had his leg amputated. "een bane Willy" (Dutch) translates to "one leg Willy." I was to meet some of his friends in Amsterdam years later, although I never did meet him.

Hanging out and roaming around Bombay was a bit too much for me while I was recovering from the hepatitis and I really felt the need to get back to Goa just to lay in my hammock and chill. So, a couple of days later we hopped aboard "the good ship Cockroach" and late the next morning we were back at our little house on Calangute beach, under the palm trees, surrounded by the happy, smiling fishing community we had become part of. Butterfly was there in his usual capacity.

Mike and I were no longer the good friends that we had been when we started off from Amsterdam. Our funds were getting pretty low and Mike was quite sullen, holding me responsible for ruining his trip to the Far East along with the scam. I was feeling pretty miserable physically and mentally. Feeling very weak now, just skin over bones and missing the camaraderie of a good friend. I was still trying to hang on to what was left of our friendship, not wanting to accept what was happening, but there came a point when I no longer cared.

One day I was laying on a thin grass mat inside of the house, needing the coolness of the cement floor, fading in and out of consciousness as the day passed and night drew closer. I lay there on the floor too weak to make it back to my hammock. Mike walked by me a couple of times, but never offered any acknowledgment. Because of his attitude toward me I sure as hell wasn't going to ask him for help. Later on Mike went to bed in the double bed where he slept, walking past me again with an air of distain.

At some point during the night, I became aware of just how ill I really was and felt like I wasn't going to make it through the night. An intense anger welled up in me. How could Mike just leave me here in this condition? I wouldn't treat my enemy like this. I'm sure it was the seething anger that gave me the strength to drag myself over to the bed where Mike was sleeping, pull myself up and tumble in beside him. I felt like this was my last gesture. I was not going to die on the floor like a dog.

Mike woke up startled and pissed "What the fuck are you doing?" he snarled.

I replied "Fuck You" and passed out.

A day later I awoke, still in my earthly body and managed to get myself together enough to eat and recover slightly. During this period I would have periods when I was functional, not really OK, but compared to how weak I could get, I was relatively OK. I could move about.

To say I was fed up with Mike, would be an understatement. As we still had to be in each other's company until money arrived from home I chose to remain civil to him, although all I wanted now was to be alone. The money arrived. A friend from home, RJ, had concealed a few hundred dollars in some packages of rolling papers, something of no value or interest to the postal people so they let it go by.

Mike was anxious to get back to Canada and that was fine with me. All I wanted to do was rest and recover and there was no better place to do it, I thought. I loved it here: friendly people, palm trees and a beautiful sandy beach, warm water… tropical paradise what more could I want?

I was feeling a bit stronger so I decided to go with Mike to Bombay and part company there. We had one last visit to the Lotus and Mike left the next day. I shook his hand goodbye and told him in no uncertain terms, that as far as I was concerned we could still be friends, to some degree, but we were no longer business partners and I would have nothing more to do with him in that regard. Mike flew back home and I took the boat back to Goa.

Chapter 20

Visions in the Sky

I must have slipped into delirium as I can hardly remember anything other than being sprawled out on the deck, too sick to move. It was here I met a girl named Love. Megan was her first name. She was on her way to Australia.

She obviously saw that I was in a bad way and came to my aid, propping me up, giving me water and comforting me.

When we arrived in Panjim she got me into a taxi and accompanied me back to my house on Calangute Beach where she helped me into Mike's bed. That's the last thing I remember before I collapsed into a comatose state for the next several days.

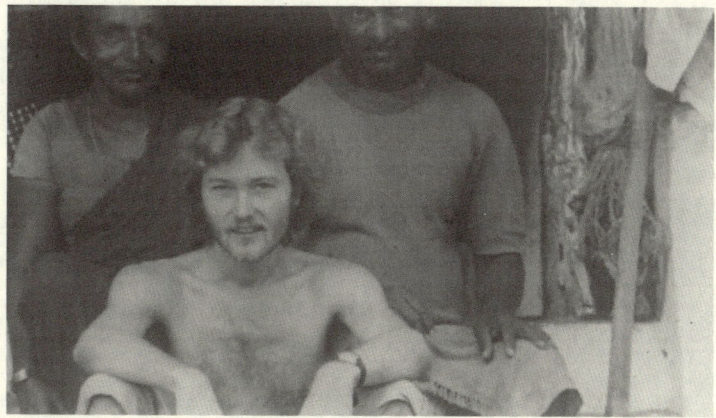

With my landlords

I don't remember much other than being conscious at times and this very cultured, high society English girl taking care of me, propping me up in the bed, feeding me soup and vegetarian food that she prepared and playing the flute. No doubt she saved my life. Without her, I'm pretty sure I would have passed out and most likely, away, in my little house and no one would have found me for days. Another fortuitous encounter.

Around day five, I started coming around and had the strength to sit up and gradually over the next few days I was up and walking about. I was too weak to make love but after a few more days of her excellent care we crossed that bridge! I had not smoked anything since I left Bombay.

One day, feeling up to it, I sauntered down toward the water. As I was walking between the palm trees, I had what I'd later learn was an *out-of-body* experience, not that uncommon I understand, among people who have had a near-death experience,

Suddenly... I viewed my own incredibly skinny, emaciated body, including my own face, from a short distance up above. In a split second I thought, "I'm dying." I was "outside" of my body. My life force was no longer like it feels now, contained within as I write these words, but rather my consciousness was up and away from myself. It was only momentary, I believe, but I remember my awareness: My body is going to collapse now as "I" am out "here" and my body was "there"-- just an empty shell.

In this same moment I felt swathed in a vast, all encompassing brightness and in that instant I was part of everything that is..or ever was... cosmic, totally connected with "the universe"... pure energy, I guess. I can only describe it as "total consciousness." It was incredible...and peaceful all at once. Bliss, perhaps...? Then, instantaneously, I was back in my body bewildered and awestruck, touching myself all over to confirm that I was really "back" while thinking, "What the hell just happened?"

I turned around and walked back up to my house got pen and paper and wrote the following poem which just came pouring out. I've wondered and thought about it ever since.

> *Charlatans, wise men, seekers of the truth...*
> *Reach you hand in through my eyeball, and I will lay down ten*
> *thousand trips about the universe, I'll take you where I've been.*
> *There are castles up on Venus, they drive chariots on Mars.*
> *On Earth they try to kill you if you refuse to buy their cars.*
> *We travel a rough road, stumble and fall*
> *and each in his journey must taste of the gall.*
> *Brothers and sisters, can you not hear my call*
> *It may be distorted due to the wall.*
> *You may gaze upon my body, hate me, rape me, spill my blood*
> *But in my hour of passing retrospect and you will find*
> *That you never even knew me or the cosmos of my mind.*

I didn't know what to make of this. I wasn't in the habit of writing poems but this just poured forth, mostly inspired by Mike, I think, and the rest I'm still pondering.

The next few days were filled with strange occurrences. Butterfly was killed when the vehicle in which he was traveling to Anjuna Beach flipped over, throwing him out and then landing on him, crushing his head. I was deeply saddened when I got the news, as we had developed a deeper connection after that night I cleaned and bandaged his foot.

Megan, my English Florence Nightingale and I went to his funeral which was held in Mapusa the next day. Butterfly was laid out in a wood-framed coffin covered with sheer, black cotton so that he was visible inside. He was dressed in an old suit that was far too big for him and his hands were covered with a pair of cheap, white cotton work-gloves and bound together with rope. His head, which had been more or less squeezed back into shape, was resting on a soiled white pillow with a large, blood / fluid stain caused by seepage from his crushed skull.

The mourners, several of the local women, including the ones he would annoy and curse on "those nights," kept removing the coffin lid while sobbing and wailing uncontrollably, as they jostled his body to the nearby graveyard.

There was a couple of times I was sure they were going to dump him out of the coffin with all the stumbling about as they clamored to touch him one last time. Talk about a most bizarre scene.

Later that night Megan and I were heading over to Anjuna to take in the monthly full-moon party. The moon provided plenty of light as we walked along Baga Beach toward the narrow river that separated us from Anjuna. The river was high, so we had to wait for it to get a bit lower before we could wade across. We made ourselves comfortable on the sand and lay there gazing up at the stars. The sky was clear, as always. I had been sleeping under the stars in my hammock for months and the one thing that always struck me about the night sky was the noticeable absence of clouds.

After awhile I waded out into the river to check the depth and was about mid-thigh when the lighting changed to an eerie glow. The water became a gunmetal/metallic color. I felt really strange all of a sudden, as if the hair on the back of my neck was standing up. When I looked up, the moon was just disappearing behind a big cloud that resembled a bust--the form of head and shoulders.

Immediately I returned to Megan where she lay in the sand and lay down beside her. "Do you see what I see?" I asked. She nodded, soberly.

Both of us lay there transfixed by the vision that unfolded before our eyes.

By now, the cloud didn't *just* resemble a bust, it *became* a bust, with well formed head, neck and shoulders, eye holes, nose and mouth formed by darker cloud and openings as the moon moved behind the forehead. Rays shone out in all directions around the head and out through the eyes like a heavenly form. We watched in awe as it continued to change.

Dark patches formed sinister eyebrows, the face narrowed, small horns of cloud formed on the shoulders and head simultaneously, followed by another larger set of horns on the outside beside each of these. The whole thing changed into the classic Devil's image with double horns before our eyes. Then, it just dissipated into a thousand tiny fragments and the sky was once again cloudless. We just lay there for some time, silent, mesmerized. Eventually we stood up and returned to Calangute without even going to Anjuna. It was the strangest thing and neither of us spoke of it again. I think we were bewildered. We had witnessed something mystical.

Megan continued preparing the most incredible vegetarian meals I had ever eaten and I'm sure it was in large part to her wonderful cooking and loving care that I recovered so well.

A week or so after the "cloud night," she set off for Bombay continuing on her journey to Australia.

Eventually I got a post card from her sent from Thailand, telling me she had gotten hepatitis. "I wonder where that came from?" she wrote on the card. I never heard from her again. I hope she's had a full and happy life. My love to you Mega, I'll never forget you. Not long before she left I asked her why she took all that time and made such effort to take care of me to which she replied that she just liked to fuck blond haired, blue-eyed guys. Lucky me!

A short time later, I got some type of insect bite on my right ankle that just would not heal. In the tropics festering is not uncommon with wounds below the knee. There's a lot of fermentation going on in the low damp areas, which makes an ideal breeding ground for germs.

After a few days a small round scab appeared over the wound and my ankle became infected. It festered to the point where I had to remain in my hammock with my leg elevated. A couple of the local women tried to help by putting mud concoctions and leaves on the wound and a German tourist who was staying nearby at Fernande's offered to put a bread poultice on it. The leaves and mud weren't doing anything so I agreed to let the German try his poultice, but the silly ass took it boiling hot from the pot and wrapped it around my ankle. I screamed and had to hit him to get it off. He scalded my bloody ankle! Nothing more. Idiot!

The wound got so bad that I could not lower my leg below the horizontal position, it throbbed so intensely. My whole leg became very swollen starting with my foot so that it resembled elephantiasis. The thickness of my lower leg was the same as my thigh. From my foot to my knee was like putty and I could make a deep indentations in it anywhere which would remain for quite some time.

I knew I had to do something, but there wasn't much medical help available and trying to get around was impossible. As soon as I lowered my leg, my ankle throbbed with such excruciating pain it felt like it was going to explode. All I could do was lay in my hammock with my leg elevated. Everyone, that is the locals whom I'd gotten to know, were deeply concerned. I needed immediate medical attention.

The son of the family I rented my house from offered to carry me to the village doctor. I agreed and the next morning before we began our journey, I smoked copious amounts of Bombay Black to deaden the pain. It was still pulsating with pain but tolerable. I slung my arm over his shoulder and he supported me as we hobbled through the village on our way to the doctor.

The doctor's "office" was a small one room shack with a dirt floor and a makeshift plywood examination table draped with a ragged, blood stained, once-white sheet. I was welcomed by the doctor, a small, thin guy about forty, with hand gestures and a wag of his head. He helped me up on the table where I lay, exhausted and sweating, thankful to have my leg raised and the intense throbbing subside.

Doc looked at my wound, hummed and muttered a bit and then announced that many other "hippies peoples" had come to him with the same problem and he would give me the "cure." The "cure" began with a shot of dubious looking brownish liquid in my arm, after which he began to force the puss out of my wound by squeezing just below the knee and working it down, all the while repeatedly encouraging me to "bear the pain, bear the pain." This torture took about fifteen minutes or so and there's no way I could have tolerated it without all that Bombay black. "Bearing the pain" was excruciating and we were both soaked in sweat, but in the end Doc managed to squeeze about a cup of orangey-white puss from the small hole in my ankle and, I dare say, in the end, he likely saved my leg and quite possibly, my life.

My helper got me back to my hammock where I collapsed exhausted. Within a few days the swelling was diminished and my leg improved to the point where I was able to take a group taxi to Panjim and visit the hospital. There they attended further to my wound and told me I was lucky to have seen the doctor when I did. I could just as easily ended up "een bane Jackie." Or worse. I hung around Goa until mid-June, a month or so into the monsoon season. I loved the warm rain. I had the entire beach to myself and would walk in the most vicious downpours that would send the local villagers scurrying for cover, looking at me as if I were mad. Most of the hippies had left by the end of May heading north to places like Nepal or back to Europe or wherever. My respite was over. I was back on my feet and needed to pick up where I had left off.

Afghanistan was on the horizon

Chapter 21

Hitch-Hiking Through the Desert

I picked a day to leave Calangute Beach wondering if I'd ever return. A lot had happened since I first set foot in Goa and now all hundred and ten pounds of me was bound, via the bedbug express, to Bombay and onward to the unknown wilds of Afghanistan and whatever might lay in store.

Hash was very cheap in Afghanistan compared to India and I figured I'd score the same primo (Le Dain quality), Masar-i-Sherif hash for about twenty dollars a kilo which I would sell back in Canada for about ten thousand a kilo and start over.

"Start over." That's a curious expression…We don't "start over," we continue on, battered and bruised perhaps, but hopefully wiser from our experience…

After a few days in Bombay at the Stiffles, getting a feel for being back in touch with the world, I decided I'd hitch-hike to Delhi just for the hell of it. Having been an avid hitch-hiker in my teens, I thought this could be a really interesting way to see the country. Always I had loved the anticipation of the unknown…never knowing where you might end up or who you may encounter. For me life was about opening up to serendipitous events, adventure and experience, whatever they might be. I never worried about misfortune on my adventures and figured that whatever came my way I'd deal with or I'd be dead and not have to...That was my philosophy.

I took a bus to the outskirts of Bombay and set out walking along the road. In 1973 there were no big highways, but rather small, narrow roads with thick, rough, asphalt tops with no centre lines.

It wasn't long before I was picked up by a lorry--this was how I would travel through central India for the next six days, being handed over from one driver to the next, an esteemed guest of their culture... it was like that...celebrity status!

As there weren't many westerners traveling around India in those days, those of us that were, were considered quite a spectacle especially by people living in the countryside away from the big cities like Bombay and Delhi. There were no TV's then, in rural India so their worlds were pretty limited to their surroundings.

I found myself bouncing along in an old, doorless Tata truck on a road that's barely wide enough for one vehicle...and *this* is the main route to Delhi...and everywhere else. "Precarious" is an enormous understatement!

The roadbed was raised up about a meter or so, angling down at a fairly steep incline to the parched ground. On top was a layer of asphalt about six inches thick with rough, jagged edges. It reminded me of icing on top of a cake. The pavement was only wide enough for one and a half vehicles, so when two vehicles approached each other head-on, one or both had to drop over the side at a perilous angle in order to pass without a head-on collision. No one wanted to drop over that jagged edge, so they drove directly at each other until the very last moment when they both *usually* veered off at the same moment to avoid a collision.

For the drivers it was a continuous game of "Chicken" to see which one could force the other off the road first. Mostly, both drivers would hold out to the very last second, either laughing hysterically or cursing a blue streak before swinging wildly to the side, two wheels dropping off the asphalt with the truck lurching at a near forty- five degree list while they tried to maintain sovereignty as close to centre as possible.

Insane! Although top speed was only about fifty kilometers or so, a head-on collision would have been deadly and sometimes, when you went off the edge, the truck came close to toppling over right on its side.

The drivers were great, perched like Hindu gods in their decorated, shrine-like cabs.

As one driver turned off in another direction he would be sure to set me up with a fellow driver heading toward Delhi; and so it went.

At night we would stop at rest areas. These stops were just very primitive open shacks under some trees. Some of them would have a very basic "restaurant" consisting of a thatched roof supported by four posts, possibly some rough wooden planks for seats and a couple of pots sitting over open flames of a rock firepit that served as a kitchen. The fare was simple vegetarian dishes served on tin plates, and, of course, there was always chai.

The drivers all carried wood frame rope beds with them on top of their trucks, which they would place around the dry, arid ground, in a cluster. There they would socialize, perhaps have a drink if they had some liquor with them, or pass on news and other information, basically just spending enjoyable nights under the stars in the company of friends.

Everyone was welcoming and friendly and there was a strong sense of community! I found Indians to be very open and hospitable people in general, especially in the countryside. It is like that in many places around the world, but India is special. It has what I would call a feeling of "open heart"--openness to trust, understanding and compassion. That was my interpretation. Perhaps it's because the culture is so old...

India...Truly...There's no place like it!

It was at these rest stops that arrangements were made for my safe and comfortable passage onward and it was, with a sense of trust and responsibility between the drivers that I was handed over for the next segment of my journey.

Sometimes I would be with a driver or his assistant who might speak decent English. There was always an "assistant" who seemed to be just along for the ride. At other times, I would be with hosts who spoke very limited English or none at all, but in all cases it was very comfortable and we managed to communicate just fine. "Open Heart."

One particular driver was a short rotund little chappy from the Punjab with an imposing, handlebar mustache. He spoke not a word of English, nor did his young Kashmiri assistant, about my age, who was completely stoned out of his head the whole time on, what else--the best Kashmiri hash. He giggled a lot and goosed me on the bum every chance he got. He didn't strike me as being gay; he just seemed to think it was funny.

The driver was also a bit out of his gourd as well, but they were both so genuine and entertaining and very good natured and I enjoyed their company for three nights, my longest ride. We enjoyed a special camaraderie as we rumbled along, slow roasting in the intense desert heat.

The truck, like most of the others on the road, had no doors and a big springy seat; elevation about seven feet above the road, before the drop-off. The inside of the cab was a virtual shrine with small sacred ornaments and Hindu gods in abundance. Ganesh, the elephant-headed God was most favored. All around the windshield were little lights strung like Christmas tree lights of various colors. You had to maintain a grip at all times for fear of being catapulted out the door opening by a sudden lurch or bump. The springy seat added significantly to the catapult affect.

There were large open wooden boxes on top of the cabs where I would sleep at night along with the driver and assistant, although in most cases the driver would use his rope bed on the ground at one of those primitive truck stops.

Sometimes I would ride up in the box in the dry parched air. Evenings were the best, when the desert heat gave way to cooler temperatures and millions of stars created a magical canopy overhead, so close you could almost reach out and touch them, especially after a *chilm* of Kashmiri hash....

The days were so unbelievably hot that the three of us would sit in the cab with soaking wet towels draped over our heads and within twenty minutes they would be bone dry! It was like being inside a clothes dryer with constant hot air whirling around the cab, parching every part of you.

I would occasionally try to describe, in that non-verbal manner of expressions and gestures, the roads and driving conditions on the 401 highway through Toronto with eighteen lanes of traffic and cars with air conditioning traveling at 120 km/hr. plus. They would give me that quizzical look, as if I had perhaps had too much sun or charas. At other times I could see in their eyes that faraway look and I knew they were imagining a Utopian Shangri-la where the streets were paved with gold and everyone was wealthy, happy and well fed.

One day as I was riding on top in the box and feeling particularly "fried," we stopped near a small village of scattered mud huts. All of the inhabitants, perhaps a hundred or so, swarmed us, surrounding the truck about six deep, staring up at me, pointing and "discussing" me as if I were some kind of weird creature on exhibit. Most of the time this didn't bother me, but on this particular day I just freaked out and started screaming at them all to "fuck off!" What the hell were they gawking at! I was livid. I think my brain was fried.

What a spectacle I must have been, up on top of the truck in the blistering heat, fried to a crisp with a wet towel draped over my head, jumping around like a lunatic. What a ranting maniac! Of course all this did was provide them with more entertainment! The more I ranted, the more entertained they were. Dejected, I just gave up and sat down, with the towel quickly drying on my head.

The next adventure came later on that same day when we stopped near another group of mud huts clustered together in a small compound-like setting, a short distance from the road. Raj, the driver, pulled over just off the side of the road and stopped. He was extremely excited, bouncing around in his seat before jumping down from the truck, hyper and grinning, motioning for me to follow him. Assistant Ajay, the Kashmiri, was all smiles and giggles, as he encouragingly motioned for me to go along with Raj.

I had no idea what was happening but followed along the dry dusty path about thirty meters or so behind Raj. As we neared the compound, a big mama in a bright yellow sari appeared with her arms outstretched toward Raj. I thought it must be his wife as I watched him spring into her arms. He was just a little guy and it looked like she was about to swallow him whole. Immediately they disappeared into what I could now see was a group of one room huts.

I found myself standing in the center of a courtyard in at least forty-degree heat with the wet towel draped over my head, surrounded by several cloth-covered openings from which women of all ages appeared smiling and ready to please. It took a moment for my sunburnt brain to clue in that these were indeed "women of service" and this was indeed a desert brothel!

When Raj finished his little visit, which didn't take long, we were on the road again with a very content driver and a still giggling assistant. They took me as far as their turnoff to Varanasi, formerly known as Banares-- the oldest living city in the world-- *where time began*, according to Hindu belief. It's where many older or ill Hindus go to die, believing that to die on the banks of the Ganges and have your ashes scattered in the sacred river is an assurance of heavenly bliss, free from reincarnation—the eternal cycle of life and death. (Samsara). I considered going to Varanasi with Raj and Ajay but decided against it.

They passed me along to another *road warrior* who would take me the rest of the way to Delhi. We were all sad to part company.

It's interesting, the connections one makes along the road of life. Some are fleeting moments, soon forgotten and others affect you in ways that last a lifetime. I wonder whatever became of those guys....good hearted, simple, fun guys. For me it was a very memorable time...I wonder if they've ever thought about me. I bet they have...

And so, I made it all the way to Delhi. Booking a room at the YMCA , a favorite place for western travelers, located off Connaught Circus, in central Delhi I started to prepare for my "mission" in Afghanistan.

Chapter 22

Conflict and Connections

A few days after I arrived I was stopped on the street by an old *Sadhu*. Sadhus are Hindu holy men dedicated to finding release from the worldly plane. They have no possessions and roam about the country sustained by the charity of others. They believe that through meditation and contemplation, one can achieve the forth and final state of life and transcend beyond the continuing cycle of rebirth, to eternal bliss...

Most of the time I passed these guys by with not much more than a nod but for some reason I decided to stop for this one. It was the look in his eyes perhaps, a look of kindness, and the open-heart connection I felt with him.

He asked me if I believed in God and if I would donate a few rupees to an orphanage he was collecting for. I robbed him and ran off!

Seriously, he told me he had something for me...like he could tell my fortune. I told him I wouldn't answer any questions other than when he asked me if I believed in God, so as not to give him any clues on which to build a story. I gave him some rupees, which he had me place between the pages of a holy book he was carrying and then he recounted my story.

He said I had come to India with a friend, *one who appeared to be a friend but wasn't* and then continued on telling me, quite accurately, about my experiences since I had arrived in India: my illness, Mike's betrayal, Butterfly's death, Megan….and this Sadhu also told me that my mother had been "sick" but "not to worry" because she was alright now and that another close relative had been near to death but not to worry about him either because he was ok now, as well.

I hadn't heard any news from home in awhile and a couple of days later I headed to the local Poste Restante.

Poste Restante, basically was a post offices general delivery where letters would be held for a period of time for the recipient to pick up. That was the way we communicated, *long-distance,* in those days. Well before the days of internet and cell phones, travelers like myself had to make arrangements for mail long before we would arrive at a destination.

We used a self contained envelope called an *aerogram* that when opened up, provided a "page" on which to write your message. Once written, the envelope was refolded and sealed by licking the glue on the appropriate spots that sealed the envelope with your message on the inside, to be opened, unfolded again and read by the recipient, somewhere, sometime.

It took a few weeks, sometimes longer, for an aerogram to reach Canada from India or from anywhere in that region of the world. You always had to tell the recipient where to send their reply, be it someplace in India or perhaps Nepal or wherever you might be heading. By the time your letter arrived and a response was written and mailed the elapsed time was at least one and a half to two months before you received a reply. Getting a letter at a Post Restante was like receiving a precious gift. One of the first things you did when you arrived at the destination was to checkP.R. for this connection to your "otherworld" and whatever news it might contain.

Well, we all know about Mike, Butterfly and Megan, but the letter awaiting me from my mother informed me that she had undergone a hysterectomy, but was fine and my Uncle Richard had survived a heart attack but was allright.

I didn't believe in fortune-tellers and sooth-sayers but I found the words of the old Sadu curious indeed...

~

My funds were low so I sold the Nikon camera and lenses that Mike and I had purchased in Amsterdam... so long ago. My total accumulated wealth was a few hundred dollars which I could easily turn into fifty to one hundred thousand back in Canada, If things worked out. The Big "IF!" I would need a place to work when I got back from Afghanistan so I rented an apartment in a fairly nice area of Maharni Bagh in the embassy district.

During the few weeks I was in Delhi, I met Maggi, and Henri. Maggi was an American girl from a very well-to-do American family whose great-great-grandfather was a prominent figure in the American Civil War and civil rights movement. Henri was her French boyfriend. We immediately hit it off--another one of those "chance encounter" serendipitous experiences. I hung out with them for a week or so while I searched for an apartment. They didn't have much money and were staying in a shit-hole in old Delhi, called the Crown Hotel occupied mostly by junkies and riffraff.

It turned out that they were heroin users, but you would never guess it. They were as normal as anyone else and functioned fine. Without the heroin, I guess it was another story.

I only knew them as addicts. They were not typical "junkies" that's for sure. They were intelligent and open and I trusted them explicitly and felt very comfortable in their company. When I was almost ready to leave for Afghanistan, I moved back into the YMCA because it was more convenient. I gave Maggi the keys to my apartment and told her and Henri they could stay there while I was away. I couldn't see them staying in that rat-infested dive of a hotel while my apartment sat empty.

As I was standing in the reception area of the "Y" a couple of days before I was to Leave for Kabul, I heard my name called and turned around to see Dan, a friend from home. What a surprise! Then he informed me that Mike was with him, along with someone else I did not know. It seemed that Mike had told Dan I was in Delhi sitting on a pile of hash with no money to transport it. He had tricked Dan and his friend into getting several thousand dollars fronted to them from friends of theirs and together they all flew over to complete a scam which I had supposedly arranged with Mike before he left India.

I told Dan that this was a big pile of bullshit and that I had nothing but a few hundred bucks and was on my way to Afghanistan to try and score some really good Mazar-I-Sherif hash and that I was going to find a way to send it home. I also told him that I had absolutely nothing more to do with Mike after we parted company in Bombay. I was done with him as far as business was concerned.

We all met at Gaylord's restaurant on Connaught Place that evening and when Mike started with his bullshit story, I said straight up that I'd have no part of it. Mike flipped out, went into a rant and stormed out of the restaurant amid the gasps and stares of shocked patrons. Gaylord's was a nice, upper class, fine dining restaurant, a landmark in Delhi at that time.

After Mike's hasty exit, Dan and his friend Brian and I continued with our meal while I explained my plan to them.

The next morning I went into the restaurant at the Y for breakfast and spotted Brian sitting with Mike. I went over and sat with them. It wasn't long before Mike got real surly and began to mouth off. I had well-enough of him by now and as he began to rise up out of his seat spouting something like "You better leave before I..." He didn't get a chance to finish his sentence because I sprang to my feet in a fit of rage and yelled in his face "Or you'll what?" I was beyond rage.

Mike quickly sat down and zipped his lip as I cursed and ranted at him to come outside: another fabulous scene in a nice, quiet, respectable Indian restaurant!

Disgusted and fed up with this asshole I'd once considered a close friend, I threw my napkin on the table and stormed outside in a frenzy......furious beyond.... Mike didn't come out.

What did these generally calm, gentle people think of these young westerners?

Uncouth, ill-bred ruffians I suppose...

That was the final straw in my relationship with Mike. I saw him a day or so later on the street outside the Y and told him in no uncertain terms what I thought of him. I was over my fit of rage--I was just done with him.

I can't imagine what he was thinking...that I would just go along with him and his bogus story, as if nothing had happened between us?

Dan offered to invest a thousand dollars with me and the following day I headed off to Kabul, Afghanistan by plane instead of overland, as had been my previous plan due to lack of funds.

Chapter 23

Afghanistan

It was late afternoon around the first of July when I stepped off the plane at Kabul airport. Dan had told me that the brother of a friend of mine from Halifax (Ray) was going to be on the same flight. After we landed, when the passengers were all waiting around for their baggage I looked everyone over and spotted the guy who must, by his appearance, be the brother of that friend.

I walked up to him and said, "With a face like that you must be Jim's brother."

This of course freaked him out. Who the hell would know him over here, half a world away, in this obscure place?

We exchanged a few words but it was pretty obvious that Ray was really uncomfortable being approached by some guy claiming to be from his home town while he was here in this remote part of the world on a clandestine mission that no one, especially from home, should know anything about! What are the chances?

I grabbed my bag and bid Ray and his girlfriend Sue farewell and headed off into Kabul not expecting to see either of them again. I got a room in a small hotel complex near the center of town and after settling in I walked around, checking out the area a bit and then returned to my room for an early night.

Early the next morning after a light breakfast I went for another walk about and ran into Ray. Ray was a bit more relaxed now, having gotten over his initial shock and paranoia. We went to a small cafe where we had tea and got to feel each other out a bit. After establishing that we were both there for the same purpose, we discussed the idea of pooling our resources and working together.

Ray and Sue had a camper van which they had driven from Amsterdam and left in storage in Kabul a month earlier while they traveled to India. They also had a local contact for hash.

A young houseboy at their hotel had two families, one, in a nearby village where he lived most of the time and the other outside of Mazar-i-Sherif in the northern hash region close to the border with Uzbekistan, and...his father was a hash farmer. How convenient!

We agreed to rendezvous for dinner that evening and I met Ray and Sue at a nice outdoor garden restaurant where we got to know each other better over dinner while discussing the best ways to smuggle hash back to Canada.

The price we would be paying for the absolute best quality would be around twenty dollars per Kilogram. Back home this quality would be worth ten thousand dollars per kilogram. Not a bad mark-up! And, hash oil, which was a lot more compact and easier to conceal, was worth almost double that. Really not a bad mark-up!!!!

So oil seemed the way to go. We decided to give it a shot.

It was a relatively simple process to extract the oil from the unpressed pollen as well. All you had to do was soak the pollen in ethyl alcohol for several hours and the hash oil would separate from the pollen and float to the top combined with the alcohol which you would then scoop off and reduce to the desired consistency either over a heat source, or naturally, under the sun. We preferred the "sun" method. And we would have the use of a house with a walled compound and a private garden in a village close to Kabul.

All we needed now was the alcohol...and condoms.

But these two items were not so easy to acquire in a Muslim country as we were about to find out.

Ray's job would be to procure the alcohol. Sue and I would purchase all the condoms we could find. Condoms were one of the preferred methods of storage and transport in those days. People would swallow five and ten gram "condom balls" of hash oil (or heroin) on an empty stomach, jump on a plane, fly back to Europe or North America, clear customs, get somewhere secure and shit the balls out and "win the game." Occasionally though, a condom would burst and the person would arrive "Late," as in D.O.A. Dead on Arrival.

We had no intention of doing anything like that, but we still liked the idea of the condoms as a way to store and handle the sticky goo. This was well before storage bag days...

We met the next morning of another bright and sunny day.

Kabul was a small, ancient city of mainly dirt streets with lots of dust...it reminded me of a Wild West town, especially when a group of Pashtun tribesmen would come riding up wildly on horses and dismount nearby. For the most part they were big guys, over six feet tall, dressed in their rough and smelly goat-hide coats with antique rifles and bandoleers slung over their shoulders. Fighting was their main thing. It was their tradition. It was said of them, "If they weren't fighting a common enemy, they were fighting amongst themselves."

According to plan, Ray would use the van and go wherever he had to to get the alcohol and Sue and I would shop for condoms and we would meet up later.

Our first stop was a pharmacy/general store where we causally walked up to the counter and I asked the shopkeeper if he might have any condoms for sale. Luckily for me he understood "condoms."

Anyone who knows anything about the Muslim culture knows that this would never happen--a Muslim woman asking a man for condoms, let alone be anywhere around where such an encounter was taking place, especially in those days .

I did the asking, while Sue just hung out a bit in the background, as nonchalant as possible.

The shopkeeper looked at me, then gave an awkward glance in Sue's direction and reached way under the counter, drew out a foil-wrapped condom and dropped it on the counter.

Elated, I said "Great, but I need a lot more." I tried to explain mostly by hand motions. The shopkeeper gave me a kind of solemn look, then reached under the counter again and brought out another two and dropped them next to the first one. His English was almost non-existent and I kept trying to explain my needs by way of gestures and expressions...more , more...He looked at me like I was deranged or something. "What's with this guy?" he must have been thinking, then he'd glance over at Sue who was just standing there, appearing rather indifferent to the scene unfolding at the counter.

Finally, he brought out about a dozen or so which, he indicated, was all he had. I smiled and purchased them all and then Sue and I set off in search of the next shops to repeat the scene over and over again.

It got to be rather ridiculous going from shop to shop demanding all their condoms and waiting for their reactions. I can't imagine what was going through their minds. They must have been thinking "this must be one horny dude." I have no idea what they must have thought of Sue--maybe that she was "demanding." It was so funny to watch their eyes shift to Sue and then quickly back to me--sometimes it took all of our control not to burst out laughing in their faces.

When we finally had purchased all of the condoms in Kabul, we headed back to the hotel to find Ray sitting there under a big dark cloud, depressed because he was unable to get alcohol anywhere. Everywhere he tried to buy it, they refused to sell it to him because they thought he was going to drink it.

The following day Ray got all spiffied up, this time using the approach that he was with the university and needed alcohol for a research project. It took a few attempts, until he met a sympathetic shopkeeper who sold him several gallons and with that we were all set. Alcohol and condoms! What a party we were going to have! Early the next day we set out for Mazar-i-Sherif along with Assaf, the young Afghani boy, son of the farmer.

I was sick as a dog. The previous night after a tiring day of condom shopping, I decided to celebrate my good fortune with meat. I had been mainly vegetarian for the past several months in India because of my condition. Roast lamb on the menu sounded so good...visions of home....I hoed in... big mistake.

Whether the meat was rancid or due to a combination of things, I was violently ill all night, vomiting and shitting the same yellow/brown bile, all the while sweating profusely and shivering uncontrollably.

I had awoken in the middle of the night feeling right out of it; extremely sick, dizzy, weak and disoriented. This was not a fancy place, just a typical mud-brick structure painted green with several basic rooms built around a common courtyard that shared a couple of rough toilet stalls, more like outhouses than up to western standards, although they did have sit-on toilets, not just two footprints in front of a hole in the ground which was most common. There was no running water, so you had to flush the toilet by dumping in pails of water that you dipped from a large plastic barrel nearby.

I was in bad shape as I bolted from my room staggering like a drunken sailor to the toilet not sure whether I was going to shit myself or throw up first. I chose the latter and as soon as I barfed I quickly had to shift to the sitting position shitting what appeared to be the same bile, then switching back to barfing. Back and forth it went. It was the grossest thing I've ever experienced. (Sorry for the graphic description).

This continued throughout the night and by morning I was exhausted. When they came to get me, both Ray and Sue had to help me into the van, I was that weak from the ordeal. I just flopped in the back and we drove away, Sue at the wheel.

We weren't too far along the road from Kabul when all of a sudden a cow came out of nowhere and ran right in front of us. Sue tried to swerve, but the embankment was too steep and she had no choice but to hit the cow straight on in the hind quarter.

The cow went down and slid along the road and off the side embankment enough that Sue was able to maneuver around it and we got away with just a minor dent. The cow got up and ran off, a bit bruised and battered but otherwise it looked OK. It could very well have been the end of our journey. Again!

It took all day to get to Mazar-i-Sherif driving through the rugged, dry, harsh landscape. The sun had just about set as Assaf directed us into a camping area behind a big hotel complex, assuring us that everything was cool. No need to have any concerns; his father was good friends with the police, with the hotel owner and with just about everyone in Mazar-i-Sherif it seemed.

Mazar-i-Sharif, is renowned for its hashish. This was what I had smoked, compliments of the LeDain Commission back in Halifax, and this was my mission: to bring back the very best for my special customers and friends.

Buzkashi, the national sport of Afghanistan is very popular here."Buzkashi " meaning "Goat Grabbing" is an ancient sport of horsemen, dating back to the thirteenth century.

Twenty horsemen, on very specially trained horses, bitterly fight for the beheaded goat while galloping at high speeds and colliding together in rampaging clusters trying to tear the dead, headless goat, weighing at least seventy kilos, from the grip of the one who has it. It's played on the open steppes with lots of space to maneuver. A spot is chosen and the objective is to snatch the goat carcass off the ground while traveling at a fast gallop and get it to the drop zone. Anything goes, whipping, punching, kicking, whatever; broken bones and serious injuries are fairly common. These are rugged men, considered to be among the very best horsemen in the world along with their legendary horses. Unfortunately for us, it wasn't Buzkashi season.

We should just make ourselves comfortable, Assaf suggested and he would be back in three days with fifty kilos of top quality hash, some pressed but mostly pollen that we would soak in the alcohol.

The camping area was a natural, peaceful setting of trees, grass and flowers with inviting open campfires at night. We hung around the area watching cock fights or checking out the famous Blue Mosque, built in the 15th century to replace the earlier one that was destroyed by Genghis Kanh around 1220, or wandering about the town to the markets and other interesting sites, biding our time as we waited for Assaf's return...all the while getting anxious to get to a safe place and move our project along.

On the evening of the third day we were sitting around our campfire just relaxing and wondering what was happening with Assaf, when there was a big uproar in the driveway of the hotel. A huge transport truck with attached flatbed about thirty feet long was making its way slowly into the camping area with yellow lights flashing and air brakes hissing. The flatbed was empty except for a huge white cloth sack and a set of antique scales right in the middle of it. It stopped right in front of our site.

We wondered what the hell was going on when Assaf jumped out of the passenger side with a big ear-to-ear grin. He walked along the side of the flatbed, reached up and hauled off the big white sack and the scales and then waved the driver farewell. Ray, Sue and I stood there in total disbelief as the truck pulled away, with yellow lights flashing and air-brakes hissing. This could not be happening!

"Be cool" instructed Assaf, as we tried to keep our composure.

"Is this guy out of his mind?" we were thinking, while being reassured by Assaf that everything was fine. "No problem." Everything was "No Fucking Problem!" After a few minutes of recovery time, we settled down from the initial shock and adrenaline rush of the delivery scene and broke into a major laughing fit at the absurdity of this whole adventure!

Here we were being super careful, low key, and perhaps even a bit paranoid so as not to attract attention to ourselves and then this happens! Assaf's theory was "Just do it in the open, make no mind of it and no one will pay any attention." Hmmmm.....

We all slept in the van that night, Assaf soundly, not so for us. In the morning with fifty kilos of hash stashed in a storage compartment, we set off toward Kabul and Assaf's other home.

Chapter 24

Dangerous Circumstances

With no mishaps or roadblocks along the way, we arrived at the small village not far from Kabul late in the afternoon and were guided to a two-story mud and wood house surrounded by a ten foot high mud and stone wall. The place belonged to a village elder, a friend of Assaf's family. There was a big garden area within the walls about fifty feet by fifty feet with lots of sun exposure and no prying eyes. Perfect.

We off–loaded our equipment and supplies and the hash pollen, of course, and then returned to Kabul to drop off the van (with twenty kg. of pressed hash) and pick up a few more things. We all returned by taxi, after dark, including Assaf, because there was no electricity and he wanted to make sure we got the oil lamps going properly and we were settled in comfortably before he returned to Kabul.

The house was cozy, especially the upper level which was decorated with beautiful, hand made carpets, pillows and low furniture. We sat on the carpets and dined on low tables. There was also a lovely, wide balcony running the width of the house, overlooked the garden.

In the morning after a breakfast of tea with bread and jam, we got busy setting up our operation, arranging large glass bowls and various vessels in an area of the garden that would get good sun exposure most of the day. We then mixed the pollen with the alcohol and placed it in the vessels. It was fascinating to watch the process unfold as the black oily substance separated from the golden brown pollen and rose to the surface with the alcohol.

This process took a few hours. Then we scooped off the black mixture with a ladle and placed it in large shallow glass bowls to allow the sun to do its work. There was nothing for us to do but enjoy the day and wait for the tar to thicken to the consistency we desired. Pure hash oil of the very best quality... $$$

We spent the next two days in peace and comfort and very stoned. We didn't really need to smoke anything--we were getting so stoned just working with the pollen, hanging over it and fussing with it all day long. But then again...it was very tasty hash rolled in a joint with a bit of tobacco.

On the third day Ray and I were in the garden attending to phase two of our project, which was coming along vey well. Sue had returned to the hotel in Kabul to keep an eye on the van and the twenty or so kilos of pressed hash stashed in a big trunk we bought along the way.

We had a few kilos of the very best primero hash oil and several bowls of half-evaporated oil mixture laying around our workspace, when we heard a car racing along and coming to an abrupt stop in front of our compound, followed by loud, urgent pounding on the door...Ray opened it and in burst Assaf all afluster in a swirl of dust, babbling incoherently about I.A.C. or A.I.C., desperately trying to tell us in a frantic combination of Afghani and broken English that there's an emergency and we had to grab what we could and leave immediately.

Being as stoned as we were, we really couldn't grasp what Assaf was so panicked about. Finally we got him calmed down enough so that we could understand what he was trying to tell us: Someone from the village had seen us walking around the upper veranda last evening and that person told someone who told someone else and it got back to the police and right now the American I.C.A. police were on their way here.

Ray and I looked at each other in disbelief. "C.I.A.!" we both shouted at the same time. Holy Shit!

Scrambling like mad to collect what we could of our production materials and dumping the rest, we were gone in a flash. With hearts a-thumping, we jumped in the taxi Assaf had waiting and blasted off across the barren landscape heading the other way as we observed three cars and a dust trail on the opposite side of the little village heading toward the compound.

We were lucky, "escaping by the skin of our teeth" as the saying goes.

Because of all the hash, opium and heroin smuggling going on in Afghanistan in those days, there was a heavy international police presence, from America, Canada, Germany, England and other countries. Each country had members of their secret, undercover police lurking about, trying to stop the flow...

Arriving back at the hotel with our oily mixtures, we explained the situation to Sue. We were in a predicament. What to do now without the privacy of the compound walls?

We'd have to look for a secluded place to continue our processing, somewhere not too far from Kabul, as traveling around with our contraband would be very risky.

Early the next day we set out driving along the road toward Pakistan and within twenty kilometers or so, we came across a small dirt track that took us back from the main road enough to give us the privacy we required.

There was a nice flat area beside a small stream that provided an ideal camping spot and that's where we set up shop.

Ray and I dragged the trunk with the hash out of the van along with a couple of small carpets he and Sue had purchased in India. Sue got busy setting up the stove outside of the van, in front of the open double side doors in order to heat the mixture of alcohol and pollen that Ray and I had poured into big jars. We had to keep it near the camper in case someone came snooping and we had to hide it quickly.

Everything set, we began heating the mixture slowly, patiently waiting for the alcohol to evaporate.

Things were going along well. Ray and I had taken a few kilos of the pressed hash out of the trunk and were playing around with it, moulding it into shapes and thinking of ways to disguise it for shipping back to Canada. It was incredible stuff. The best of the best. We were going to make a lot of money!

All of a sudden...KA-BOOM ! the van exploded. Flames and smoke were shooting out the side door opening where the stove had been. The big propane gas tank was on the ground, covered in flaming hash oil. Ray and I both jumped at the tank in the same instant and managed to get the fire out before that exploded as well. But it only took those few minutes for the entire van to be engulfed. Huge flames were spewing out all the doors and windows and the back of the van as well. The windshield exploded as the flames reached a height of twenty feet.

The van was done for, but all we were concerned with at that moment was the hash. People and police would soon be arriving and we had to get rid of the evidence—pronto!

The three of us started grabbing handfuls of hash and throwing it as far away from the scene as possible, into the stream, into the forest, wherever.... "Ten thousand dollars" Ray yelled as the heaved a big glob. "Another ten thousand" I shouted as I flung a handful. Sue got into the act as well and we all laughed our asses off as we threw away our fortune before any of the local passer-bys started arriving, which they did within a very short period.

I think we were all just beyond belief at this point. After all the adventure and risk we had been through, now this! All we could do was laugh at the absurdity of it all.

A bus had stopped, attracted by the flames shooting up over the trees. Within ten minutes people were pouring into the area to witness the spectacle.

We had managed to get rid of everything that was laying around and just stood there stunned, surrounded by the locals while the camper and everything in it burned— All of Ray and Sue's personal things, photos, clothing, our precious hash oil, all of it destroyed.

Before long, a truckload of police arrived. These guys were not the friendliest in the world. Dressed in ill-fitting, old, grey, German army uniforms they were all the more intimidating.

The only requirement to be a policeman in Afghanistan in those days was age. Besides being nasty and intimidating they could be pretty ignorant and stupid as well. Most of the Afghani people we had encountered were very gracious people like you find anywhere, but these policemen were a different breed. As soon as we encountered them we knew they were trouble--very unfriendly and suspicious of us, as they were. There were at least a dozen of them all milling around, poking at the still burning van.

I felt like I could have been in Nazi Germany during the war and these guys were Gestapo. As the flames died down, there was a lot of stuff smoldering on the ground around the van and in the mess I spotted a large stainless bowl filthy with residual hash oil amongst the rubble.

Shit ! Oh Fuck !

As nonchalantly as possible I sauntered over and picked it up, not sure what I was going to do with it to make it disappear when a policeman came from behind and ripped the bowl out of my hands.

"We're done" I thought. But the policeman just stared at me and then bent down and scooped dirt into the bowl and began dumping in on the smoldering embers looking up at me with a big, self satisfied smile! Unbelievable! Really... UNBELIEVABLE !

The next occurrence was not so nice....Another policeman, this one, a big, surly type picked up an empty gas can that was laying nearby and shook it at me while shouting "benzine, benzine" the German word for gasoline.

I was aware that the can was there but it was empty so I said to him "neit benzine"...no gas...empty. This set him right off--Looking really nasty and super agitated now, he got right up on top of me, hysterically shaking the can at me, screaming "BENZINE! BENZINE!" I had no fucking idea what he was ranting on about and just shook my head and made that universal gesture, shrugging my shoulders with arms extended, palms up and repeated "Neit benzine," thinking "what's your problem, man?"

This made the hateful bastard even more insane and he screamed at me, more agitated than ever "BENZINE, BENZINE , BENZINE" furiously, shaking the can right in my face. I thought he was going to hit me with it.

I kept thinking "this guy's insane," until it hit me. This screaming maniac was thinking we burned the van on purpose so we wouldn't have to go through the hassle of exporting it out of Afghanistan because that could be a real problem if there were any paperwork problems or not enough money to pay for permits and such. This is what travelers reverted to sometimes when all the hassles attached to a vehicle got to be too much. Shit! Shit! and MAJOR SHIT! All I could do was look at the guy and shrug at him with that gesture. "I don't know, I can't help you."

Meanwhile all the rest of these soldier/policemen were gathered around poking inside the van and stirring the still smoldering ashes. It was then that we realized the trunk these guys were sitting on and resting their feet on still had around fifteen or so kilos of primo hash inside! Any one of them, at any moment, could decide to flip the lid and that would be it for us.

Talk about an elephant in the room!

Somehow that didn't happen and eventually, the police decided they were going to take the owner of the van, which would be Ray, back to the police station in Kabul to fill out a report.

Sue and I were suddenly on our own. They didn't care about us now.

We watched as Ray was offered a seat in the police van that had arrived during this time with a couple of senior officers who were much more amicable. Two of the policemen loaded the trunk and two carpets salvaged from the fire into the back of their van and Ray and the officers drove off. Ray was forlornly looking at us, waving goodbye through the back window, sure he was done for, as did we. "Well," both Sue and I said at the same time, "That's the end of Ray." We agreed that once they got back to the station the police would surely open the trunk, discover the hash and then come looking for us as well.

The best plan we could think of was to get back to the hotel as fast as possible, gather whatever we needed and get the hell out of there and across the border, then hire a lawyer for Ray and begin proceedings with the Canadian embassy to get him out of jail.

We got a drive back to Kabul from one of the sympathetic spectators. I gathered my passport along with my meager belongings and quickly went to meet Sue at her hotel and "head for the hills."

We were in the driveway, on our way and in the brief time that we were there Ray showed up in a taxi. Two minutes later Sue and I would have been gone.

After he had filled out the report back at the police station, they told Ray he could leave. You can imagine how he felt! We could not believe our luck. We had really pushed it and now we were going to make a run for it because sooner or later one of them was going to open the trunk.

Just then we saw a police vehicle coming toward us as we stood there kinda frozen in time, like deer caught in the headlights. They pulled right up to us. Is this it?...Two policemen got out, walked around to the back of the vehicle, lifted out the trunk along with the two carpets and set them on the ground. We were just gobsmacked as we thanked the policemen, even shaking hands with them. All smiles and giggles we watched them drive off! Unbelievable! Really! It seemed impossible that we were not all behind bars.

Quickly Ray and I got the trunk into their room. We all decided, then and there, we were done with Afghanistan. I was done with everything...I was just done--period. I needed to go home now. I had been through enough.

I said I was going to throw a couple of kilos into a suitcase and head back to India by bus and train. There was a bus to Peshawar, Pakistan leaving in the morning and I was going to be on it. I weighed a little over 100 pounds. I had lost everything and had cheated death and disaster several times...and now this!

Ray and Sue still had to deal with the camper. They needed to arrange to have the burned out hulk transported to the border and that would take them at least another day.

I cut the lining inside of a crappy old suitcase I had gotten at a market and wrapped two kilos in plastic, formed it to fit and glued the lining back in place. It was a shitty, basic job that would not pass a close inspection but at this point I don't think I knew what I was doing anymore and I didn't care. I just wanted to be gone from there.

I gave them the address of the apartment I had rented in Delhi and with luck they would meet me there in a few days. Insha Allah!

The next morning I was on a dilapidated old bus jammed with locals. Our luggage was packed on top in the roof rack as we set off for Pakistan. About twenty kilometers out, we passed the place where the van had exploded and there, by the side of the road, sat the blackened hulk where it had been towed and left, like a stark warning I thought. It all seemed surreal.

Our journey in that lopsided wreck of a bus took several hours in the hot mid day sun to arrive at the Pakistani border crossing just before the Khyber pass.

When our wreck pulled up in a cloud of dust, the driver was instructed to unload all of the luggage from up top and then all of us passengers were instructed to take our bags into the customs building for inspection. When the bag-man passed my suitcase down to me I wasn't sure if I smelled hash or if I was just being paranoid so I moved away from the crowd, set the bag down, opened it and almost fell over from the strong odour of hash! Sitting in the hot sun all day... it was "ripe."

Panic, whirled through my brain.... What to do? I wanted to throw it away--just pretend it didn't exist, hope no one would notice it, but I knew all of that was impossible with the driver and all the other passengers standing right there. I had no choice. I would have to take my bag inside for inspection along with all the other passengers. My mind was racing as I entered the building.

As luck, Karma or whatever you choose to call it would have it, inside the building in the large inspection room were big fans on floor stands positioned around. I quickly went to one, dropped and opened my suitcase directly in front of it and heaved a sigh of relief as the smell instantly dissipated. This was my only hope. If it was checked closely, the jig would be up then and there.

The guard was moving along the line of passengers, briefly sifting through the contents of their bags and when he got to mine he did the same, briefly stirring the clothing around with his hand and indicating with a flick of his wrist that I had passed examination and was good to go!

Moments like this are so surreal: you are on the edge and your very life hangs in the balance. If the guard was focused at all and removed some items, he would have seen immediately that things were not kosher.

I was out of there in a flash and had my bag stored back up on top of the bus and was relieved to be on our way again... next stop Peshawar, Pakistan.

We would be traveling through the infamous Khyber Pass, a twisty old road about three meters wide that hairpins almost constantly as it skirts the edge of the mountain. It's one of the oldest known routes and still one of those "dangerous places." It snakes through the lawless tribal regions of the Spin Ghar Mountains bordering Afghanistan and Pakistan and was an integral part of the spice road as well as the invasion route of such notables as Alexander the Great and Genghis Khan. At this time it was the domain of the Pashtun tribal people and they were known for attacking travelers, buses or any type of convoy, if they had a mind to. Fortunately we made it through without incidence.

Peshawar was a congested, noisy, wild, dust-blown trading center where you could buy or trade anything from a small boy to a sub-machine gun. I quickly made my way from the bus station to the train station eager to depart this den of inequity on the first available train. Luckily, I didn't have to wait long to board a train bound for Lahore. This was to be another endurance trip of several hours, jammed into a second class car totally overloaded with little brown bodies. I hooked up with a small group of westerners like myself. We always gravitated together for that safety-in-numbers security where we could watch each other's backs.

There were three Americans-two guys and a girl; a German girl, Dutch guy, English guy, and me. We clustered together in one car and as the train rolled along, a railway policeman made his way through the cars, hassling people. The requirement for some of these occupations must have been nastiness because thats how a lot of them were: nasty pricks.

When he got to our group this unfriendly, aggressive asshole demanded to inspect our bags. These guys made a particular habit of hassling hippies because they knew there was a good chance of finding drugs and then they could extort a bribe under threat of arrest. In some cases people were fined and arrested, after which they had the opportunity to buy their freedom and their drugs back, if they had enough money.

The American guys started yelling at him telling him to "Fuck off." We all joined in cursing him and shooing him away. Bombarded with all of the verbal assault, he left, albeit a bit sullen, flinging curses back at us as he lumbered off.... but, thankfully, he did fuck off! I wondered what the Americans had in their bags...

We were left alone for the rest of the trip and made it safely to Lahore several hours later where I got a cheap room for the night and consulted my copy of the I Ching. This book had been introduced to me by Noah, my Israeli friend and I had dragged it along with me all the way from Amsterdam, consulting it from time to time when I was in the mood.

I found the I Ching to be a most fascinating book--many consider it to be an oracle, actually. Every time I consulted it I got pertinent information and guidance that seemed to make a lot of sense and fit my particular circumstance at the time.

Very curious book the I Ching... Wisdom of the ages and the old Chinese sages...I had consulted it just before I left

Kabul and the gist of the passage I got after *throwing the coins* (sort of like rolling dice) was "treading on the tiger's tail but will not get bitten."

It's a bit complicated to explain, but there are sixty-four different passages or *hexagrams* and you access them by chance upon throwing the three coins. The chances of getting the same one twice in a row are very rare, almost impossible.

Now, sitting in my hotel room here in Lahore I got the exact same passage as in Kabul.

"Treading on the tiger's tail"....

I had one more border to cross at Amritsar, India. After an almost sleepless night I got up, had some tea and with my suitcase in hand, I headed to the nearby bus stop. I had come this far and was in it, for better or for worse. I didn't care. It was a Kamikaze mission, no turning back now.

Chapter 25
Amritsar

It's really hazy... It was all so surreal. I was near the bus station in Lahore. It was early morning and I was going to catch the bus that would take me to the border crossing at Amritsar, India. The only thing I clearly remember is that it was a bright, sunny morning and a French couple about my age pulled up in a faded old red VW camper and offered me a lift to India, changing my destiny and probably saving my life. *Again*.

Simple words but they mean so much.

What I do remember thinking was, "This is great," because traveling by bus is much riskier as my previous experience at the Afghan-Pakistan border proved. When it's only you and your bag there's not much room for error, but with a camper, there's the camper itself, which is more apt to be suspect, and more likely to be the main target of interest for the border police. Luggage would be a secondary consideration.

As fortune would have it...

We arrived at the border crossing where we were directed to the "inspection area." The thing I was most concerned with was the smell. I had poured cheap perfume all over the inside of my suitcase but It was still fairly obvious. As soon as the suitcase was opened, the unmistakable smell of hashish would seal my fate.

Because the French couple did not have a valid *carne de passage*, a special document that permitted vehicle travel between countries, the low ranking guards who were supposed to search the van were stymied. It would be up to the next level of authority to decide if the van could proceed to Amritsar city, about twenty kilometers away and have the *carne* processed there. Or, would they refuse entry and send the French couple and their van back to Pakistan. The young couple argued and pleaded but to no avail.

I was informed that If the van was turned back, I would be required to have my bags searched inside the customs building and then walk with my luggage the hundred or so meters through this "No Man's Land" to the actual frontier.

It was around ten a.m., the sunlight was golden, with a temperature of about thirty degrees. All around us were Indian border guards dressed in their khaki garb, equipped with assorted rifles and other military paraphernalia. Interesting, intriguing- looking, dark-skinned people wearing turbans and wrapped in long sheets, hung about hoping to be of use in some way.

We waited. "Waiting" was the number one activity or non-activity at that time in India. "Waiting" has actually developed into an "art" in India.

On a couple of occasions during this period, a randomly passing guard would, more out of boredom than anything, ask why we were here and sometimes suggest that I take my bags inside to have them checked and then walk to the frontier. I always said I'd wait because it was too long a walk in the heat with my bag.

At one point, around one o'clock I was told that I must go into the "building" for passport inspection. I think they were all just bored and found us hippie-types to be curiosities more than anything. For the most part my take on these border guards was that they couldn't care less about the drug thing, they were of the mind "if you want to kill yourself with drugs go right ahead, just don't make a problem for us."

Anyway, I clearly remember standing in the "building" which was a huge open room with a high roof supported by a few posts. There was a long counter, about ten meters in length, near one wall where luggage was inspected. Against the opposite wall were the offices, of which the Commandant's was one. He was a tall, slender, turbaned, bearded Sikh, clad in a spotless, stiffly starched khaki uniform, imposing in his appearance and air of authority. He approached the old wooden bench in the "waiting area" where I had been directed to sit and wait for my "interview."

The commandant, a very important person, in his own mind at least, directed me into his office and motioned for me to sit opposite him in front of his huge desk. After a few pleasantries, he began with his "interview."

"What is your mission? What are you doing here? Where are you coming from? Where are you going?" Casual questions, after which he told me to follow him outside to the waiting area bench again where we were joined by a middle aged, overweight lady wrapped in a sari who was introduced to me as a medium--one who could read minds. She would know if I was lying when he questioned me. She sat right next to me on the bench drilling into my brain with her piercing eyes.

Again the Commandant asked: "What are you doing here? Do you take drugs? Are you smuggling drugs? Do you know what happens to people who smuggle drugs into India?" This line of questioning went on for five minutes or so in a strangely pleasant, agreeable, friendly manner.

I just answered his questions and I guess my brain was so fried by this point that the medium couldn't get a "reading." After awhile the commandant must have decided I was just another burnt out hippie who had been through a rough time and was just homeward bound. He told me he didn't think they were going to permit the camper to enter India.

Apparently satisfied, the psychic got up off the bench and they both sauntered back to his office leaving me sitting there to stew in my own juice, as it were.

I was alone with my thoughts. I clearly remember standing by myself in that big room staring at the rich woodwork trim around the windows and the pale yellow walls, and the redish-brown hardwood rails edging the long counter with the beautiful hand- rubbed patina that glowed so softly in the golden sunlight that streamed in the window... and the fly that landed on the window ledge...

My sense of awareness was intensely acute. I could see the life of the fly, the vivid details of everything around me, all so beautiful and perfect and I was struck by the feeling of wonder at just being alive and so conscious of everything that was playing on the big screen of my life as I stood there savoring these last moments of freedom before I was to be executed. It was like being awake inside of a dream.

An officer walked up to me and informed me that the van was indeed, not being permitted to enter India so I had better grab my belongings and bring them in for inspection. That was it. I was fucked. I could stall no longer. Reality struck me. If I was busted here It would be the end of the road for me. I would die here. The cheap, horrible smelling perfume I had poured all over the inside of my suitcase would not save me here.

I weighed in at most one hundred and ten pounds. I had been one-eighty or so before the insidious scourge of hepatitis had its way with me, ravaging my body and soul five months earlier. At this point I was so strung out and stretched to the limit--I had nothing left. I thought I was different but I was just like so many others of my genre in that time and place; young adventurers who had journeyed into the unknown seeking their fortunes only to end up wasting away, sinking into oblivion in one way or another.

It's a bit of a blur here, but I remember walking out, as if on someone else's legs. I got my things from the van, bidding a forlorn farewell to the French couple, and slowly trudging back into the "building" burdened by the weight of my entire sojourn and a very heavy heart.

The long counter stretched out before me, distorted like a photo from a fisheye lens or the effects of LSD. Besides the officer who had sent me for my bags, there was another very tall, stern-looking, turbaned, bearded, khaki-uniformed Sikh standing right at the centre of the counter waiting for me, like an executioner waiting for his victim.

There was nothing I could do, I had no options. At the gesture from the officer I walked over to the guard and lifted my suitcase up on top of the counter. The sunlight was still streaming in the window and lighting up the reddish-brown patina of the wooden rails, which seemed to be my centre of focus. As he peeled back the first of two straps I could see and feel the most wonderful loving experiences of my life, my parents, my close childhood friends... I was strangely at peace, and felt a deeply profound, combined sense of love and sorrow as he began to open the second strap. In a moment he would let go of the strap and open the suitcase and it would be all over for me; the *coup de gras*...

Just at that exact moment the Commandant appeared and said, "We are going to permit the van to go to Amritsar so you can either finish your inspection here and carry your bags or put them back in the van and we will search them there."

Unbelievable! Come on! My life just turned on a dime... again. How can this be?

A second or two later and It would have been too late. My life was hanging by a thread...Right on the very edge! If you've ever been there you know how it feels.

The kaleidoscopic roller-coaster I had just been riding came to an abrupt halt and I zoned back into the reality of the moment with the correct response: "I'll go with the van," at which point the inspector re-buckled the strap he had his hand on and then the other one as I stood there in a state of suspended euphoria. I then carried my things back out to the van like nothing happened...How can all of these events all be random?

I was still in extreme danger and I knew I had to do something to at least get rid of the smell, or I *would* be busted. Back in the van I had a few moments alone—I opened the offending suitcase. phew! The smell of Afghani hash overpowered the cheap, shitty smelling perfume. I frantically fanned it as best I could and shook my clothes and spread them around. That was all I could do. If I could only let out a great, disgusting overpowering fart!!!

The French couple approached with three guards. I had all the doors and windows opened and sat as nonchalantly as possible in the back with my bag opened beside me.

The guards, all mumbling to each other in Punjabi, gave the back of the van, including my bag, a brief, cursory search with one of them actually sticking his hand in my suitcase and kind of stirring my clothes around a bit before he moved on. They looked under the van and tapped it here and there and then they searched under the front seat where they found a damaged old clay jar that seemed to pique their interest. They discussed, I'm assuming, how it might somehow be related to smuggling. That was soon discarded and we were, thus far, cleared to go.

The couple left with the guards and returned twenty minutes later with another rather intense-looking turbaned official in an equally, stiffly starched khaki uniform. He was going to escort us to Amritsar. He jumped in the passenger seat, while the girl got in the back area with me and away we went, the French guy driving, heading to the town of Amritsar.

As we drove along the official would occasionally, slowly turn his turbaned head around and stare right at me in the most unnerving manner. I was just barely keeping it together at this point and paranoid as hell about the smell. Can he smell the hash? I kept thinking. Is he waiting for me to bribe him? What should I do? What a hellish ride as I wracked my brain for the right solution. He did this head swivel and intense gaze that felt like he was boring right into my brain at least three more times before we got to Amritsar.

I decided that the best thing I could do was nothing. If I offered him a bribe and he wasn't aware I would blow the whole thing. I'd wait for him to make the move.

I remember clearly drawing up in front of the customs building in Amritsar and just before he got out, this intense turbaned sikh official turned and nailed me with one last penetrating stare, driving those piercing eyes right through my brain like red-hot needles, a final time before walking away with the French couple.

Was this my last opportunity? I was thinking. What excruciating turmoil I was in!

I waited, calmly on the outside but truly writhing with anxiety, for another hour or so, expecting at any moment to see several armed guards descend on the van and hear the official say, "You had your chance."

The French couple finally returned and joyfully told me they had the *carne de passage* and we were bound for Delhi, free and clear! I had made it! I was given a new lease on life... I had danced on the tiger's tail but I had not got bitten.

Driving through the Punjab on the way back to Delhi was like driving through a movie set. At one point along the road we stopped to watch several huge vultures ripping apart the bloated carcass of a cow lying nearby. Hideous, jet black creatures about four or five feet in height with hunched up wings leapt about, spreading their wings slightly to give themselves a lift off. They would take turns hopping up on the carcass and digging in with long taloned feet as they ripped long strips of hide and tissue from it with grotesque looking, bloodied hooked beaks attached to similarly hideous bald reddish heads with ghastly bloodshot eyes--a most vile and loathsome spectacle to witness!

We arrived in Delhi and for some reason or other I can't remember, they dropped me off at Connaught Circus telling me they would return shortly. I can't imagine why I let them drive off with my bags, especially after everything I'd been through since leaving Kabul.

It didn't seem odd at first but after some time I began to feel very unwell, thinking that maybe they had smelled the hash and I wouldn't be seeing them again. But such was not the case and they did return shortly and then dropped me off at my Maharni Bagh apartment and drove out of my life, just like that.

It was like we had a scripted encounter and what a most incredible part they played in my life. It was *only* because of them that I didn't end up in the Amritsar prison where I likely would have met my end, one way or another. Can all of these critically timed encounters just be random, meaningless happenstance? I have to wonder to this day.

I walked into my apartment where Maggi and Henri were hanging out shooting up heroin. Great to be home!

I had been through the valley of the shadow of death…and here I was.

Chapter 26

Delhi

To say I was "fried" would be a huge understatement. I was not in good shape physically or mentally. By *Devine Providence* or call it what you will, I had made it through the gauntlet all the way from Kabul.

Now I was back in Delhi, almost broke, waiting for money to come from Canada so at least I could return home. I was done with the East, I had to get out of here. I had the hash that I had carried all the way from Afghanistan and I had spent the last of my money to package it up and send it home. At least I'd have a few dollars to start over with ....hopefully.

It was unbearably hot, well over one hundred degrees Fahrenheit and you couldn't move around too much outside. Inside, if you turned off the ceiling fan, sweat would drip off of you almost immediately. You had to be very quick to roll a joint as dripping sweat ruined many an effort. In less than a minute after shutting off the fan you would begin to sweat and very soon it would be rolling down your face and actually dripping on a book or newspaper, letter you might be trying to write or a joint. Maggi and Henri coped by shooting up heroin and I coped by smoking hash. We just hung out and waited.

Three days after I arrived, Sue showed up with a small hawk, but without Ray. Ray was in the Amritsar jail. They had gotten busted at that same long customs counter I had just come through the day before, only they weren't so lucky.

Arriving on the bus from Lahore their luggage was properly searched and that was it. Ray took the rap, as they say, and was hauled off in chains and thrown into a hot, smelly cell about three meters by five meters with a foul smelling latrine hole in the centre of it. He shared this space with eight other prisoners; all hard core Indian, Pakistani, Afghanni, and not one Westerner. They were in for everything from robbery to murder. As Sue described it, the stench was unbearable and the heat intolerable. Ray fully expected to see me in there, and they were both bewildered as to why I was not there. They even asked for me! Sue was not charged and was allowed to continue on her way. She came right to Delhi, to my address which I had given them before I left Kabul. They had no money and I was the only person she knew. She was desperate, totally freaked out!

Before I had left for Afghanistan I had met another Canadian(Brian) who had been busted several months earlier at the same Amritsar Border crossing. He was smuggling gold, which was considered a much worse offence than smuggling hash. Brian had been released on bail, but his passport was confiscated and he had spent several months working with lawyers, finding his way around the system and making connections which included the Chief Prosecutor in Amritsar. (Ah! India)

I took Sue to meet Brian and he became instrumental in setting her up with the people she needed to help her, namely, the Chief Prosecutor for Amritsar. Because Sue was so desperate I gave her the three hundred dollars I had just received from home to help with Ray's situation.

Meanwhile Maggie had decided to do a smuggling run to Germany and Henri moved to the Crown Hotel Annex in Old Delhi. The Crown was bad enough ...but the Annex.... that really was the end of the line; The last stop for junkies and wasted souls. This decrepit, rat-infested hovel was located at the end of the infamous Chandi Chowk, a main thoroughfare meandering through Old Delhi. Outside of the Annex was a smorgasbord of destitution, inhabited by some of humanity's most decrepit creatures. Weird looking, one-eyed men with grotesquely deformed limbs, legless beggars on skateboards, lepers without noses, lips or limbs: filthy, ragged street urchins, child prostitutes, freaky old painted up prostitutes, drug addled misfits from everywhere...these dystopian street-dwellers comprised a slice of the most bizarre collection of humans on the planet, I'm sure. Fellini would have been impressed.

Sue had made the contacts she needed and had returned to Amritsar to work on Ray's release. I still had my apartment rent paid up for another week and was wondering what I was going to do when my time was up, but that decision was made quite simple when the time came, as I had nowhere to go but to the Crown Annex and crash with Henri. I was completely wasted, physically, mentally, spiritually...my entire trip to the East had turned into disaster--the whole situation with Mike, becoming deathly ill with hepatitis, all of that weirdness in Goa, my leg infection, being chased by the CIA in Afghanistan, the van exploding, losing everything, Ray in jail...I had endured so much and here I was.... again sinking into oblivion. Heaviness and despair clung to me like a huge ape on my back.

After a few days in this depressing, shit-hole, in the stifling heat, surrounded by stoned out junkies and the dregs of humanity, I succumbed and sank to the lowest point in my life. I felt as though I had crossed some line. I didn't even recognize myself.

It was as if I was in some twilight world, watching it all unfold but not really there. I sought escape. I had to step out of this bizarre nightmare if even just for a brief period.

I asked Henri to hit me up. I was on my bed, leaning back against the wall. The ceiling fan was slowly stirring the hot sticky air. Rats crawled along the rafters. Street noise was wafting in through the openings. Henri stuck the needle in my arm. Everything went spinning slowly, the whole room swayed. I felt myself drifting into a vortex, suddenly feeling like I was going to be sick. My head fell forward. I was powerless to move. I swooned and floated, probably coming close to overdosing the first time.

I couldn't move or lift my head off my chest. I didn't care anymore...I had become just another one of the lost souls, those other travelers like myself from various parts of the world who ended up wasting away, overcome by whatever experiences had rendered their worlds unrecognizable. It was like I was watching someone else. This was not me. I couldn't possibly be one of those young carefree kids who set out to see what was on *The Other Side* and never returned.

But here I was, truly at the bottom of humanity's ladder... ravaged and swirling around in a decrepit piss-hole....going down, down, down the drain...nothing left...I didn't even care about the rats that shared my space, climbing along the rafters or running across the floor.

I languished here in this sorry stupor for a few days before Maggi returned. She took one look at me propped up against a wall, wasted, with my head hanging down on my chest and said "You've got to go home." Even though she didn't know me that well, she went right out and bought me a plane ticket back to Canada, cleaned me up and marched me straight out to the airport. The next thing I knew, I was walking across the hot tarmac of Delhi International and climbing up the two tier stairway pressed against the outside of the gigantic Boeing 747 airplane.

I remember the day well. Maggi grabbed a taxi in the street outside of the Annex and came right out to the airport with me. She wasn't taking any chances.

I was wearing a clean shirt and pair of jeans that I had brought with me from Canada so long ago and had never worn because of the heat. The jeans were like waist size thirty-six and I was now waist size twenty eight, so they were all bunched up and belted with what was left of my belt. I must have been a sight, emaciated and freaked out. I felt completely out of place surrounded by all of those clean, well-fed, well-dressed, proper western tourists.

Before stepping into the gigantic, silver, space capsule that would transport me to across the world, I paused to take one last, lingering look from the top of the stairway back at this world that had so chewed me up.

The airplane seat seemed so big, I felt like a little kid whose feet couldn't touch the floor. Taking up only half the seat, I felt very insignificant. The humongous 747 lumbered down the runway and lifted off. I felt as if I was being transported in a time machine....all of the things I had experienced and endured left me feeling like I was in a waking dream striding two worlds.

Transfixed, I watched the parched landscape below dissolving into the past. I saw the Taj Mahal, painted by the hazy, orange-golden glow of the late afternoon sun, fade in the distance. It was all surreal, like my body was here on this magic carpet flying ship but my soul was left behind...I was not the same person ....

Slowly gliding over Pakistan, Afghanistan, The Middle East, Turkey, Europe...another world...another life...It felt like more than a lifetime had passed since I'd traveled through these countries. My head, my heart, my emotions...my entire phyche had been shredded by the conflicting anguish of friendship and betrayal, cruelty and kindness, suffering and salvation, life and death...

What Maggi did for me was huge. Three hundred dollars was a lot of money for our circumstances in those days and not to be taken lightly considering that a relatively small amount of money really could mean the difference between life and death. She probably saved my life. (Again). I had given up and was heading to a place that I don't think I would have returned from.

I had traded my lifeline for Ray's life and now I was being thrown a lifeline. Could it be Karma? Perhaps. Life is such an amazing, puzzling journey... Is it true...what goes around comes around...?

I changed planes in London; next stop Toronto.

Arriving in Toronto was like landing on another planet. Culture shock hit me full force, much more intense than anything I had encountered in the East. Everything appeared futuristic. I took the new, clean, almost empty, airport bus downtown to the Royal York Hotel and from there got a taxi to my brother's place in Forest Hills.

The cab ride was unbelievable. I was all alone in the expansive back seat of a huge American car. It seemed abnormally big, especially after all the group taxis with multiple bodies crammed into a space half the size! The springs! The shocks! It was like I was in some monstrous floating machine and as we made our way through the downtown area, I was apprehensive about the seeming lack of people.

Were was everyone? Was something wrong? The city looked deserted as if the population had vanished, decimated perhaps by some kind of disaster. I anxiously kept looking around for the people. I had come to regard the overcrowded conditions of India as normal. This felt very strange.

I was welcomed at my brother's, as usual. He shared the upper level of a big old house with another guy (Michael) and I hung out there for a few days, getting readjusted to the Western world.

I explained my plight to my brother and told him that before I could do anything else I had to send that money to Maggi. Three hundred dollars was a lot in those days. Although he didn't just have it lying around he could see that I was desperate so he got it for me and I promised to repay him asap, which I did.

I immediately American Expressed the money to Maggi and got confirmation within a couple of days that she received it. Then I was O K. I could relax.

My brother also helped me get a drive-away car to deliver to Nova Scotia and shortly thereafter I was on my way back home to Halifax to try and put the fragmented pieces of my life back together.

PART TWO

Chapter 27
Back to Canada

The drive back to Nova Scotia was unlike any other I had experienced. Because I was, I believe, experiencing culture shock, everything appeared enhanced. I had never before distinguished such a difference in the shades of the green between the regions. It was like I saw the emerald green of Nova Scotia for the first time.

Settling back in was difficult. I felt estranged from everyone, including my family. I felt strange just being here in general, like I was out of place, like I didn't belong.....I felt isolated. All my friends thought I was dying. I looked like I was dying at just over one hundred pounds. The last time they saw me I was about one-eighty or so.

Mort and I got back on track. He had moved out from Sandy *again* and was living in a house with two other guys, Ben and Jim. Ben had a friend who worked in a strategic area of the post office and could intercept international packages up to five kilos before they went to customs. We discussed it and Mort agreed to go to Amsterdam and send hash back and I would take care of things here. I would help him get set up, return home and take over his room and his big Cadillac El Dorado while he was away.

We flew to Amsterdam and rented an apartment in a nice neighborhood near the Hilton Hotel. Next we made ourselves a press out of half inch plate steel and a ten ton jack and purchased the rest of the materials Mort would need. I flew back to Halifax. And Mort sent the hash.

We followed this program for a few months and all was well. Except for me...I was not well. I was hugely depressed. I struggled to make it through each day. By now it was late fall and all the leaves had disappeared and the landscape was bleak. I felt very alone and isolated. I had a wonderful family and great friends but no one I could relate to, or so it seemed. I felt alienated from everyone. I was emotionally bankrupt, you might say. I was miserable.

I hid my fucked-up feelings as best I could. I didn't talk about Mike or a lot of the experiences I'd had. I tried to pretend that all was well, but I was coming apart at the seams. I guess it was the combination of things. Eddie was dead now two years, Mort and I had gone through our stuff and he was living away. It didn't feel right to be spending time with Sandy without Mort around. I was coming down sideways from the totality of my past years' experiences.

The house I now shared with Ben and Jim was like a central hangout. There were lots of parties but I struggled to be there. I had no zip. I felt like an empty shell. In the daytime I would drive around taking care of business. Often I gazed at the bare trees against the grey background and thought that the branches looked like my nervous system...all frayed networks of nerve endings. Life was so colorless and bleak and everyday my desolation seemed worse than the day before. I wanted to die. I begged for death to take me...

Before this I had never experienced anything like depression in my life.. I had been through some bad times and hit some rough patches but this was unlike anything I had ever experienced. Eddie's death was the first glimpse into that world.

I could barely get through each day, just hanging on until it was time for bed. I would lay down in my dark room and actually pray to God that I wouldn't wake up. I didn't have the strength to endure another day of this emotional torture. Eventually I would pass out from exhaustion and wake up to face another day and have to deal with it all over again.

Just simply talking to people was agonizing. It's hard to explain unless you've ever been there. Major depression. Detachment. Anxiety. Unfeeling.

I was the walking dead. It was like I had no soul. I was a lifeless shell void of feelings yet my whole being writhed in intense emotional turmoil. I couldn't feel love, just pain and anguish... tormented. I couldn't feel, yet I felt ...adrift...like I didn't belong--anywhere.

For the first time I understood why someone would actually commit suicide. If you had never experienced love in your life, had no close human contact and existed in a void as I did, there would be absolutely no reason to live. You are the walking dead.

I was lucky. I had experienced lots of love and deep connections throughout my life thus far, and I held on to the belief that it had to be there again....I knew it was real. I believed that whatever was happening to me would pass. I told myself I would just have to endure it until it did--If I could just hang on ... one day at a time. If I got hit by a train I would have been happy with that but I would never purposely take my own life,

I knew that. I just had make it through one day at a time, that's what I'd do. I'd just hang on.

Chapter 28

European Re-Connect

This emotional torture continued on into winter. In January I flew over to Amsterdam to see Mort and look up Johan, the lanky Dutchman I had met on the Herengracht bridge days before I left for India....a lifetime ago.

We reconnected like old, trusted friends and I introduced him to Mort and he introduced us to his brother-in-law Max, and the four of us hit it off. I stayed in the apartment with Mort. Johan and Max would drop over and we all got to know each other better. I felt more at ease here. Depression still had me in its grip, but I seemed to be able to handle it better. Mort and I had some pretty deep discussions about all that had happened between us over the years and if anything, our relationship deepened.

Mort had purchased another VW van which we used to haul stuff around. We made false bottom crates and shipped them back to Canada from Belgium. We would drive to Brussels with the not-so-empty crate and shop for nice, fragile, art glass and ceramics to fill it and then send it off to a willing accomplice at home.

Shipping from Belgium was important. The image of Belgium was straight and clean. Nothing ever happened in

Belgium, especially in those days... But Amsterdam...Now, that was a different story. It was all about perception. Every little aspect that would deflect suspicion was important. There was never a problem. I would fly back and forth to Halifax on occasion to handle our affairs.

We were hanging out with Israeli Noah and English Dave as well. Sometimes we would go visit Noah's friend Abe whom I mentioned earlier. We continued going there occasionally for those Sunday dinners and parties. Sarah was an energetic graphic designer and Abe was pretty mellow, smoking hash and listening to music was his thing, but as Abe got heavier into cocaine his personality changed as often happens with extended coke use and abuse. He became somewhat paranoid and very aggressive...a different person from the laid back hash smoker I knew.

As I mentioned earlier, I tried many times to caution and warn him and the other friends that were part of this group. I would go to parties at some of their homes where they would spread long, thick, continuous lines of coke on a mirror and pass it around, everyone snorting huge amounts. This would continue all night long, not just once or twice. It was serious abuse.

Cocaine is an insidious and highly addictive, dangerous, narcotic drug. It's a stimulant that works through the central nervous system and *prolonged use will cause severe damage to your body and brain*, damaging your internal organs, bringing on paranoid psychosis and even death. It's quite unlike cannabis which is relatively harmless and considered a mild, non-lethal hallucinogen. No one has ever died as a direct result of cannabis abuse. Many have died from cocaine overdose and many a relationship has been destroyed because of it... Including that of my dear friend Syb...

I tried to warn my friends, when it became popular in Amsterdam and they started getting heavily into it. Most of them really weren't aware or concerned about its properties and the harmful, deadly affects. They were just interested in the immediate, wonderful, euphoric, energetic buzz of feeling ten feet tall and bulletproof. They would dismiss what I was saying as pooh-pooh and carry on. I continued trying to caution them because I had seen and experienced the negative, destructive side of that vile, soul-destroying drug back in Ottawa and it was obvious to me that only bad things were going to come from such abuse. They would wave me off like I was crying wolf. *They just didn't want to know.*

Eventually it got so bad that one of the crew, Dari, an Afghani, couldn't even talk coherently any more--he just babbled on and continued snorting. Abe ended up killing his wife in a fit of rage. The group eventually scattered and I would hear sad stories over the years about some of them either doing time in jail somewhere--or dead.

Over the course of many years in the underworld drug trade I have witnessed a number of people who ruined their marriages, family ties and their lives because of cocaine, and each and every one of them thought they had it under control. The Big Lie, as it's known. I had several offers over the years to make lots of money dealing this drug but there was no amount of money that could ever persuade me to do business with cocaine or the people who were involved with it. We all draw our own lines and some of us don't have any lines at all.

English Dave suggested that we do a scam to Stockholm. He had a contact there and I thought it would be fun to see

Sweden and perhaps meet some of those beautiful, fun-loving "liberated" Swedish girls I'd heard so much about, so... we built a stash for ten kilos of hash in our van and Dave and I drove up to Stockholm on a test run while Mort remained in Amsterdam taking care of business as usual.

It took us a few days to get to Sweden, driving through Germany and Denmark. It was winter with lots of snow and cold temperatures. Also, this was during the so called "oil crises" of '73-'74 and it took us an extra day because we got stranded in Denmark where we couldn't buy gas on the particular day we arrived.

In Sweden Dave's contact (Erik) found us a rental chalet in a secluded, forested area about twenty kilometers from Stockholm where we were safely able to dismantle our stash and get it ready for delivery. He warned us several times about the efficient and highly-trained police.

It was quite tense in Stockholm; police were in abundance. You would see them walking in pairs, or in groups of four, going by in cars, more in vans, it seemed like they were everywhere--a very high police presence like I'd never seen before meant you really had to be on your toes. This was no place to be unaware.

We had a rendezvous arranged with Erik and were heading in along the country road with the hash in a suitcase in back when Dave said he needed to pee. There was no traffic on this little back road so I just pulled over a bit and stopped. Dave stepped out of the van and the next thing he was nowhere to be seen. The van had lots of windows so this was really strange. It was as if he had been snatched by aliens or something. He had vanished. I was getting really concerned when I saw him about twenty meters in front of me scrambling up the side of the embankment all covered in snow.

When he stepped out of the van and shut the door he immediately slipped on the icy surface and went straight down the embankment--about a ten foot slope of sheer ice. Too funny... good thing he had a great sense of humour!

At the rendezvous everything went without a hitch. We gave Erik the suitcase on his promise to deliver the money two days later. True to his word, two days later he brought the money changed into large bills for us, and Dave and I drove back to Amsterdam. Fait accompli!

Back in Amsterdam Johan mentioned that he had a contact in Sweden as well and perhaps we could do another run. We agreed, but this time we needed a bigger stash to make it worthwhile so Mort and I bought a big Ford motorhome with English registration at the American Express market. English plates were good, England being a relatively non-suspect country. Dutch plates were never a consideration because of Amsterdam. The Ford was a conservative-looking camper that could sleep six. It presented the perfect image and offered lots of stash possibilities.

We did a *build-in* for thirty kilos and Johan knew a straight-looking American girl who would present a perfect image as "the wife" and Mort would drive. Appearances...Image...the all-important aspects of smuggling...

Mort and Sheila left for Stockholm and Johan and I flew up. We rented a car and drove to Linkoping, a small town where his female contact lived, about an hour away from Stockholm.

We met Elsa and her boyfriend in a local restaurant, slipping into the opposite side of their booth. Elsa was a classic blond Swedish beauty and the whole time we were in the restaurant she kept "giving me the eye" and kicking me under the table and reaching across to touch my knee. I didn't know what to do. Was this her "for real" boyfriend or just some guy she knew? I felt very uncomfortable. She had a buzz on from alcohol and obviously enjoyed teasing me.

The next day she drove with Johan and me to Stockholm, where we hooked up with Mort and Sheila. We met them in the centrum while Elsa went off to arrange her part of the deal and a rendezvous for the next day. I reserved the secluded chalet again and off the four of us went to the safety of the forest. We would meet Elsa again the next afternoon at two p.m. I was looking forward to that. We had gotten to know each other a little on the drive and no, that wasn't her boyfriend.

Johan and I drove the rental car to the rendezvous, leaving Mort and Sheila and the camper back at the chalet. Elsa had arranged the meeting, explaining the extreme need for caution, of which we were well aware. There would be no phone contact and only pre-arranged meetings. Johan knew her well and she had his trust. The hash business was a trust game all the way for us, and that was the beauty of it. In the circles we traveled it was all about integrity.

Elsa explained that It would take a few days for the money to be collected and they would do their best to get us large bills but no guarantee. Elsa would connect us to her friend Peter, who would take care of everything and she would oversee the transfer.

She had to go make the final arrangements and see if Peter had any money he could give up front when he met with us tomorrow.

We parted company and Johan and I enjoyed a great meal in a fine restaurant where Johan tried his hardest to get me to eat fish, which I hadn't eaten for years…bones, ugh, they made me gag. After a delicious dinner we returned to the chalet and crashed for the night.

This was a real "cloak and dagger" affair. It was a high stakes game and you couldn't slack off. The excitement was being on the edge. You had to be vigilant, aware and focused...totally in the moment. That was the buzz. It is addictive.

The next day we all went to town--Johan and I in the rental car and Mort and Sheila in the camper, with the hash in a couple of suitcases ready to go.

Elsa met us and laid out the plans for the pick-up and just nonchalantly, while we were sitting in the car, asked me if I'd stay the night with her in a hotel. I was delighted...a bit surprised by her directness, I mean, when she asked me, I did a double take...I wasn't used to girls making the moves on me, especially so directly...it was usually the other way around! I was, however, delighted indeed... Love those liberated Swedish women!

She showed me the hotel nearby and said she'd see me later on, after the transfer was taken care of. She had to go meet Peter's friend and tell him where the Camper was so he could get the hash and that would be that. No telephone contact.

Johan would hook up with Mort and Sheila and I went and got a room.

Elsa showed up around six o'clock and after some wild sex we went out to a lovely restaurant for a nice celebration meal after which we spent a wonderful night together. One of those "special times." In the morning she returned to her village. I thought I'd see her again but I never went back to Sweden. I wonder sometimes how my life might have unfolded had I made different choices at different times. I think we all wonder about that. Life really is curious. A fork in the road can change everything...

Mort and Sheila headed back to Amsterdam and Johan and I got another room and met with Peter to get what money he had and to make arrangements for the rest. It would be be another two days. There was no need for both of us to stay and Johan had family to attend to so he booked a flight back to Amsterdam late the following day. We changed what money we had into the large bills that Johan would take with him and I would see to the rest.

We had another great dinner that night, where I succumbed to Johan's eager persuasion and was introduced to *Sole Meuniere* which would become one of my all- time favorite fish dishes.

I drove Johan to the airport, returned to my hotel and waited for Peter to contact me. He came by the next day with two big brown bags full of money. There was a problem with changing it and he was all apologetic, but it was what it was. I would have to change it myself using several banks, changing small amounts each time. So be it.

In Sweden, the smaller the denomination, the smaller the bill, starting with one about the size of monopoly money and progressing to something the size of a place- mat, so big the bank gave it to you folded in three.

I was a bit paranoid about having all this money. There was nothing to do but put it in my suitcase and spread my clothes over it. After all the warnings about the police I was not taking any shortcuts--Stockholm was not a place to be slack.

That night, after smoking a joint with a towel rolled up and placed on the floor against the door and the window wide open, I made sure everything was totally cleaned with no traces of ash or anything in the ashtray and went to bed.

Very early in the morning, like five o'clock or so, I was awakened *at my bed* by some guy in a short work jacket and workman's pants, like a plumber--that being the first thought that came to mind. He was flashing a badge and identified himself as "Police." Another *plumber* was leaning against the table where my suitcase sat, full of money. It was a soft, duffle type bag with a zipper the length of it and the zipper was open exposing my clothes with the money just underneath. All the guy had to do was reach behind and stick his hand down in the clothes for the prize.

The next thing I thought was "These guys are good!" All the stories I had heard about the Swedish police and how thorough they were, were true. I went right into script, acting very surprised and bewildered.

"What is this about?" I asked. They said nothing other than asking for my passport, which was beside my suitcase in a briefcase. I shrugged, acting just slightly annoyed, got up, walked across the room in my underwear, got my passport and handed it to Plumber # 1 and got back in bed.

They asked me what I was doing here and I told them my story; tourist...Then I asked them if it was normal to wake everybody up like this, or was I a special case. They ignored my question and obviously had no sense of humor. After a few more questions, they seemed satisfied that I was of no interest and left. Heavy duty! That was close. I hopped around the room a bit in my underwear drawing a few deep breaths. That was the warning! I knew I had to be extra on top of my game.

Most of the day was spent going around to banks changing a few thousand dollars at a time, then taking the large, place-mat like bills, back to my room where I stashed them in my briefcase.

My flight back to Amsterdam was at five p.m. and by the time I had gotten all the small bills replaced with the larger bills there just enough time to make it. Checking out of the hotel, I threw my suitcase in the trunk and placed my briefcase, full of money, on the passenger seat beside me and headed toward the airport.

I thought I'd better stop and take the money from my briefcase and stuff it down my western style boots, just in case. This was the era before body searches, so I thought my boots would be the safest place to stash the cash. Pulling over to the shoulder, I stopped and adjusted my mirror so I could see behind me at a glance and started to remove the money from the briefcase. When I looked up to check the mirror there was a cop already stopped behind me getting out of his car!

I couldn't believe it. How did he appear so quickly? It was less than a minute since I stopped. I tossed the money under my seat as there was no time for anything else, pretending that I was looking for my passport when he "surprised" me at my window with a rap.

I jumped, acting startled and immediately started babbling to him that I thought I left my passport in my hotel room and frantically tried to explain that I was late for my flight while at the same time continuing to dig around for my passport, which I came up with just then.

Obviously relieved, I calmed down and apologized for my frantic behavior and said I was OK now, I'd make my flight. He looked at me somewhat suspiciously and glanced around the car attentively, professionally, but was obviously convinced that things were as they appeared. So, after checking my passport he told me to go ahead and walked back to his car.

Oh, that tingle!... the thrill of it all! Life on the edge...

I drove straight to the airport parking lot and jammed the large notes down my boots, returned the car, and boarded my flight without further ado. Adios Sweeden!

Chapter 29

Spring '74

Back in Amsterdam Johan, Max, Mort and I were developing deeper, trusting relationships. It's been my experience that significant, intense situations can deepen relationships to the same extent, perhaps even deeper, than the years it takes to develop that kind of solid friendship and trust in ordinary, mundane, if you will, relationships where trust or dependence may never be tested. When it comes to money matters and personal sacrifice--that's when the depths of friendships are revealed.

Max had a friend whose uncle had a hash farm in Ketama, Morocco. Johan and Max offered Mort and I a fifty-fifty proposition. We would, between us, build a stash in our camper for two hundred kilos of the best hash and they would arrange everything else.

Johan found us a safe, secure place just outside the small town of Deventer, a charming little town situated on the banks of the Ijssel River about two hours drive from Amsterdam.

A friend of Johan's had recently bought an old, abandoned lightning rod factory building in a rural setting along a narrow road that ran beside the river. It was lovely and private, about two kilometers from the town. He had converted it into a vacation home. It also had an attached garage accessible from the main building--perfect for our project.

Mort and I moved into the house, complete with indoor fish pond, parked the camper inside the very perfect garage and shortly thereafter commenced our project.

Working together with Johan and Max, we completely dismantled the interior of the camper, raised the floor two centimeters and covered it with a false floor made of several 4 mm. stainless steel plates which we drilled and screwed down to the frame. We then covered that with a nice carpet and took the same amount of two centimeters off the bottom of the built-in cabinets and reinstalled them. It looked perfect. It would take a lot to find this stash.

During the months that we worked on the camper, Johan and Max would stop by frequently and one day, early on, Johan brought another friend by the name of Franz along. Franz was interested in doing the run from Morocco. We liked him immediately. Later on we would also meet his wife Hannah and newborn baby, Evi.

A solid family man, Franz was just out of jail where he had been serving time for passing fraudulent cheques. He came into our circle of friends along with his brother-in-law Jan who was skilled in plumbing and metalwork. They both helped us build the stash. We had a great time working on this project while really getting to know each other. I loved the honest, straight-forwardness of the Dutch. They stayed with us and occasionally Hannah and Evi would join us for a few days as well.

The adventure and intrigue....The Life...the quality of friendships was mainly what it was all about for me. The money was great, don't get me wrong, it was nice to have the financial means to go anywhere and do anything I wished but I was never very materialistic so I never gave it much thought. I wasn't interested in amassing a great fortune. There was nothing in particular I desired, beside the freedom it brought which allowed me to travel the world at my leisure enjoying and photographing those people, places and things I most enjoyed and valued.. that was enough.

A few close friends would visit from Canada and stay with us now and then. We'd walk to town and shop and visit the restaurants and bars ...

The author in Vondelpark Amsterdam circa 1974

The hidden valleys of Ketama with our farm on the right

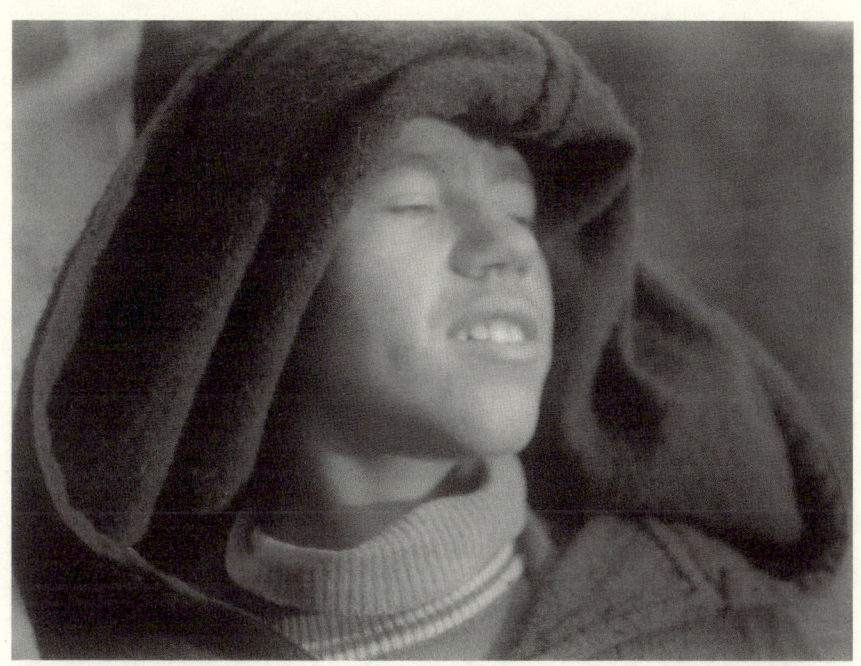

Early spring arrived and the camper was ready to roll. Franz and Hannah were anxious to get going, portraying the image of the typical young, clean cut family going off on a big family adventure to explore some of the African continent in their camper.

Johan and Max flew down to Morocco during this time to make the arrangements with the farmer. Once things were all set down in Ketama we just had to get the camper there.

A rendezvous was set up with the hash farmer in the foothill town of Chaouen about half way between Ketama and the coastal city of Tangier. Chaouen is a beautiful little town in the Rif Mountains known for its blue-washed buildings, weaving workshops and leather crafts. It's also not far from the infamous Ketama region of legendary hash producers.

Mort, Johan and I flew to Tangier while Max went on ahead to make further arrangements with the farmer. After a day or so checking out Tangier, we rented a car and drove to Al Hoceima, a small resort area on the northern coast across the Strait of Gibraltar from Spain, where we had a prearranged rendezvous with Franz and Hannah. We found them in a beautiful Moorish style hotel complex near the beach.

During those months of working together on the camper and visiting Franz and Hannah in Amsterdam, we had become very close and I was deeply concerned for their welfare, naturally. Hannah chided me one time about the money being my main concern. I told her straight up--I was more concerned about them. To hell with the money. Money could always be replaced. Their welfare was most important to me.

The next day we had to be in Chaouen for our prearranged meeting with Max. Hassan, the farmer, would be there along with his young son, Max and Max's friend. They were all decked out in *djellabas,* the hooded, woolen Berber robes worn by everyone. It's the traditional dress of this northern Moroccan region which we would soon adopt, making it easy to blend in with the crowd. Hooded hobbits all.

We met at a small cafe and enjoyed several glasses of mint tea. After receiving detailed directions to the hash farm and establishing meeting times, we parted company. Several hours of driving were ahead of us and we had to time it so we arrived at a certain dirt road a few kilometers past the little town of Ketama in the region of the same name at three o'clock in the morning. Max and his friend Mohammed would be waiting for us there. We would follow them up a very narrow, dark, winding, extremely treacherous mountain pass for ten kilometers.

Shortly after leaving Chaouen, we came across the scene of an accident. A young American guy was lying on the roadside near the crash site where his friends, two American women and a man were hovering over him while waiting for an ambulance to arrive. We all stopped, Franz in the camper and us in our rental car and offering our assistance but there was nothing we could do. After ten minutes of hovering over their friend and showing our concern, we continued on.

I always wondered if that young American guy made it....he didn't look too good laying there unconscious by the side of the road...

Johan, Mort and I decided to go on ahead. It was about five hours driving through the mountain roads and we would wait for Franz a few miles before the town of Ketama. Franz had given us some Spanish amphetamines called bustijd to keep us awake. They did the trick all right!

Johan was driving and as he started getting high on the amphetamine he began driving way too fast, jamming on the brakes as the road disappeared in the darkness around a sharp turn, leaving nothing before us but a sheer drop of thousands of feet. Mort and I yelled at him but that did no good and he continued scaring the shit out of us for several miles. It was pitch dark as we sped along that mountain road.

Then it was Mort's turn at the wheel and he wasn't much better. It was misty as well, with wisps of fog that also played havoc with us, blinding us for seconds when seconds could mean the difference between life and death. Our yelling and cursing at him had no effect, of course.

Finally it was my turn, "Now you bastards, it's payback time!" I was so pissed off, I did the same thing. We were all stoned like crazy on that stuff and I drove as fast as I could, braking just at the last second and wheeling around blind corners with those two freaking out and yelling curses at me. "Not so funny now, is it you assholes!"

By the time we got to Ketama, about two-thirty a.m., the effects of that drug had worn off for the most part. We waited at a place where Franz couldn't miss us and when he arrived we told him to follow us through the town without stopping for anything as we continued all the way out to the turn-off road where Max waited.

As we drove through the near deserted town, a few stragglers in djellabas appeared out of nowhere, running after us shouting "Hashish, Hashish ...The best one!" We just ignored them and kept on motoring until we were well away from the town and into the dead quiet again.

When we got to the rendezvous spot at precisely three a.m., Max gave Franz brief instructions and cautioned him about the treacherous, half-washed out road. Max led the way, Franz followed him and Mort, Johan and I followed behind as we headed ever deeper into the remote area of the Rif mountains.

The road was more of a dirt track used by trucks and horse carts, rutted all to hell, narrow, with big chunks of the outer edge washed away in places. We would be crawling along this ascending path for about ten kilometers. Roads would branch off every now and then like limbs of a tree. It was probably a good thing that it was totally dark so we couldn't see just how dangerous it really was.

Several times we had to get out and remove boulders or other debris that blocked the road. At places, the road was so narrow that the back outer double tire of the camper was right on the very edge. On one patch of road we had to cross a washed away area jury rigged with big lumber that had been laid across the missing section.

Hannah and Evi got out of the camper and we checked the stability of the ten foot beams across the chasm as Franz took a deep breath and inched his way across while the rest of us guided him, all of us engrossed by the extreme tension. One mistake and Franz would plummet straight down at least one thousand feet. We, in the smaller cars could manage by hugging the inside of the cliff but it was still dicey.

Finally, an hour after that nerve-wracking crawl, we arrived at a set of huge, rusty looking, steel double doors built into the side of a cliff. A shadowy figure appeared out of the dark, like a hobbit in his *djellaba*, and flung open the big twelve-foot-high doors and motioned for Franz to drive in. It reminded me of Ali Baba's cave. There was also room for our rental. It was all very clandestine ... everything must be hidden from the prying eyes of police informants and jealous competitors.

So... with the camper tucked away safely we were told to grab our bags and whatever we needed and follow Mr. Hobbit in the dark. It was four a.m.

We couldn't see much because it was so very dark without the moon, and we only had a couple flashlights between us as we trudged along a narrow foot-path cut into the edge of the mountain.

We walked like this, single file for about half an hour and finally arrived at Hassan's farm where we were ushered into a guest house consisting of a two-storey building made of thick, solid rock and mud walls.

The four of us, Max, Johan, Mort and I had the ground level which had a small wooden door in the side of the wall that opened into a carved out trench about three feet wide that ran the width of the building. On the right side of the trench, about three feet high and made of the stone that was carved-out from where we stood, was the kitchen and prep area which ran the width of the interior as well.

On the left about the same height was the open interior living area about four meters by six meters, completely covered with hand made Berber carpets. A narrow wooden bench ran along the three sides. There was only one small shuttered window, which, when closed created absolute darkness.

We would spend the next week lying around on these carpets or leaning against the benches drinking copious amounts of sweet mint tea. Franz and family were ushered to the upper apartment which was similar and just as comfortable.

We were all exhausted and just crashed on top of the carpets under the weight of sleeping bags and blankets and slept soundly until the roosters started crowing at dawn. Mort was sleeping near the open window and sleepily commented on the soothing sound of the distant crowing when, like a gunshot, one of the roosters let go right outside the window next to him! He jumped about ten feet and let out a fierce yell.! We laughed our asses off. Mort always was a bit jumpy, by nature. (Remember Miami airport!)

As we stepped out in the early morning light we found ourselves perched high up on a plateau that jutted out from the side of the mountain. A six-hundred-year-old family village consisting of a dozen small buildings, also made of rocks and dirt dug out from the mountainside, shared the inner side of the plateau. They housed everything from people to animals to crops and whatever.

There was no running water in any of the buildings. The only water came from the nearby stream below us. There were no toilets of course. No outhouse either.

Mort and I got coffee from our personal attendant, Absalum, who came with the place, and then we went for a stroll past the other structures, following the path that led through the farm. Shortly after passing through the little cluster of buildings we arrived at the edge of the plateau.

A panoramic vista opened up and far below lay this incredible, hidden, Shangri-La valley stretching off into the distant mountains as far as we could see. Scattered all over were hash farms joined only by meandering little donkey trails. It was truly mind blowing ...a faraway place...not seen by many outsiders....

Franz, Hannah and little Evi joined us in our guest quarters and we all enjoyed a most delicious breakfast of fried eggs with deep amber-colored yolks, as fresh out of the hens as could be. Along with this we had thick, round, heavy bread cooked in an open fire clay oven. There were fruits and jams, coffee and of course... mint tea. We were treated like royalty. Muslim hospitality, as I have experienced it, is second to none.

Around mid-morning Hassan came to welcome us and check to see that we were comfortable. Then he asked us what we wanted to do.

He gave us a nice big piece of zero-zero, the *cream-de-la-cream* of their hash to enjoy, while he made preparations for our two hundred kilos of premiro hash, (the # 1 grade after Zero-Zero), to be sifted and made ready for pressing. We spent the day relaxing, hiking around the area, smoking zero-zero in small pipes called *sebsis*, and drinking more mint tea. We met Hassan's young sons and just settled in to the adventure, the hospitality and our exotic surroundings.

After enjoying our day off, we feasted on another sumptuous meal prepared by Hassan's wife and daughter on the outside wood-fired oven and delivered to us by the male servants. After a social visit later on in the evening from Hassan and his young son Mohammed we all retired to our respective places to sleep.

The next day, except for Franz and Hannah, the rest of us would hike back to the garage, dismantle the camper and retrieve our supplies. We all agreed it would be better if they didn't see the camper apart now with the exposed stash, just for the psychological benefits. Every little advantage helps when you are smuggling contraband across borders. You need to psych yourself into believing that you are what you are projecting.

After another sumptuous breakfast, the four of us, Johan, Mort, Max and I followed Hassan and a couple of his workers along with a pack mule back along the path we had followed a couple of nights ago in the pitch dark.

It was quite different walking back along that narrow trail in the daylight. There were some tricky areas and you had to pay close attention. The path was cut right along the edge of the mountain and any misstep would likely have you hurtling a significant distance down a steeply inclined rocky slope, or worse.

Arriving back at "Ali Baba's cave," we dismantled the camper, which took a couple of hours, then we retrieved our supplies from the stash. These included packing tape, thick cellophane sheets, cotton sacks, staplers and staples, cash, and the various parts of our ten-ton steel press. We loaded all of this onto the mule and made our way back to the farm.

We spent the next few days inspecting our pollen as the group of older men sat around inside one of the buildings beating the buds with sticks and shaking them through fine screens. Zero-Zero, is the real sticky resin that's scraped off the workers hands and collected on the sieves. It's sweet like honey and we only ever got about a kilo for personal because that's all there ever was.

Once we had enough *premiro* pollen, we would start the pressing, in the comfort of our guest house.

The workers converged with us and we all joined in measuring out two-hundred-and-fifty gram amounts of pollen to fill our appropriately-sized cotton bags. The mouths of these bags were folded over three times and stapled across with five staples. When we got all the bags filled and stapled we steamed them and pressed them in our homemade press consisting of heavy side plates bolted together with big stainless steel bolts and a thick base on which stood a ten ton hydraulic jack. On top we fastened another thick plate and resting on the jack was another. The bag was filled and flattened by hand so that the pollen was evenly distributed. This was steamed and then pressure was brought to bear on it until it was pressed to one centimeter thickness. Two bags together would give us the exact thickness we needed for the stash. We would cut some of these up in long narrow pieces and others short and wide to fill in the gaps.

It was fun interacting with the workers. We didn't speak the same language, theirs being Arabic, but we certainly communicated and made jokes and showed signs of appreciation and respect toward each other, transcending language and cultural barriers.

Meal-times were great. We would all, workers included, sit around in a circle on our carpets. To begin, our main servant, Absalum, assisted by a helper, would pass around a big silver washing bowl with a bar of soap on a central pedestal. You would pick up the soap and the servant would pour warm water over your hands from what looked like a big silver tea pot. Once your hands were washed and rinsed. you were offered, what we referred to as the *"everything rag."* This was a piece of cloth Absalum used for everything--from wiping up spills to wiping off his shoes and blowing his nose...seriously "everything!" The workers all used it, but we all passed.

Next a huge platter of succulent roasted lamb or chicken in a thick gravy with couscous and vegetables was placed in the middle of our circle along with loaves of that most delicious bread. Each of us tore off pieces of bread and dug in with our right hands. No knives or forks here. This was communal feasting at its best.

In a Muslim culture the left hand is considered "unclean" so everyone dug in with their right hand, also, you had to be aware not to offend anyone by passing them anything with your left hand. This is considered an insult.

The meals were so tasty, my mouth still waters just thinking about it. I can almost taste the lamb stew! After the meal we would all have more mint tea, some sweet biscuits, perhaps a *sebsi* and, after a brief respite we would resume our work in progress.

There were no women present except for Hannah and baby Evi. The local women all kept their distance and if you happened to get too close to them they ran away, mostly in a laughing, light-hearted manner. They prepared the meals and tended to the sheep and gardens. They hand-washed laundry in the river below, beating the clothes against the rocks. They also gathered firewood and all other such mundane, necessary tasks …

After all the handling of the hash, which went on for two full days, we would clear up all residual clutter and then prepare a clean work area. There we would wrap two slabs of hash together with a couple of layers of cellophane and then, further wrap wide cello packaging tape around each package at least three times to ensure that it would be smell-proof from any sniffer-dogs. Sloppy packaging and carelessness had cost many people their freedom. Not us. We were professional all the way. There were no shortcuts.

When all the wrapping was done and wiped clean again, the workers placed our valuable cargo in big burlap bags and loaded them on donkeys. Mort, Johan, Max and I followed the procession back along the trail again to the secret garage, where, over the next day, we filled the stash and reassembled the camper as good as new.

The only thing left to do now was to pick a time for Franz's departure. We were all concerned about the condition of that treacherous piece of road out of the mountains so we decided to wait two nights for the a full moon and the advantage of the best light for Franz and Hannah to make their way back down to the main road.

Hassan and some of the other farmers had repaired that really treacherous spot over the past week, but who knew what they considered "repaired?" We checked it out and it was considerably better, but still not what we would call ideal.

Departure night came. It was clear with a canopy of stars and the moon high in the sky, illuminating our way back to the "cave." Earlier we had packed up the van with their bedding and most of their clothing and personal items, so we had little to carry when the time came to leave. Around midnight Franz and Hannah and little Evi were comfortably ensconced in the camper, ready to roll.

Everything was set. About ten kilometers away and two thousand feet below, at the end of the long chasm, was the main road through the area. A few kilometers further along from the turn-off, was a bridge across the river and from our vantage point high up on the mountain, we could see a light flashed from the bridge. That was our signal. Hassan's men were down there watching for police patrols that roamed the area. When Franz reached that bridge, he would flash us twice and we would know he was safely out of the mountains and on his way.

The police patrols passed at certain intervals and Hassan's man would signal when the last patrol for the night went by. Franz would then drive out of the mountainside cave doors, like Batman leaving his lair, and begin his nerve-wracking journey out of there.

I remember so vividly standing on the mountain top in the light of the full moon with Johan waiting for the signal, our parting hugs with Franz and Hannah, and then resuming our positions to watch and wait as Franz slowly and carefully wormed his way back down over that fucked-up, washed-out, rutted track to the highway.

We would catch glimpses of their headlights as they rounded a mountainside twist and came into view for a few seconds or a few minutes as they inched along hugging the cliff on their descent. Then for long periods there would be nothing as they disappeared from our line of vision. Those were the tense moments. Then we'd catch another glimpse of their lights and so it went until, finally, there on the bridge we saw their much-anticipated double flash--all is OK signal, and we could heave a sigh of relief. They had made it out of the mountains safely... now they needed to get clear of Ketama.

Johan, and I hugged each other with the full moon shining down on us, like a scene out of a movie. The next time we would see Franz, Hannah, baby Evi and the camper, we would all be in Amsterdam. Insha Allah...

They shouldn't see any police patrols again until they were well away from Ketama and then they would be on easy street, so to speak. But anything can happen at anytime. Such is the nature of the beast.

Everything was really well done. They looked the part of their role: intelligent, clean cut and wholesome, your straight-looking, conservative neighbors anywhere, typical, tourist types in a straight-looking family camper. They had the mental aptitude to deal with whatever situations might arise. Johan and I walked back to our guesthouse where Max and Mort were sleeping. They had said their goodbyes to Franz and Hannah earlier as there was no need for all of us to cluster at the send-off.

The four of us left the following day, driving out in daylight. It didn't matter if anyone hassled us now. We had no cash and we had no urgency so we drove into the Ketama market where we were assailed by a legion of hash hustlers, mostly aggressive older teenage boys who did everything in their power (short of physically dragging us away) to persuade us to "Come to my father's, uncle's, brother's hash farm for as many hundreds of kilos as you would like. No problems."

Some of them were legit, no doubt, and some of them were bandits, no doubt, who would rob us if they thought they could. With these people you always had to show your macho side because they could be quite pugnacious and any sign of weakness could invite conflict. We entertained our entourage for awhile and then drove away followed by by a carload of youths who trailed us for several miles before they gave up.

Continuing on to Tangier, this time in daylight, we saw the reality of the twisty mountain road and the many sheer drop-offs that might easily have claimed our lives that *night of the bustijdes* a week or so ago.

Each of us had a small piece of zero-zero because Franz wouldn't be back in Amsterdam for awhile as he was taking a more circuitous route through Algeria and Tunisia, from where they would cross over to Italy by boat, rather than go through the *lion's gate* of Algeciras Spain, a notorious place for drug busts of all sorts.

When we arrived at the Tangier airport for our flight back to Amsterdam we were prepared to be searched. Body searches weren't common in North America and Europe but here it was more the norm. There was always a heavily armed police presence.

I had carefully placed my flattened twenty grams, sealed in cellophane,(now two, ten-gram form-fitting pieces) in both insteps, inside my socks. My bag was searched after which I was escorted into a private office and patted down by a plain-clothed, higher ranking police official, who was obviously suspicious of me. He was friendly enough, very polite and all and I felt pretty confident because he had already patted me down and was engaging me in some light banter, but then unexpectedly he told me to take off my shoes.

Oh Shit! This was a new experience. He closed his complete hand over the top of my foot and squeezed. The tip of one of his fingers must have touched the edge of the hash but obviously not enough to feel. He smiled and said I was good to go. That was close! That was a rush I didn't need…

It seems foolish to take such a risk for such a small prize, but that was the life- living on the edge, adrenaline pumped, all senses on high alert! It's something like a coke high only natural. You're in the zone, keenly aware… intensely in the moment, like with scuba diving …you are locked and loaded into your immediate situation. I loved it…too much, I'm afraid, this challenge and battle of wits. I liked to keep my Guardian Angel busy. It made me feel alive. I guess part of me aligned with the great Wallenda, the famous high wire walker of the early 1900's who said life for him "was on the wire, all the rest was waiting." I wouldn't go that far, but I did relate…

Back in Amsterdam we waited. I hated this part because Franz and Hannah had become close friends and now they were in harm's way. Even though the camper was very well put together and they were solid about what they were doing, there's always the chance of the unforeseen happening and I worried about them getting busted in some awful place. It was that gnawing guilt feeling. Even though they were adults and had made their own choice, I felt responsible for them. I don't know what I would have done if they ended up in some horrible Moroccan or Tunisian jail. It might as well be me driving the camper, I thought.

That's the one aspect of smuggling I really didn't like, therefore I took every safeguard and precaution and never got lazy or greedy, over confident or big mouthed...I watched my P's and Q's.

About a week after leaving Ketama they arrived. We got a call from them just across the Dutch border in Germany. They were almost home. Safe. Whew, we could all breathe a sigh of relief. What a celebration we had later that evening when they came rolling in the driveway.

Hannah's brother Hans was with us, along with a couple of other close (involved) friends when they arrived. We all hugged and kissed and broke out the champagne and passed the pipe filled with the finest zero-zero. What a party !

The next day we opened the stash and gave it to Noah in exchange for several hundred thousand of those nice looking Dutch Guilders. Gone in one fell swoop! We were rolling in the dough!

Mort went back to Canada to rejoin his wife, Sandy again, as their on-again-off-again relationship was on-again--this time for good--we hoped. Franz and I went searching for a farm ....

Chapter 30

Adventures in Ketama

Johan and I had developed a deep friendship and I knew his wife and children well and had gotten to know a number of his friends. We thought it would be fun to rent a farm where we could live together, work on our campers, set up a darkroom, as we were both into photography, and just enjoy a quiet, private space outside of crowded Amsterdam.

Franz and I found a comfortable old farmhouse about twenty kilometers from Amsterdam, located on a small canal outside of the tiny village of Wilnes. It was perfect for our needs; nice and private with a large area where we could work on our vehicles, unobserved. There was a gated entrance at the beginning of the driveway alongside the house. The land was actually about meter and a half below the water level of the canal, protected by a *dijk,* which is common in Holland. Attached to the farmhouse was a long barn type building, which previously housed thirty cows.

Our usable land was an area about fifty meters by eighty meters bordered by the narrow country road that ran along the *dijk* in front of the farm and on either side by two small canals that created the property boundaries. At the far end a large fence set the rear boundary. Behind the property were hundreds hectares of pasture land for neighboring cows.

Next to the cow barn on our driveway side was an adjustable metal roof about ten meters by fifteen meters suspended by four metal corner posts designed for hay storage. It had a wenching system that enabled us to raise or lower the roof to any desired height. We enclosed the area with heavy, commercial tarps which which gave us our "workshop" where we could dismantle our campers.

We also discovered a built-in stash place in the house big enough to hold any load we might have, on occasion. One day, not long after moving in, Max was slouching low on the couch in the living room and noticed that a section of the back of the built-in bookcase, under the bottom shelf, appeared to be falling forward. Closer inspection revealed a removable section of boards that concealed a hiding place big enough for about five or six people to hide, which is exactly what what it was used for during the Nazi occupation of Holland, we were to learn later on.

The house was designed with a few different levels, in such a way so that this hiding place was virtually undetectable. Made to order for us, you might say.

We had a great time getting settled in and having friends and family by. In early March we thought it was time for another run to Ketama. This time we would use an old blue Citroen van that Johan and Max owned. Max would drive, accompanied by the same American girl who had done the Sweden trip with Mort.

As prearranged, Johan and I met Max and Sheila in Tangier and drove together up to Ketama.

A short distance out of Tangier as we approached a roadblock I took a photo of the soldiers through the windshield. Well, that was a big mistake!

One of them, a rather nasty-looking fellow, came storming over to my window, freaking out, shaking his automatic rifle in my face and yelling a blue streak of Arabic curses at me. He was livid and I quickly understood that he wanted the camera. I opened the back to expose the film, but that wasn't going to do. He reached in and grabbed the film, yanking it out of my camera, exposing the whole roll and then he threw it in the dirt, all the while staring daggers at me and cursing me out. I thought he was going to have a heart attack, or shoot me, or both.

If I hadn't had a good grip on my Nikon F when he yanked out the film it would have gone too. As it was, I was lucky he didn't grab my camera. Holy Shit!

Satisfied that he had taught me a lesson I wouldn't soon forget, he returned to his post and motioned us through the roadblock still seething with anger and glaring at me like he still might shoot me any second.

We were relieved to see them receding into the distance as Max and Johan rattled on at me for committing "the crime of the century." I loved the way we could all yell and fight with each other "You stupid asshole bla ,bla , bla" then it would be all forgotten and we'd be laughing and carrying on as usual. It was all part of that ever deepening camaraderie between true friends, that made my world spin the right way.

We met the farmer's man in Chaouen and arranged the rendezvous for the usual time at the designated place on the far side of Ketama.

We arrived at the spot at three a.m. and, guided by our contact, slowly made our way up that treacherous mountain pass to the mountainside cave/garage where another cloaked and hooded figure waited for us in the shadows, ready to guide us along the footpath to the farm.

It took us a week to press and package another two hundred kilos of *premiro* whereupon Johan and I saw Max and Sheila off at the appointed hour and watched again from our mountaintop vantage point as the headlights snaked their way down into the deep crevasse and eventually signaled us from the highway bridge. The most treacherous part of that mountain road had been more properly repaired, but it still left a lot to be desired. There were no guardrails or anything like that on this route.

Johan and I awoke the next morning to a deep snowfall with more snow continuing throughout the day to the tune of about fifty centimeters. We were storm-stayed. There was no way we were going to hike out of there in just our shoes and socks.

It was beautiful however, with pristine snow covering everything and we were quite comfortable in our surroundings. We were well fed, had the best zero-zero to smoke so we just hunkered down and made the best of it, enjoying the tranquility, reading, relaxing, enjoying Hassan's great hospitality and the beauty and serenity of this hidden valley. I felt privileged to be here in this timeless Shangri-La witnessing life as it has existed here, virtually unchanged for hundreds of years. It was truly awe inspiring.

On the fourth day we decided to get going or we might end up getting stuck here for weeks. Max would be arriving back in Holland in a few more days and we should be there. After another hearty breakfast, we donned knee-high rubber boots provided by Hassan and set off in the deep snow.

Walking the entire ten kilometers out of the mountains along that poor excuse for a road we marveled at places where there was almost no road at all to support a vehicle. In some places the snow was waist-high and proved to be hard slogging but we finally managed to stumble out onto the main road where we were able to snag a bus heading toward Chaouen.

Talk about a harrowing ride!

The driver was an aggressive asshole and the bus was a decrepit, lopsided old wreck, which he drove much too fast, screeching around blind corners with rocks and dirt flying over the edge. If we'd have met another vehicle coming in the opposite direction on one of these turns it would have been all over with one big bang and us careening out over the edge, to our deaths.

I don't know if the driver was driving so wildly for our benefit or not, but he scared the crap out of us if that was his purpose! It was one of the worst driving experiences of my life and made *the night of the bustijdes* seem like a Sunday drive. The bus was half full and it was obvious that most of the passengers weren't enjoying this terrifying ride. We politely tried to get the driver to slow down but he was obviously stupid and wanted to exert his power so he arrogantly dismissed us.

When we got to Chaouen, we told him what an asshole he truly was. Although we didn't speak his language he got the message, little that he cared. It was just sport to him. Another bus with a much better driver took us the rest of the way to Tangier and the next day KLM took us back to Holland, just a day before Max and Sheila rolled in ...another successful mission complete. Another celebration, more money, life was golden!

Johan, his wife Marieke, their three small kids and I were all settled in on the farm feeling very comfortable.

Franz and I had also become close friends by now and Johan's sister, Hennie, was a good friend of Hannah and soon Hennie and I started hanging out. They were at the farm a lot along with other friends of Johan's who were quickly becoming my friends as well. What a great time it was. We were all in our prime living lives of adventure and travel. We had lots of money and nothing was routine. Every day was interesting and intriguing as Johan brought me into his circle of friends. Most of the people I met were entrepreneurs, involved in some sort of nefarious activity or artists of one kind or another. We spent quality time hanging out with these people, while I pursued my photography skills.

One fellow, Daman, lived in a gypsy wagon on the outskirts of Amsterdam. The setting was like Mad Max's gypsy camp with four gypsy caravans scattered among wild vegetation and strange figures created out of scrap metal. Daman had a huge warehouse that he used as his studio to weld together his unique creations, many of which he sold to Dutch towns and villages to be positioned in places of honor for public viewing.

He was another one who believed that cannabis was not harmful if used in moderation especially if the user was mature enough to benefit from the experience on a more spiritual level.

Like many other Amsterdam Dutch, Daman was open to change and experimentation. Over the years he would occasionally be linked to huge shipments of grass or hash busted in Rotterdam harbor. He was never jailed for anything but would have to appear in court sometimes to give a statement. That was about it. And we're talking about shipments of ten tons or so.

The police also held the same view--that hash and grass were at the bottom of the scale of harmful drugs as were, typically, the types who dealt in it. For the most part these dealers were nothing like the gangsters who dealt in cocaine, heroin and the other dangerous drugs. These hard drug / criminal types were a different breed altogether with little or no regard for their fellow man. The hard-core criminal types were all about the money and violence, including murder could be part of their creed, if need be.

Gotta love the pragmatic Dutch. The Dutch police spent their time going after these criminal types and didn't bother the smokers or cannabis dealers too much. They had the same open-minded attitude with their driving laws. If you did dangerous and stupid things, they would bring down the hammer, but controlled speeding when traffic and weather conditions were favorable or ignoring traffic signals or driving the wrong way on one way streets at times when there was little or no traffic was ok. They took the common sense approach. It just made community living so much more agreeable.

The Rijks Polite patrolled the highways in Porche 911 convertibles in those days. They stopped a Canadian friend of mine one day in his Porche 911. After having a few words with him and checking out his car they challenged him to a race! Only in Holland!

Chapter 31

Morocco-Holland Connection
Summer & Fall '74

I always loved spring and summer in Nova Scotia so I headed home mainly to see family and friends and enjoy the area. Unfortunately, it wasn't long before I descended back into despair. I could't seem to shake the awful feeling, that heaviness, emptiness and lack of soul.

Ben and his woman Geri had broken up over the winter. I had gotten to know Geri a bit at parties or when she spent time around the house I shared with Ben and Jim. I bumped into her one day and a week later we met for a coffee and started hanging out together. We talked a lot and she knew what a hard time I was going through with my re-entry and one day as we were walking in a park in Halifax, I stopped to rest against a picnic table.

Typically I was fumbling about trying to explain my dilemma--that I felt like I was coming apart at the seams when she looked me straight in the eyes and said point blank "You are the most fucked-up person I've ever met!"

Her words hit me like a shock wave. I don't know why, exactly. Perhaps because they were delivered straight from the heart with love and brutal honesty...all I know is that the effect was immediate.

The very air before me rippled and it was like the reverse of my out-of-body experience in Goa. Many will think this a fantasy, but I felt and saw waves of energy rippling over me. It felt like my soul, my essence, if you will, was returning to my empty shell of a body. I know it sounds crazy but all I can do is describe what I experienced, real or imaginary. For me it was real, the same as the out-of-body experience in Goa was real for me, and that's actually all that matters. To quote the French philosopher, Descartes, "I think, therefore I am."

I grabbed Geri and squeezed her with all my might. The sky suddenly appeared a little bluer and I got a little spring back in my step. The veil was lifted. I was through the tunnel of darkness and heading back to the light and the land of the living. My condition would only improve now, I knew it. I had crossed a threshold and the valuable lessons I had learned from that desperate time would help me throughout life.

For anyone who has never suffered such despair or depression it's hard to imagine the anguish of just being in the world. Each day is an excruciating, emotional ordeal.

Death truly is preferable to this kind of existence, if there is no hope.

Geri and I hung out together for the summer. Mort had moved back in with Sandy months ago when he left Amsterdam and all seemed well in our worlds.

I rented an apartment in Halifax and took a few road trips from Halifax to Toronto to Ottawa and back to Halifax just visiting friends. It was great to feel truly whole again.

In September I returned to Holland with a big Alaska Malamute I had bought in Ontario on my second road trip.

We now had six dogs on the farm: a Malamute, a German Shepherd, a Belgian Shepherd, a Bouvier, a Saint Bernard and a ballsy little Cocker Spaniel named Alex, who kept all of the big dogs at bay.

It was comical to watch this feisty little mutt growling and snapping at these huge monsters that could have easily chomped him in half with one bite. They had the run of the house until we had enough, then we would shoo them out to the barn where they were fed. Meal-time was quite the scene! The dogs would go crazy, jumping around, whining and barking trying to get at their food. As soon as the bowls hit the ground, little Alex would run to his, snarling and growling which kept the other dogs back, whining and fussing until Alex was finished eating. As soon as he moved away from his dish they would all charge their bowls in a mad frenzy...It was too funny to see.

I had made arrangements for a friend from home, RJ, to do a run to Morocco. He found a lady companion, Cindy, to play the role of the "wife" and they flew to Amsterdam. We set them up in the Ford motorhome with all the necessary maps and such and specific directions to the lovely seaside town of Al Hoceima and our favorite hotel, La Cabilla. We would meet them there the next week for our usual middle of the night run deep into to the mountains.

Everything went without a hitch. Johan and I flew down, rented a car in Tangier, drove to Al Hoceima, rendezvoused with them and then drove on ahead to confirm everything with Hassan at the usual cafe in Chaouen. After that we met RJ at a designated place a few kilometers before Ketama and then we blasted through town in the usual fashion, made the three a.m. rendezvous with our guide and onward and upward we went.

When we awoke in the morning and stepped out of our guest house we were greeted by the most incredible vista. All of the farms throughout the valley were in full bloom, just about to be harvested. The various shades of green and the huge marijuana plants were breathtaking. We spent a week there, as usual, drinking lots of mint tea and doing our press and wrap and finally loading up the camper.

RJ and Cindy threaded their way along the edge of the mountain in the darkness and signaled us from the bridge below. They were safely on their way, or so we thought, but that was not so. RJ clipped the next steel bridge and rolled back the thin metal siding of the van, actually exposing the stash.

We, of course didn't have any way of knowing this and left the farm later in the day to head back down to Tangier and home.

When we finally saw him back in Holland, RJ described it as looking like someone had peeled back the side the camper with a can opener. With this huge curled flap blowing in the wind, he drove to the first good-sized town he came to but couldn't find anyone to repair it, so he had the whole outer side skin removed. The camper was cheaply made, with just thin metal sheeting stretched over a light wooden frame. What you saw now was the exposed wooden frame, the backside of the thin interior plywood wall and some insulation. But the worst thing was that you could actually see the exposed edge of the metal plate that covered the solid hash floor! An alert border guard might have questioned it but none did, lucky for all of us.

RJ got food poisoning in Tunisia and was miserable most of the trip. That, combined with the damaged camper must have garnered sympathy from the border guards he encountered along the way because they all let him pass unhindered. Lucky guy!

We couldn't believe it that day when he pulled into the farm with the whole side of the van missing. Another successful run from Morocco with everyone safe and sound! We were flying high!

A Dutch guy Franz had met in jail was now out and looking for some quick cash. Franz asked me if I'd be interested in having him and his wife do a run. We met with Tomas and I felt good about it so I agreed. The Ford was repaired and readied again and Tomas and his wife Marion and their four-year-old daughter drove off to Morocco in late October.

Again, the trip was successful. The money was piling up and we were spending it fast and furious on fine dining, photo equipment, trips, helping people out, ... whatever we wanted, as well as investing in other people's scams, some of which worked out and some of which didn't. Fast money--it comes quick and can go just as quick, depending on what you want. For me it was mostly about freedom.

Johan was approached to do a trip by an older couple he knew so he and Max outfitted them in their Citroen and they went off to Morocco while I went back to Canada for Christmas.

Disaster struck! Their stash was discovered at the Algerian border and the old couple were thrown in jail, there to remain for the next ten years. They were only in their fifties but "old" to us at the time. I was thankful that I wasn't involved. But one couldn't help feeling responsible even if it was their decision and they knew the consequences.

Johan and Max remained faithful to them. They hired lawyers and did everything possible to secure their release but they were to remain in jail for the full ten years. All the while Johan and Max continued working with lawyers on their behalf, sending them medical supplies, food, money and whatever else they needed to sustain themselves over the years.

Just about the same time some other friends of Johan's from Amsterdam, Joop and Peter, were doing a similar run with a camper. Ignoring the fact that the border at Algeciras, Spain had become increasingly more dangerous, they still decided to go directly through the Lion's gate instead of taking the longer, generally safer route through Algeria and Tunisia.

It was a Kamikaze run. I know we all felt invincible in those days, but going directly from Tangier, Morocco to Algeciras, Spain was indeed stepping on the tiger's tail... and they got bitten, badly. The stash was discovered and they were both thrown in jail with a seven-year sentence attached. And in Spain there is no early release for good behavior. Seven years meant seven long years! They did escape, but that's another story...

≈

RJ had decided to stay in Amsterdam. He had integrated into the group, found an apartment in the centrum and brought his real girlfriend over from Halifax.

Cindy was long gone by now.

It was the end of January, 1975. Franz and I went shopping in London for another camper with "respectable" English plates which we found and drove back to the farm to begin a conversion.

During this time RJ and Franz thought they'd send a small shipment to Canada. RJ had his own contacts in Halifax and he and Franz put something together but things went awry as they were shipping it from the Antwerp airport. They aroused the suspicion of the local customs agents and it was only by the skin of their teeth that they were able to talk their way out of a bad situation.

The customs officers were going to smash open their big ceramic art object but Franz managed to convince them not to. They also managed to talk their way out of the immediate situation but had to leave the package behind. They were free for the moment, but.... I suppose a Dutch guy from Amsterdam, the drug capital of Europe, and a Canadian guy shipping a big crated object from Belgium, was a bit suspicious...

They beat it like hell over the border into Holland before the thing was smashed open and the hash found.

Dutch and Canadian police were informed and that incident would come to haunt me and a few other friends from Halifax. Thanks to RJ and Franz the police in Halifax started an investigation of RJ and his associates and a couple of years later when I was spending more time in Nova Scotia, it was "guilt by association." Of course.

It didn't take a genius to figure out that Mort and I were more than likely involved with RJ along with a couple of others who also came under suspicion. We were all associated to some degree and all seemed to live a free lifestyle often traveling to Amsterdam, maybe not together, but still.... This group didn't have regular jobs that would show income, which, of course, would add fuel to the fire. Halifax was a small place back then and connecting the dots would have been quite simple.

Chapter 32

Enjoying the Life 74-75

Things were really heating up at all of the borders so we decided to take some time off and slowly work on the new camper and get it ready for the future.

During this period Johan, Franz, Mort and I took some great trips. Franz and Johan flew to Halifax, then we all went to Toronto where they met my dearest friend "Syb," and his wife BB. After a few days hanging out with them, my brother and a few other friends, the four of us flew down to Montego Bay, Jamaica. After a wild night there we rented a car and drove to Negril where we rented a cottage on the cliffs near the infamous Rick's Cafe.

Of course we scored some of that world famous *ganga* known as Lamb's Breath. We had a great time eating, drinking, smoking and making merry, diving off the cliffs at Rick's, swimming and snorkeling around the reefs...lots of fun, lots of laughs....living the high life...

Franz headed back to Holland after two weeks. Dedicated family man that he was, he didn't want to be away from Hannah and their toddler for too long. I loved and respected that about him.

Mort, Johan and I flew to the Yucatan in Mexico and explored much of that remote and undeveloped coastal region, which has been over-developed and commercialized since then and known now as the Mayan Riveria.

Back then, in most of that area south of Playa De Carmen there was nowhere to stay except for hammocks strung under *palapas* on the beach. We traveled around by local buses and ended up one afternoon at the ancient Mayan ruins of Tulum where we met a group of archeologists from the Smithsonian Institute who were exploring the as- yet-unexplored jungle nearby. There were eight of them, all dressed in khaki, safari-type clothing, lounging around a campfire, and all armed with hand guns in holsters.

We hung out with them that evening while they told us of their mission, which was to go deep into the jungle around the ruins, guided by a special high priest of the Mayans who they had made contact with the previous year. At that time there were still some dangerous activities going on with descendants of the ancient Mayans, isolated deep in the jungle…hence the special guide and the guns.

The only accommodation was a few kilometers away down on the beach, so we left this group and made our way to a small cluster of decrepit thatched huts where we rented three hammocks for the equivalent of a dollar-fifty each and spent the night shivering without any blankets to protect us from the chilly night air blowing directly at us from the ocean.

After Mexico I returned briefly to Halifax. Mort remained there with his family while Johan and I went off to explore Portugal where he would later buy an old farmhouse in the Algarve. We were having a ball spending our ill-gotten gains.

SAMSARA

One particular memorable experience was in London where we stayed at the Waldorf Hilton, one of the top hotels, along with another Hans from Amsterdam. We were chauffeured around town in a Rolls Royce Silver Shadow and ended up at some exclusive nightclub drinking five-hundred dollar bottles of champagne with the beautiful and charming hostess who ended up coming back with us to our hotel. I do believe we had a very good time, but it certainly is a blur....

Chapter 33

The Big Time

It turned out that Franz's friend Tomas had some very serious connections in the hash world and within a few months he and Franz were flying all over the world facilitating the disposal of very large loads of hash that Tomas's Indian connection arranged to have delivered. These loads, usually around a ton, were "customs cleared" into various countries such as Denmark, Germany, Australia, Canada and a few others.

It was April and I was back in Canada, driving from Toronto where I had been to see my dear friends Syb and BB. About two o'clock in the afternoon. I was en route to Ottawa to see another old friend Tom, and pick up some money he owed me from another scam, when I experienced the strangest sensation. As I was driving along, a most powerful feeling came over me that something was very wrong at home. My first thought was that my mother had died. It felt like a strong energy, a life force had suddenly left me. I thought "this is nuts" and tried to shake off the uneasy feeling. When I arrived in Ottawa, a couple of hours later, my friend Linda greeted me at the door and said I had to call Geri at home immediately.

Now I knew someone had died. When Geri answered the phone I just said "Who was it?" She told me my father had died earlier that afternoon of a heart attack and my mom had found him when she returned home from work.

The news knocked the breath out of me. I went for a long walk, then called my mom who told me not to drive back as I had just driven up a few days ago. I said not to worry. I then went to Tom's to pick up the money he owed me. It was all very strange.

I drove all night and the next day, arriving back home that evening at supper time. My father was buried with a great send-off at the packed church. A couple of his close priest buddies said the mass and we buried him in the same graveyard as Eddie, just a few rows away.

I hung around Halifax for awhile as my mom wasn't doing so well. She had no appetite and was losing weight. Living alone in the big empty house was not good for her.

Mom's brother Richard, with the foreign embassy, had just been offered a transfer to Minneapolis. He asked Mom if she would like to move into their house in Ottawa and take care of two of his three children who were attending school/university there. We all thought it a good idea, so she moved in June and I went back to Holland for a visit.

At this same time, Franz asked me if I had any contacts in Canada who could handle one of their large loads and if I'd be interested. I said I did and I was. So I flew back to Canada and contacted Tom in Ottawa. He was in. No problem.

The shipment was arranged for September. I invited Johan to help me with it and off we went and rented a beautiful sprawling farm on the outskirts of Ottawa.

This was working out well. I was going to be close to my mother for what source of comfort I might be and not far Syb and BB and my brother and friends in Toronto.

A week before the load was due, Johan and Franz arrived at the Ottawa farm to help me prepare things. We dug some big holes in a couple of the out buildings in which we buried big plastic containers, covering them over with wood and dirt so they were virtually undetectable.

Everything was set when the first load arrived. Tom and his partner, Jake, provided a van and driver to transport the load from Toronto airport to another secluded farm outside Ottawa not far from ours. The hash was hidden in bolts of cloth.

The van was handed over to Frank, (Franz and Tomas's) liaison, who actually picked up the load after the faux customs inspection, and then dropped it off in the parking lot of a near-by hotel where Tom's driver would retrieve it and drive it back to Ottawa.

Johan and I were in one car and Tom and Jake were in another as we followed the van at a distance switching positions and doing other maneuvers to make sure it wasn't being followed.

After traveling over many miles of highway and unpaved back country roads all appeared well and Jake's people were there waiting for us as we arrived at their farm. To our great alarm, out came a bunch of Uzi style machine guns. Jake was somewhat paranoid. He was also involved in some other nasty businesses involving cocaine, Satan's Choice, heavy, criminal types from the Montreal underworld, and who knows what else, I was to find out later.

Johan and I were strongly opposed to the idea of guns...this was a real game changer for us.

As the gunmen stood guard, the rest of us unpacked the load and Johan and I took it the last few miles through the back roads to our farm and the waiting underground stashes we had prepared.

We had been promised top quality by Franz and Tomas but a large part of the shipment was crap. There was some good hash mixed in but most of it was poor quality and It took a few months to dispose of--a lot longer than good quality. I never would have gotten involved with this kind of bullshit. I prided myself on quality and it made for bad feelings between different factions of the operation. Jake especially, let us know that everyone involved was less than happy. I felt shitty because they were good friends of mine, especially Tom whom I knew from Halifax.

We never saw anyone except for Tom, Jake and Sam (the bag man), who I knew from earlier times. He would show up with hundreds of thousands of dollars in brown paper bags every now and then. There were times when we had so much money stashed all over the farm that we would lose track of it. It would be in every denomination and hundreds of thousands of paper dollars takes up a lot of room.

A large, hard shell Samsonite suitcase would hold about three-hundred-fifty-thousand dollars on average and we would usually take two of these at a time, by train or car, to our money drop contact in Toronto.

Geri and I had stopped seeing each other shortly before I moved to Ottawa and I was now involved with Sidney, a young, Quebec French lady I had met in Amsterdam through mutual friends. She had a similar history to mine and we fell in lust and now she was living on the farm with me and helping out with things.

One cold, snowy, December night when Franz and Tomas, Johan, Sidney and I were hanging out on the farm getting money ready to transport to Toronto, we discovered that one bag of hundred-dollar bills had gotten very wet and dirty so we began drying them out by the wood stove in the living room. Tomas had some LSD that he said was quite special so we all took a hit.

It wasn't long before things got twisted. The money was blowing around due to a small vent fan and occasionally a hundred-dollar bill would blow right into the fire. After that happened a couple of times we figured we had better stop with the drying and put the wet bills away for another time.

From this point on things went completely sideways. This is the real danger of fooling around with drugs like LSD. It can be very powerful and it can take you to places you don't want to go and from where you might never return. We all pretty much "lost it" meaning, to the uninitiated, that we lost sight of the fact that we were tripping on acid and actual*ly became* our hallucinations. I went on my particular "trip" where I thought Johan, Tomas and Franz were my children and Sidney, my wife.

Then, In an instant, I watched them all age ten years, then in another blink of the eye, ten more years and again until they were transformed into old men in their sixties and Sidney and I were in our nineties. *This was so very real.* I was experiencing my life passing. It was okay though. It was a very natural experience…life, passing.

I started to feel the cold hand of death upon me and felt that my time was near.

I felt pleased with my life because the only thing that mattered was that *my children* were all here with me, seemingly happy and healthy. It felt like life had passed in an instant but I felt at peace with everything and said I was going to go lie down now (and die). They all followed me into the bedroom, and gathered around my bed as I lay there. There wasn't much verbal communication…everything was just flowing…I lay on the bed waiting for the cold to creep up my body and take me away while mumbling about how happy I was that they (my children) were all there. They, of course didn't have a clue as to what was up with me so eventually they left, puzzled, and went back into the living room. After some time, I have no idea how long, I snapped out of it and came to realize that I wasn't dying and they weren't my kids and I thought, what kind of nonsense is this?

Nobody knew what I was experiencing, as I would find out later, because they were all stoned out of their gourds, as well, and having their own individual experiences.

Annoyed, I flung the blankets aside, jumped out of bed and walked into the living room where I immediately went off on another rocket ride. I didn't know where I was or who anyone was, except for Sidney, who I thought was my granddaughter!

I sat down on a chair near the wood stove and Sidney, wearing a bright red kimono, came and sat on the floor beside me, draping her arm over my leg.

Thinking I was her grandfather, I was having a terrible time of it because I knew we had been sleeping together and I thought I must be really depraved. Then Tomas leaned toward me and offered me a pill saying they had all taken one. I didn't have a clue who he was but his watch started dripping off his arm like a Salvadore Dali image. Then I got it! He had been in the other "lives" I had experienced and so I figured he must be Father Time. I remember pointing my finger at him and saying "I know who you are". "I know who you are," very suspiciously...

Next I saw this comfortable cedar home with all new, expensive furniture turn into a dilapidated old shack with ragged old furniture and the wood stove being the only source of heat. I had no idea who Johan and Franz were, only that Tomas was Father Time...

Somehow Sidney got through to me and suddenly I snapped back in touch with reality long enough for her to tell me that they had all taken Valium to bring themselves down because the acid was way too strong. I managed to slip one in my mouth before leaving on my next trip.

Sidney and I were standing in the kitchen and I could feel myself going and it was only Sidney's voice which sounded way off in the distance saying "Come back, come back" that brought me back. We all managed to hang on to reality while we continued tripping throughout the night until way after the sun came up.

Even the house looked "bent" the next morning when we went for a walk outside in nature where, at one point, Johan told me he had seen me and Sidney as himself and his wife. Whew! Lucky...Dodged another bullet...

Years later I would meet the guy who actually made this acid from a recipe he got from Timothy Leary. He told me he never took it. He got so stoned just making it, that was enough.

Chapter 34

Bad Times

I didn't like to meet anyone involved in these deals that I didn't know, so usually Johan would meet this little Pakistani man known to us as *Mr. Smith*, in some underground hotel parking garage where Johan would hand over the suitcases full of cash to him. Mr. Smith was tiny and slightly built and couldn't lift the suitcases, so Johan would actually have to place the cases into the trunk of his car for him.

Anytime I was in Toronto I was usually at Syb's and sometimes Johan and I would leave the suitcases jammed full of cash with him until we could arrange a rendezvous with Mr. Smith. Thinking back, it was probably torture for Syb. He loved to open the suitcases and fantasize. He'd tell me about stacking it up and playing around with it. Fantasizing...Poor Syb...My brother...I know I tortured him.

A couple of times Mad Syb, as we called him now, dropped the suitcases off for us if we were not there. I remember him telling me of one time he went to deliver two suitcases at The Royal York Hotel but he didn't have a cent to pay the parking attendant. He had to drive around with all this money in his trunk and try and find a quiet, private place to stop where he could safely peel off a twenty from one of the bundles in order to pay the guy. When you're involved in this sort of thing, the craziest shit happens.

As you may recall, Syb and I were best friends from childhood. His young bride BB and I also became best friends in our early teenage years and they were my true extended family. I was always welcomed with open arms whenever I arrived at Syb and BB's, and whoever was with me was also warmly welcomed. We had a very special relationship.

Syb was a lunatic. He was a natural comedian even as a kid and we shared many good times over the years. He thought I was completely "mad" as well. Which I was, looking back. Many are the times I would show up with friends from Amsterdam or Halifax or wherever and we would party hearty. BB was wonderful to put up with all of our shenanigans. She would join us, of course, but always in moderation, being a very responsible mom, caring for three small children. Thank you so ever much BB for everything. A special place exists for you.

Syb never got involved in the hash business, although he could easily have done so. He was content to live his life as a very successful electronics salesman, take care of his family and observe all the madness of our lifestyles. My friends became his friends and we shared a wonderful, fun and very connected, close brotherhood. As the saying goes "Brothers from different mothers"...it was truly so.

It wasn't fair to stay at their place all the time and we needed our own space as well, so quite often we stayed at one of the big hotels like the Intercontinental, Hyatt or our favorite, the Harbour Castle Hotel on the Toronto waterfront.

Syb and BB, my brother and his wife, and another close friend (Keith) would often join us for an evening of fine dining at the best restaurants. These were the days of wine and roses, indeed. Money of course, was no object.

The load was finally gone by mid-December, without incident and another load was offered for the New year. This one, Top Quality assured. Apparently the wrong load was shipped last time.

Johan, Tom, Franz and I discussed it. I was pretty sore about all the aggravation they had caused me and my friends. Now that this one was behind us we agreed that a load of really good shit would make up for all the problems of the last one. I decided to go for it. In this world your word is golden. Integrity is everything. I wanted to redeem myself.

Sidney and I had Christmas at the farm with Syb and BB and their kids, along with close friend Keith, my brother and his wife, my mother and my cousins who were living in the Ottawa area with my mother. We had a fabulous time after which Sidney and I flew down to Cozumel, Mexico for New Years, 1976.

Upon our return in mid-January, the second load was ready to be shipped. Tom's driver was lined up to transport it after Frank got it from Customs. The weather was not great and the roads were slippery. The transfer from Frank went smoothly but just as we were leaving the city, Al, our van driver, slammed on his brakes as we were going over a highway crossing. Following behind I hit my brakes but slid on the icy road stopping just a few centimeters from his bumper. At that exact moment wasn't there a RCMP car coming the opposite way who saw the whole thing. He gave me a stern look, but continued on his way.

Had I hit the van it could have been a bad situation. Whew! Close call! Again!...Anything can happen...it's always the unforeseen happenstance that can change everything. The one you don't see coming. Stepping on the Tigers Tail is a dangerous and uncertain game. It's sort of like playing Russian Roulette.

We made it back safely to Al's back road home. At Al's country home, (there were no guns or any of that bullshit this time). We were not far from our farm on the back roads so I took the van the rest of the way.

Johan had gone on ahead and I had the strangest ride. The wind was blowing and the road was all drifted in snow sweeps across the way like giant, pointed witches fingers trying to grab my wheels and spin me into a larger drift. In one particular section the lamp posts were all leaning over at a weird angle to the road. It was dark and with the blowing snow the visibility was very limited just to the area of my headlights.

One particular stretch of road was dead straight for a couple of miles and with the slanted lamp posts, and repetitious snow drifts and whirling snow continuing on for such for a long time, I seemed to be moving but not going anywhere. It was an optical illusion and weird as hell, as if I was inside of one of those snow globes you see around at Christmas time. I thought I had entered the "Twilight Zone." And, I was straight at the time!

Finally I made it back to our farm, where Johan and Sidney and I spent the next several hours unpacking the stuff. To our extreme dismay it was more of the same shit, even worse than the first load! We were totally disgusted.

I was pissed. We had taken all this risk, had that close call with the RCMP and now this. After we had been assured top quality by Tomas and Franz, I felt used and abused.

Distribution on this level involves a lot of people and those I was dealing with were already pretty upset about the reputation they were earning from the last load. More bad quality meant more risk and bad feelings all down the line.

This is a business based on trust. Quite often transfers occur in places where it's dangerous to stand around checking out the goods, so you rely on your supplier to tell you exactly what you're getting. After the deal is done and the risk is behind you, nobody wants to have to re-handle it again. This is double jeopardy. Needless risk. Very bad on all accounts.

I told Franz and Tomas how upset we were along with everyone else but they just said to give it back. No one wanted to "give it back" after all the risk was taken. That was total bullshit. We reluctantly agreed to get rid of it at a lower price. I had a bad feeling about everything and it got worse.

This became a turning point for me. Franz, who had become such a close friend over the previous years in Amsterdam was totally unconcerned that I would have to sit on this crap for the next few months, which meant extra exposure and risk. Also I had promised my friends good hash, to make up for that last fiasco, plus, I had a reputation to uphold. I was blown away by his cavalier attitude. This was no way to treat a friend.

Good hash sold fast and things generally went smoothly. Shit quality hash came with its own set of problems. I was fucked.

Further situations occurred. Franz was doing other deals as well, I'm not sure what, but they involved him driving back and forth to Montreal where he would visit Hymie, a well known gangster connected to the old Israeli crew from Amsterdam. Franz would leave Hymie's house in Montreal and drive directly to my place. This happened a few times over a period of months, whenever Franz returned to Canada to take care of his part of the business. Franz and Tomas had other shipments going to Western Canada as well.

I had it out with him several times. I was really pissed that he would have so little regard for my safety. If he was under suspicion and being followed, he would lead the police right to me. He continued acting very cavalier about the whole situation. Fine for him, he was from another country but I was the one who would end up in prison for a very long time if he led the police to me and I got busted with the hash. That Franz wasn't followed probably had as much to do with luck as anything.

It took forever to get rid of the garbage, which is what I considered this hash to be. At one point, I actually got a couple hundred pounds back that was unsalable. That was a first for me. This was real bullshit. I was beyond upset! I didn't even bother to weigh it. I felt like burning it but took it and buried it under a tree on the neighbors property late that evening after dark.

That was another weird experience. Big John was a trusted friend of Tom and Jake's and I had met him years before. He was about six foot-six, and over three-hundred pounds. There was just Sidney and me on the farm the night Big John arrived with the stuff. I didn't want to take any chances. I wanted to be rid of it quickly. I would have been especially pissed off if I got busted with that crap after everything else that had taken place.

After loading the stuff in a wheelbarrow we got three shovels and made our way down to the creek that divided the properties. I led the way with John pushing the wheelbarrow behind us.

Crossing over the creek on to the neighbors property we located a big tree that served as a landmark and began digging a hole nearby. It was a cloudy night with a full moon and the light kept changing with the clouds. We had just finished digging the hole and were putting the hash in the ground when an eerie mist started rising and floating over the creek. It began to feel very spooky.

It presented a strange scene indeed: little Sidney and me, and Big John looking like Frankenstein, standing there with his shovel in the moonlight. Sidney got freaked right out. She just wanted to leave everything and get the hell outta there. It was like a scene from a horror movie where they were burying a corpse and in the next scene the big giant appears and beats the couple to death with his shovel. It was unnerving for sure. Creepy! We closed in the hole and got the hell out of there.

While all this was going on, Franz and Tomas and their families rented a house in Toronto and received another load which they took to their house and unpacked and which was more of the same, I was told. I refused to have anything more to do with it so they had their western contacts come and get it. All I wanted was to be finished with the bad situation I was already immersed in.

Then other things started to go wrong. One of the cash drop-offs to Mr. Smith supposedly came up forty-thousand dollars short. We were certain it was all there when we handed over the suitcases. Then it happened a second time. Another significant amount missing.

When we received bags of cash, it was all banded in ten-thousand dollar bundles same as from the bank. All we did was count the bundles, just checking the odd ones. For a business based on "trust," there were a lot of trust problems developing.

Franz and Tomas went back to Holland leaving their rented house unheated in the middle of winter. The basement was full of rolls of cloth which the hash was shipped in. They called me at some point and asked If Syb could arrange to clear it out. They would pay him well. He asked a friend with a truck to give him a hand but when they arrived at the house they found that a pipe had burst, flooding the basement. Most of the cloth was soaking wet, making it heavy and very hard to move. They got it all out and Syb salvaged what he could, putting the fabric in his garage under the front of his townhouse. He began selling it cheaply to his neighbors and friends.

Johan and I finally finished with everything around May and I was never so glad to get the hell out of there. All the negativity was really getting to me. Franz had become a real jerk, ego tripping, "walking on big feet" as the Dutch say, continuing to commute occasionally between Hymie's house and mine.

All this time Franz kept promising me he would provide me with a superior quality load to make up for all the hassles. Then Jake found out through the grapevine that a good half-ton load had arrived and Franz had given it Hymie, who he was trying to impress.

That could have got me shot. The only reason I wasn't severely mangled or possibly killed was because Tom knew me and he knew I would never have any part of this deception. Jake was a wild character, and if he thought anyone was screwing him around...watch out. He was beside himself when he found out that Franz had done this. He didn't know whether to believe me or not that I knew nothing about it.

That sneaky deal on Franz's part caused me a lot of grief. I had it out with Franz,I was livid. And he didn't give a shit. That was the worst part for me. Friendship for me meant we had each other's backs. He was out of there making millions and would never see any of these people again. It was different for me. I lived here and these guys, especially Tom, was a good trusted friend with whom I shared a lot of history, trust and respect, but now that was badly shaken. Nice play Franz.

They say money changes people and it's true. I watched Franz go from a regular guy, a good head, lots of fun, empathetic, to an arrogant, self-important kingpin who thought he was so smart because he had made so much money so quickly that he didnt want to be bothered by our concerns. It really turned me off to the point where, when later on, I lost a lot of my take investing in other deals that didn't work out, I was actually glad to be rid of it. To me it had become dirty money, bad Karma money.

Sidney and I were through now. It was more of an infatuation between us and those relationships are usually short lived. We had fun with each other and parted on good terms.

I spent the summer in Nova Scotia where I purchased a home by the ocean and spent I the summer months mulling over this bad experience. I still had to deal with the two hundred pounds of garbage that I had buried under the tree, back in Ottawa and I had to clear out of the farm by the end of September. If you can believe it, Franz asked me if I wanted to handle another load. You know what I told him.

My friends from the Afghanistan adventure, Ray and Sue were back home. Ray had been released after a few months in the Amritsar jail, thanks to connections Sue had made through that Canadian gold smuggler I had set her up with back in India. They were looking for a place to stay for the winter so I let them use my newly acquired home as I was planning to be away for several months.

Johan and I had made plans to head east to India with our campers in the fall, just to take a long, well needed vacation.

Returning to Ottawa the first week of September I made arrangements to get rid of the old hash. I couldn't believe anyone would want it but the Big Cheese from India who was behind it all wanted it redistributed. Good luck with that, I thought.

I was sure that something bad was going to happen because handling stuff again and again was a sure-fire way to get busted. However I passed it on to other people that Franz had made arrangements with, and I was finally done with it once and for all.

Or so I thought…

It was never my intention to be a "big dealer" in business with gangsters and the like. All I ever wanted was the thrill and adventure of running in places like Morocco and India with good friends I could count on, and to make enough money to support my travel habit and a decent lifestyle. The friendships, camaraderie and adventure were, for me, the best part. The money came second. It was always about life experience, owning each day, being free to make my own decisions, meeting interesting people, discovering other cultures and opening up to other perspectives of life.

I had always been particular about the hash I sold and tried to provide good hash at a good price so that everyone was happy. This business model was no fun at all. The ones putting this trip together didn't care a shit about the hash quality or the people involved, they only wanted as much money as possible. Nothing else mattered.

Apparently the Indian who organized the whole thing owned hotels all over the world and had "more money than God" and this was his little ego game, his entertainment.

About a week after I got rid of the crap, there was a big bust at the Toronto International Airport. It was the largest hash bust in Canada at that time. Guess what was displayed on national television by the proud RCMP officers…a huge pile of cloth bolts just like the ones Syb had in his garage! Several people were busted....Holly shit! Was I lucky... Again....

Johan and I cleaned up all the stashes and put everything back in order, but I left that place wondering if we missed a stash of fifty-thousand or so. To this day I still think there might be some old $20s,$50s and $100s buried up there. It's probably disappeared in a subdivision by now. Who knows?

Chapter 35

Heading East From Amsterdam

Back in Amsterdam, Johan and I readied our campers for the trip. As he had four kids now, he bought a ten meter long Winnebago. I had a much smaller camper, the one Franz and I had bought last year in England and converted to a smuggle van, which was never used for that purpose. I invited Geri to join me as we had reconnected in the summer when I was back in Nova Scotia.

Before we left Amsterdam I was invited over to Tomas's one night. Some men were there I had never seen before, along with Franz and Johan. Johan and I didn't know it, but this was a sort of tribunal to determine if we, or one of us had ripped off the money or the hash. It appeared that as well as the missing money, the hash I had handed over was light by fifty pounds.

It was all done very subtly during the course of the evening over dinner, drinks and tokes. I was led into conversation with an older Lebanese guy, Abdul, who was another major hash dealer. The conversation came around to the two hundred pounds of hash. My attitude was that it was such crap and I was so pissed off and disgusted I didn't give a shit, so I didn't weigh it therefore I really couldn't say for certain what I had handed over. As far as I was concerned, it should have been burnt because it was such worthless crap anyway.

I had nothing to hide so I spoke freely about everything and I was believed because they could tell I was on the level and not some slime-ball thief. If they hadn't believed me, I could have ended up in one of the canals with a hole in my head, I suppose. As much fun as he was, Tomas was scrappy, and would not be a guy to cross. All was fine in the end and I had made a new friend in Abdul.

Franz and Tomas and their families were heading to India as well in campers and we had planned to travel together but Johan and I were held up so they went on ahead fearing to get caught in snowstorms in Iran and Afghanistan. By the time Johan and family and Geri and I left Holland it was late in October and already winter was closing in.

We stopped in Cannes to visit Abdul, who had extended us a warm invitation to visit that night at Tomas's. He was a fine gentleman and great host and I enjoyed the use of his big BMW which he freely gave me and Geri to tool around Cannes. After an enjoyable couple of days there we headed to Italy and slowly made our way down through the country to Brendisi at the very bottom of "the boot" from where we caught a ferry to Peloponnese, Greece.

By the time we arrived in Greece, winter had hit Turkey and Afghanistan and travel through there now would be far too dangerous, so we decided to just hang out there on the Peloponnese coast. The weather was nice, the food was great. We had scuba diving gear, our own air compressor, a zodiac and everything necessary for a great vacation, so we were happy to stay put and enjoy Greece rather than risk traveling through the mountains.

As fate would have it we ended up at this campsite where an English guy, it appeared after some time, seemed to be under the thumb of the strange, Greek owner of the campground. As we got to know them it turned out that the Englishman was a mercenary who had been in the employ of Idi Amin, the maniac Ugandan dictator, and was now hiding out from English authorities because of the atrocities committed by Amin and his soldiers.

The Greek was another story. He was definitely twisted. He told us one night when we were having a few drinks with them, that he was from a wealthy family who had disowned him. After revealing all these strange tales, he tried to convince Johan and me to ferry him across the sea in our Zodiac to an island, so he could reclaim his family's ancient artifacts that really belonged to him, so he said. We thought the guy was totally wacko and didn't want any part of his crazy scheme.

Whatever was going on between the English mercenary and this Greek character was strange indeed. It was obvious that the Englishman was very resentful of the Greek, yet stayed and did his bidding, appearing more like a slave than an employee. We figured the Greek was blackmailing him, perhaps threatening to turn him in to the British authorities, who knows.

They intrigued us as curiosities for awhile and then we moved on. We stayed in Greece for a month or so and then decided to head back to Holland via Austria and Switzerland. I had checked out the Professional Association of Diving Instructors (PADI) college in Jacksonville Florida and a three month, live in, Instructors course was being offered in January, so I decided to go there as our trip East was cancelled.

Chapter 36
PADI 1977

We made our way back to Amsterdam through Yugoslavia, Austria, Switzerland..

At one point Johan lost his brakes going down a steep mountain pass. I was behind him with two of his kids in my camper when I saw that he was going a bit too fast for the conditions. Then I saw the smoke pouring from his wheels. If he couldn't get this heavy, ten meter bundle of steel under control, he was in grave danger of going right over the cliff and plummeting into eternity. Magically, there appeared a pull-off area designed for such emergencies and he was able to come to a stop. Lucky! He let the brakes cool off and from there we continued slowly to the bottom of the mountain and completed our journey back to Holland.

I left my camper at the farm and Geri and I returned to Canada for Christmas. Just after New Years I left for Jacksonville, Florida and PADI College, where I would spend the next three months training to be an open water scuba diving instructor.

The college consisted a main building with a classroom, a dive shop and six small bungalows on the campus.

I bunked in with three American guys, Bob from Atlanta, Georgia, Kaz from Buffalo NY and Sam from Maine. Bob, Kaz and I always went diving together on our days off and frequented the local bars whenever we could. We became close friends.

Bob's whole upper back thigh was really torn up. I though he had been attacked by a shark when I first saw the scars. Not the case. A decorated Viet Nam veteran about my age, he had been a platoon leader and one of five survivors of an Ambush that had virtually wiped out his entire company of ninety-five.

He told us one night the story of how he lay in a burned out area of the jungle, severely wounded, among a few hundred dead bodies. For three days he lay there waiting to be rescued, hitting himself up with vials of morphine a medic had left him, wondering if some Viet Cong would stumble along and kill him. I always wonder what it would have felt like when he saw his US rescue helicopter arrive….Life turns on a dime…some win, some lose…and if you're lucky, life goes on.

It was quite an experience diving in the ocean with sharks and barracudas and going deep inside of freshwater caves and experiencing many other aspects of the underwater world.

Nitrogen narcosis is a diving disease caused by excess nitrogen in your blood from being at depth. It has a narcotic effect. Being stoned underwater from excess nitrogen was quite another experience.

Diving, was my absolute most wonderful life experience of all..(thank you Jaques Yves Costeau), for inventing the Aqua Lung! The experience was especially intense in underwater caves, down sixty feet or so and two, three, four-hundred feet into a labyrinth. It's as black as black can be, illuminated only by your diving lights. You are in another world. If you have a problem, you can't just "go up." You are dependent on your "buddy" for your very survival. That's trust.

It's hard to describe, gliding weightlessly around inside these cave systems or inside of a shipwreck. You are totally focused and present, which is the best part of it. You are totally in the NOW, on the edge, but comfortable and relaxed...flying underwater, breathing underwater from air bottles strapped to your back,...absolute silence but for your bubbles. It's inner space, it's freedom, intense. experiential...life in full bloom. I loved it, I felt so alive...looking back, I think perhaps I was a "thrill junkie." I always wanted to jam as much life as I could into my years...

At the end of March I completed the course, becoming a certified PADI open water instructor and returned to Nova Scotia, sad to leave my new friends and the camaraderie we had developed but happy to arrive at my riverside home.

Ray and Sue had recently moved into Sue's mother's summer place half an hour away.

My Ottawa furniture was in storage along with a 1953 Buick convertible I had bought at an auction the year before. I flew to Ottawa, picked up the car and then drove to Toronto to see Mad Syb. He and I drove out to a dog kennel where I bought a Golden Retriever puppy that I named Sherpa. I then arranged for the delivery of my furniture to Nova Scotia and Sherpa and I drove there in the Buick to meet the movers when they arrived.

The RCMP were on to me now, thanks to Franz and RJ. Everyone who came to visit me that summer was put under surveillance to one degree or another. Mad Syb was pulled over in the nearby town of Lunenburg and had his car searched, for no apparent reason. Keith, was also pulled over on the highway near-by, searched, and questioned about his relationship with me. The RCMP even contacted his office in Toronto to inquire about the purpose of his visit to Nova Scotia.

Lots of strange happenings took place around my new home, including out-of- place strangers walking along the quiet little road I lived on, and *fishermen* staking out my house from a small boat, for days, just down the river from me.

It seems they thought we were up to no good..., oceanfront property on the infamous rum-running / modern day smuggling coast of Nova Scotia and all...hmm, O'Brian must be smuggling hash in by sea... Oh Yea! I would find out all about this a couple of years later on from a friend of a friend who's best friend was a Mountie.

When I was introduced to Allan he said "Jack O'Brian, I know all about you. I read a forty page report on you, I even know your dog's name."

I had been informed, previous to this, that my name had been flashed to some of the Canadian Embassies abroad by Interpol and the RCMP. My uncle Richard, who worked with the Canadian embassy in London, England in the late seventies, was shocked one day to see my name come across his desk. He contacted my older brother to advise him that I was involved in things I shouldn't be and told him to get on my case and "straighten him out."

I had started using aliases by now. To some I was Jeff to others I was George. Lots of people used aliases or nicknames. You never really knew who anyone was and it took a lot of mental organization to keep things straight.

Very little could be written down and anything that was had to be in code. There were hundreds of thousands of Dutch Guilders and Canadian dollars changing hands without receipts of any kind, all based on trust and... memory. There were phone calls coming to certain pay phones all over the place, none close to home, and all at different times and time zones.

All discussions were in code as well, and each pay phone had a reference like "the gym" or the "showroom" or "the garage".. for example, to designate where I wanted to be contacted the next time. Contacts were always prearranged and the calls kept to a minimum. I knew my phone was tapped and just assumed that just about everyone with whom I was in close contact had their phones tapped as well which proved to be the case. Paranoid or careful...sometimes there's a fine line between the two. Better to be safe, was always my motto.

When I first moved into my new home back in March of "77 I had the phone company there to install some new phone jacks. The tech who was outside working on the line informed me that he could hear every sound inside the house, not just me talking on the phone, but every sound, from footsteps to shuffling papers paper at my desk. I made a joke about "Watergate" but it just confirmed my suspicions and verified my need for extreme caution. It wasn't Sweden, but not far off.

I never talked "business" in my house, ever, because I had researched the latest technology in the spy and espionage world, as a matter of interest, and was aware of all the modern capabilities available. As always I thought it wiser to err on the side of caution. Because I was not only motivated by money I believe that made a world of difference for me. If something didn't feel right I would pass on it rather than take a risk.

Whenever I needed to discuss something with someone local, which wasn't very often, we would arrange a meeting, in code, from a payphone and always meet at some open place like a park or graveyard where we could walk and talk and be safe from eavesdroppers as well as being able to see everywhere around us for suspicious characters. After our discussions, if necessary we would arrange our next meetings in order to keep our phone contact at a minimum.

My number one rule was never to call anyone involved in the business from my home, ever, no matter what, or have anyone *ever* call me from their home phone. This was cardinal. All of this cloak and dagger stuff was fun and exciting, although it could be tedious at times, but that was just part of the game and you had to play by the rules if you didn't want to get busted.

The years from 1977 to the mid-eighties I spent traveling around the world developing legitimate import business with a photo-journalism approach. Many things including relationships, had changed and I was more interested in doing straight business now. I didn't want to become an old hash dealer dependent on the next load.

When I started down this road of discovery, my intention was to explore some other cultures, have some adventure, make a few dollars, meet interesting and fun people and return to university. I never set out to become a big time international hash smuggler...

I discovered along the way that I could make decent money importing a variety of things from Morocco, Turkey, India and other places and selling them in Holland, or Canada or England.

I had contacts for many things and enjoyed the import business and still got to travel and still maintain much the same lifestyle. Sometimes I tried to get Johan and a few of my other Dutch smuggler friends to join me in this, which they did to a small degree, but they were more interested in smuggling hash because it was more exciting, the money was great and all of the contacts were well established and everything ran like a well oiled machine. They didn't have to work at it. The main difference was, I didn't want to become a "career criminal" as it were, whereas they didn't feel the same as me. They didn't have any moral problem with it. Maybe it was my Catholic upbringing...

Because Johan and I were still close friends and I still enjoyed the camaraderie of others whom I had met in Holland, I kept in touch and on occasion would go along on an adventure just for the hell of it if I was going that way.

Ronald, another old friend of Johan's from Amsterdam had done a successful camper scam from India to Australia back in the early seventies and had settled in Bali, Indonesia, married a lovely Balinese girl and opened a restaurant in the small seaside town of Kuta on this (then), island paradise. He was becoming quite well-known over the years from his ever-expanding restaurant. Johan thought it would be fun to visit him and check out Bali. I agreed.

Thus In 1980 Johan and I flew to Bali as a side trip on our way to India, where Johan was going to join in another camper scam. I had long wanted to return to Goa and try and find Maggi.

When Johan and I arrived in January of 1980 Kuta was just a-rockin with all night bars and discos and beautiful women and handsome men from all over the world. It was a hedonist's dream.

The main mode of transportation was motorcycle or rental car/jeep. There wasn't much in the way of public transportation, just very few *bemos* (small open back trucks with wooden benches) and equally few horse-drawn carts, also with wooden bench seats. It truly was a paradise for young people, especially in the days before AIDS and world terrorism.

Fashion designers from all over the world were living/working/partying here and the most gorgeous women were parading around in the most sensuous, sexy, skimpy clothing. I didn't know anything about fashion but I was certain there wasn't a woman I knew anywhere who would not go crazy for this stuff.

Ronald, Johan's friend, dabbled in the fashion business as well, and put me in contact with his suppliers and I was suddenly involved in the "rag trade" as they referred to it. I ordered a bunch of these beautiful garments and made arrangements for them to be shipped back to Canada.

After a few enjoyable weeks of Bali, Johan and I flew to Bombay where Johan's camper was all loaded up and ready to go. He just had to check things over and make a few final arrangements in Bombay and then on we went to Goa. It seemed a lifetime ago since my last visit there, and it was with mixed emotions that I returned. So much had happened to me in Goa back when... I was kind of apprehensive.

We flew from Bombay to Panjim on a local Indian Airlines plane that was so overloaded with cargo that it barely got off the ground. This time we took a private taxi, not a group taxi that we would have to cram ourselves into with ten other bodies!

Tomas and Franz had spent a lot of time there with their campers over the past few years and had briefly met an American girl one time who sounded a lot like my old friend Maggi. I was anxious to see if it really was her and reconnect.

We went to Baga beach, at the far end of Calangute and there she was, after all this time, living in a small beach house with her new French husband, Louis. I was sad to learn that Henri had died of cancer a few years earlier. He had been cremated and Maggi had scattered his ashes over the Ganges. Louis and I hit it off and became friends also. It was great to reconnect with Maggi and experience India again, this time under much different circumstances.

Some other people we knew from Amsterdam were also staying in Goa. Tomas was living in a house a few miles away up at the other end of Calangute Beach, closer to where my house had been. Johan and I found a comfortable little place nearby and hung around for a week or so until it was time for Johan to get back to Amsterdam. I ended up taking a trip down to Cochin, much further south, with Maggi and Louis...

This was an insane trip.

We took a taxi to Panjim where we got a train part way down the coast to some town where we were told that the only transportation south toward Cochin was by bus. I hated Indian busses because they were uncomfortable, hot, crowded wrecks, with no air conditioning, but mostly because they were often commandeered by crazy lunatics who thought it great fun to see how close they could come to having head on collisions with oncoming vehicles.

We tried to buy rows, one row of two spaces for each of us but that was impossible, so we had to settle for individual seats.

Maggi and Louis got two seats together and I was across the isle, one row behind them. It was early evening by the time we got underway. They took some opium because they knew how horrible the trip was going to be, but I thought if I was going to be killed by a crazy bus driver at least I wanted to be aware of it, so I declined their offer to partake.

As expected, the bus was a jam-packed, lopsided wreck and the driver was a young Kamikazi with wild eyes who looked insane, accompanied by an equally insane looking assistant who sat up on a perch next to him.

They looked at us, the only foreigners on the bus, with excitement. You just knew they were thrilled at the prospect of being able to show off their driving skills. The death defying drive went on for several hours as I gripped the handrail on the seat in front of me and tried in vain to relax. How does one relax when your driver is constantly driving much too fast for the narrow little road and playing "chicken" with every oncoming vehicle? Maybe a little opium wouldn't have been such a bad idea after all.

It was late at night and relatively quiet. Most of the passengers were asleep, when all of a sudden all hell broke loose. Maggi was on her feet yelling at a small Indian man in the seat behind her, "How dare you touch me, I'm a foreign lady traveling in your country!" while hammering him repeatedly over the head with her purse as he tried to defend himself from her indignant onslaught.

All the lights in the bus came on as the driver jammed on his brakes. Meanwhile the little Indian fellow was trying to wedge himself under his seat, while Maggi continued to wail away at him. The bus driver and his assistant were suddenly in the middle of the ruckus trying to determine what was happening.

Maggi, hugely upset, explained that the little man had reached his hand down the front of her t-shirt as she slept. Immediately the driver added his outrage to Maggi's and began striking the culprit as well, as he tried to squirm away. At this point I was feeling sorry for the poor little guy.

Apparently he had been overcome by the sight of Maggi's voluptuous breasts bouncing about as they were jiggled by the motion of the bus. She was wearing a scooped top t-shirt that revealed a lovely looking cleavage and it appeared that the poor chap had been leaning forward, resting his chin on the back of her seat and had become enthralled by the sight of her beaconing breasts. As both she and Louis appeared to be asleep I guess he didn't see any harm in just sliding his hand down inside the top of her bra and giving them a little caress.

Well, Maggi wasn't asleep, more like in a drifting semi-sleep dream state from the opium when she felt the hand caressing her. At first she thought it was Louis and wondered what he was doing fondling her breasts, then she realized he was asleep and thus began the ruckus.

It was pretty funny, or so I thought. Maggi didn't find any humor in it at all....Anyway after Maggi and the bus driver finished their tirade, the admonished offender was back in his seat looking totally sheepish, embarrassed and ashamed. We continued on our hellish, death-defying journey of near head-on collisions, passing the corpses of several buses and trucks along the way, remnants of bad accidents that were left to rot and be scavenged by locals. I swore that if I got off of this bus alive I would never get on another Indian bus.

In Cochin, I spent a few days with Maggi and Louis checking out various merchandise and then flew back to Bombay where I spent several more days savoring my good fortune as I revisited my past life-altering experiences before boarding a plane and heading back to Canada.

I had seen all kinds of grotesque deformities and unimaginable oddities in India during my previous travels--dead bodies on the street, armless people threading needles with their toes, lepers with rotting faces, fingers, toes and much more, but it was during this trip that I saw the most horribly deformed, yet at the same time, the most beautiful creature all in one.

While I was making my way through a crowded street market one evening, photographing the sights, the crowd parted to make way and I saw, coming toward me on a low skate board affair that leg amputees often use, the most hideously deformed creature. He looked more like a huge insect than human, with his emaciated arms and legs all twisted up at weird angles. One bone-thin leg bent backwards over his shoulder and the other was bent so that his knee-cap was under his chin. He looked more like a giant grasshopper than a human being.

After the initial shock, my first reaction was to photograph him. As I began to raise my camera, he smiled up at me with the most beautiful, radiant look of pure love. It was as if he was glowing. I was awestruck, humbled like never before in my life. I felt spiritually poor and somehow inferior in his presence. In the same instance I felt as if I was receiving a most wonderful gift of acknowledgement and love.

This all took place in a matter of moments as he passed by and I realized that he must have been deeply loved and cared for by the people in his life who obviously took care of him and thus in my interpretation, he was rich in ways many of us will never know.

I never took the picture...I couldn't. To do so would have been a gross insult to him and to the moment, and even to the concept of respect itself.

I have the image locked in my mind and continue to recall it whenever I wish. Sometimes it brings tears to my eyes, sometimes it gives me a great feeling of joy, but always I recognize it as a gift from... the universe, perhaps.

India is, or was, like that-a land of extremes and contradictions. Extreme poverty exists alongside outlandish, opulent wealth, exquisite beauty beside horrible deformity; anything and everything is there. To quote that old Air India ad again, "India, there's no place like it!" That's for sure!

≈

Back in Canada, I had what you'd call a "personal attendant" from the RCMP, one Sergeant Wallace, who had been assigned to my case way back in '77 and was determined to catch me and hang me out to dry, I would learn as time went on.

When my seventeen large boxes of clothing from Bali arrived at Toronto International Airport a month later and I went to collect them, the boxes had been taped back together in a careless manner and some of the clothing was soiled from being strewn about the dirty warehouse floor.

I was, of course, pissed off and asked the warehouse attendant what had happened, to which he explained that the RCMP and customs had ripped all of the boxes apart and strewn the clothing all over the place. He told me not to feel bad because these same people had also destroyed some guy's very expensive carvings and furniture from Africa by drilling holes in several of the pieces.

Nothing could be done about it. Customs didn't assume any responsibility for damage incurred from inspecting imported goods. All you could do was just grin and bear it, as they say...

In 1981 I was on my way back to Bali at the same time Johan was doing another run from India to Holland using an old army vehicle he had converted to hold four hundred kilos of hash in the roof.

He had the tricky part done, which included buying the hash, transporting it to a safe place and the actual loading of it into the stash. This is where you are most vulnerable. Once the hash is safely stashed, the rest of the time is just spent relaxing waiting for the shipping date, or driving to another, perhaps less suspicious place, to ship from. In this case the shipping destination would be Ceylon, now known as Sri Lanka, located off the southern tip of India.

I joined Johan and Fritz, the driver, another old friend, in Madras. We stayed at a nearby resort that was billed as the "Indian Disneyland", a rather unusual place.

One day I went into the city and changed a thousand dollars with the intention of passing out hundred rupee ($10.00) notes to the "untouchables", the beggars.

Big mistake!

As I began passing the notes out the word spread like wildfire and I was swarmed. They came out of nowhere. A mob literally attacked me, trying to rip the bills from my grip, which they succeeded in doing in short order. Well...so much for good intentions...I wouldn't be trying that again.

The three of us traveled down the east coast of southern India as far as Pondicherry, sleeping on the roof-rack under the stars, enjoying each-others company and the South Indian culture.

After a couple of weeks of holidaying I continued on my way to Indonesia pursuing my straight business. Johan and Fritz were joined by Jan, another co-conspirator and member of the Dutch "gang," who had arrived to share in the adventure. They were continuing south to Tuticorin from where they would take a ferry to Colombo, Sri Lanka. The plan was to ship the camper from Colombo (much less suspicious than India).

Driving along a stretch of road, perhaps just a little too fast, not considering the added weight making the van top heavy, Fritz lost control of the camper. It started weaving all over the road until it flipped over on its side. Skidding along the asphalt surface, it came to a stop inches from a big tree. Fortunately it didn't smash into another vehicle or anything, but the camper, separate from the cab, had only a small door in the side for access and that side was down. Jan, who was riding in the camper at the time was trapped inside.

Johan and Fritz managed to extricate themselves through the driver's door and discovered that gasoline was leaking out of the gas tank and pooling under and around the vehicle. All the while local villagers began gathering around, some of them smoking cigarettes.

In a panic that they might inadvertently set the gasoline ablaze Johan and Fritz frantically tried to explain the danger and keep the gawkers away. There was a very small window in the up-facing side of the van and eventually they managed to tear it out while keeping the gawkers at bay. Jan, being a small guy, was just barely able to squeeze through the opening and escape the could-be death trap. With the help of the locals, they are able to leverage the vehicle upright and continue on their way relatively unscathed.

As I mentioned previously, things were different now. We had all made a lot of money. Some were effected more than others. Both Johan and I had been hurt by Franz's behavior but we had remained friends although that deep feeling of camaradrie was damaged.

We were all edging into our thirties now and I for one did not want to be an old drug dealer. I would check the newspapers, curious as to the ages of people who were being busted for drugs, and I always thought it rather pathetic when I read about people in their forties and older still dealing drugs. I continued bouncing back and forth to Amsterdam buying copper and brass and jewelry and searching out different markets, and hanging out with my old friends.

Chapter 37

Feet in Both Worlds

Back in Canada I was concentrating on developing my legit business but most of my money was gone now. A few ventures I had invested in went bad and I had lost heavily and just living the lifestyle flying all over the world took a lot of cash so I needed to replenish the coffers periodically over the years.

Johan put me in touch with another Dutch guy (Freddie) living in San Francisco who he thought would be a good contact.

Freddie and I spoke a few times on the phone and finally I decided to fly out and meet him. From the sound of his very deep voice I was expecting a really big, gruff guy and was so surprised when he turned out to be much smaller, wiry and thin. We would become great friends and meet up all over the world in the years ahead. He was also involved in the import-export business like myself.

I had the trust of people who would finance deals that I would facilitate now and then to replenish my coffer.

For the first deal I took a close friend, with me. Andy was in no way involved in the hash business but was willing to help be carry the money just for the free trip and adventure of it. We took three hundred thousand in cash across the border in a remote part of New Brunswick where you could just walk through the woods into the USA.

One of the isolated dirt roads that crossed the border in this area had a little customs shack that closed at six p.m. and opened again at eight a.m. the following day. There was nothing to prevent anyone from crossing either way, other than a note saying to come back when they are on duty. We thought it rather a joke at the time.

We drove to Bangor, Maine and flew from there to San Francisco to be welcomed at Freddie's house in Berkley where another good Dutch friend of mine, Joseph, was visiting at the time.

Joseph was an old friend of Johan's and one of the old crowd from Amsterdam. I had met him early on. Back in 1969 he had crossed the border from Afghanistan into Iran on his way back to Holland with a small load when he was pulled over to be searched. it appeared to be more than just a cursory search and they were likely going to find his stash.

In those days there was the death penalty for smuggling any kind of drugs into Iran. He had to make a run for it... he had no choice. This was a matter of life or death.

The keys were in the ignition of his old English Land Rover and it was about three hundred meters back across no man's land to the Afghani border. He waited for his moment to jump in the driver's seat and make a mad dash back toward Afghanistan! Immediately the Iranian guards started shooting at him as they jumped in their vehicles and chased after him in hot pursuit, firing away.

Now, the Afghanis, who didn't much like the Iranians, saw this mad pursuit and fired back at the Iranians as Joseph crossed into their territory in a flurry of dust. The Afghani guards cheered him, waving their guns in triumph as the Iranians turned and fled; and then they arrested Joseph and threw him in jail, for the hash they soon found hidden away in his vehicle. He ended up as a guest of the Afghan government for a year or so before he managed, with the help of friends, to buy his freedom.

Joseph and my non-involved friend, Andy, had a ball being tourists, driving around the California countryside and checking out the giant redwoods and other sights while Freddie and I spent three days going from bank to bank changing my Canadian bills, maximim ten-thousand dollars at a time into U.S. because of recent anti-money-laundering laws stating that any cash transactions over ten K had to be reported.

After all the exchange was taken care of Freddie arranged a runner who would carry the hash back to Bangor. These were still the days before heavy airport security and you could fly under any name and check any bags you liked without any kind of inspection, therefore a "runners" job was relatively safe, the risk mainly being from unforeseen circumstances.

Everything went smoothly and Freddie and I did a couple more scams where Freddie's runner would meet my border runners (mules) in Bangor and they would transport the hash across the border into Canada. I would meet Freddie in New York where we would change the money and make a night of it, running around to bars and all that craziness. We did this a few times without any problem.

Once my friend, Mad Syb, flew down to New York to help me change money. We spent the day walking around in overcoats with several packs of ten thousand dollars stuffed in our pockets. We hit exchange places and banks at the airports and around Manhattan, returning to the Hyatt where we would stash that money in our room, reload our pockets and do another change circuit.

My "mules" lived in the border towns of St. Stephen, New Brunswick and Calais Maine and knew most of the border guards on both sides personally, as is the case with many residents of those border towns, having families on both sides of the border that might cross back and forth several times a day.

My guys, a bit younger than me had mixed-country marriages and played hockey and baseball with a number of the guards and crossing the border was nothing for them. They were always just waved across, at most having nothing more than a personal conversation with the border guard. I would meet them at some pre arranged place around Bangor and they would transport the hash across the border and pass it off to another runner from Halifax who would drive it the rest of the way to its final destination in a specially designed stash car.

I also had contact in Montreal I was introduced to by my old English friend Dave from the Sweden days. Danny, was another far-out character who also became a good friend. As time went on I would discover that he was the guy who made the LSD that Tomas had that time in Ottawa back in 1975. It turned out that the international hash smuggling circle wasn't that big.

Danny had gotten the formula for the LSD from Timothy Leary and he told me that he never did it himself. He told me he got so stoned just making it that that was enough for him!

We enjoyed our get togethers in Montreal and had a nice simple program.

I would fly up to Montreal under an assumed name, as always, being extra careful not to be followed, I would spend the night at Danny's after going out for a nice dinner or some bar... whatever.

These trips were quite simple, I used a safe car from Danny to meet the runner from Halifax at a prearranged place where he would hand over a duffle bag full of cash that he had transported in a specially modified stash car. At the meeting he would be advised where to park the car and when to pick it up again. I then returned to Danny's where I would peel off my thirty grand or so and give the rest to Danny with the extra keys and details of the transport car and where it was parked. Then he would arrange with his people to pick up the car and place the load in the secret compartment and return it to where they picked it up. Then it was back home with my little bundle of cash.

My M.O. was to never do anything with anyone unless I was directly introduced by someone I trusted totally, who knew the new contact very well. There were a lot of undercover cops and informants out there.

It really was a whole other world. I used two aliases: George and Jeff. You wanted names somewhat similar to Jack in case you were caught off guard. For example, if I was beginning to slip out "Jack" I could easily change Ja.. to Jeff or George...little things but they are important.

The challenge was, remembering who I was George to and when I was Jeff. Not that it was really a big problem for me, unless I got confused, of course, which never seemed to happen. And even if it did we would have just laughed about it because everyone used aliases at times, I'm sure.

With no computers or cell phones everything had to be kept in your head, amounts owing, phone numbers, dates and times, different time zones, code names for certain pay phones...

code names for meeting places...the list went on. There was a lot to remember and to keep straight. Only very little could be written down in the little black book, and that, of course, had to be in code as well. It was all part of the intrigue that I enjoyed so much. It kept me sharp.

One American guy I knew (Mike--I never knew if that was his real name), had a friend (Sam), who was big-time in the business for years and even "opened doors" in the US for big shipments to clear customs undisturbed-- this, in order to gain trust within the circle, allowing him to move up the ladder where he could connect with and infiltrate the upper echelon of the international drug trade. At the end of a ten year program, Sam wrapped up his DEA undercover operation with a gigantic bust of several top level players all over the world, including my friend Mike who got six years for his part. Mike probably got off easy because of his friendship with Sam.

As we settled into the early eighties I started to feel real turmoil within. I still liked the thrill of it all and the interaction with my wild and wonderful friends, but everything was changing. Kids in grade schools were getting high; there was a proliferation of drugs on the streets everywhere and the lines were blurred between cannabis and the harder and more dangerous drugs like cocaine, heroin, methamphetamine and such.

I think a significant part of the proliferation of drugs was the fault of the authorities and educators, who more or less labelled everything the same, leading the inexperienced to believe that one drug was as dangerous or as innocuous as the other. I know this kind of mis-information led to my confusion growing up and it was part of the reason I tried the harder drugs back then. When I found out how light hash and grass really were I felt I had been lied to and was much more open to try some of the other drugs.

The "War on Drugs" along with Nancy Reagan's ridicules, "Just say no" campaign was destined to fail. Who was going to pay any attention to that? Truthful education was, and still is the most effective way to reach people and make them understand.

I intended to stop dealing altogether but was seduced by the easy money and the friendships. For years I had been flush with money, buying whatever I wanted whenever i wanted, flying all over the world, staying in the best hotels, dining in the finest restaurants. I had never paid much attention to the money mainly because it was always there, I always had "enough" and I took it for granted. If I stopped dealing altogether how and who would I be? How would I relate to my *involved* friends? What would happen to my self-identity? And, how would I continue on in the lifestyle I was accustomed to?

I was in Amsterdam visiting Johan when Franz received a small shipment of primo Afghani hash from India. It was really tasty and the speciality kind of hash I liked to deal, Super quality--LeDain quality.

My friend RJ had a contact, Ralph, who handled security for the auto port across the harbor from Halifax where cars shipped from Europe or wherever were held until they were inspected and customs cleared.

Franz and his partners were interested in a small scam so we did a trial run with fifteen kilos.

Talk about a fluke... there were fifty or sixty of the same model and color cars, little white Fiats, on board the ship when it arrived! What was the chance of something like that happening? Ralph had to search several cars to find ours!

The scam worked well but for that crazy little snag, so we were very enthusiastic and loaded the next one with sixty kilos. All was set when the ship arrived. My guys were all set with the runners in place to pick up the load after it was picked up from the port by RJ.

It was set for Friday afternoon at six but then I got a call from RJ saying there was a problem and the program was cancelled and couldn't take place till Monday. No problem. I passed the word and everyone dispersed. I went down to the country to relax for the weekend. When I arrived Ginger informed me that RJ had called and I had to call him ASAP. I knew there was an emergency because he would never call me at home.

I went to a safe pay phone and called him giving him the code where to call me back and awaited his call. I got the news that due to some internal mix up the load had to be picked up right away, it couldn't wait. I tried to reach my guy (Stan) but couldn't so I drove back to Halifax where I again tried to reach Stan, to no avail.

This was very bad. It looked like I was going to have to meet RJ and get the load myself and stash it, something I would never do, but due to circumstances I had no choice. A very dangerous situation was developing.

As luck would have it, I had been playing with a new police scanner I had just bought that no one knew about. When I met RJ to tell him I couldn't contact anyone and the new plan was for him to bring it directly to me, I gave him the scanner and told him a location where I would wait, which was a restaurant at a small shopping strip. He went off to meet Ralph and get the hash.

RJ had no idea that this was all a set up. Ralph was a "rat" and was working with the RCMP, Sgt. Wallace, in particular, for this one. I think because RJ was involved Wallace must have figured it out. It was like ten years now, on and off, I suppose, that I had been on Wallace's radar and it looked like he was finally going to get his reward. The first load was obviously permitted in order to get the big load and the guilty parties involved.

Wallace had neatly orchestrated the whole scenario with the hope that the runners would be scattered and I wouldn't be able to collect them back in time leaving me in a most vulnerable position. Good strategy indeed. It worked.

Meanwhile, RJ picked up the hash from Ralph and all was going according to Wallace's plan until RJ pulled into the parking lot of the restaurant where I was waiting. As he pulled in he heard a voice over the scanner saying "the subject's just pulling into the parking lot in a red truck." That was him. He almost shit but kept his cool and drove right through the lot and out the other side, listening as Wallace and the other under covers were freaking out. "He's leaving, don't let him get away!"

RJ beat it for the bridge to Halifax with Wallace and the others in hot pursuit. It was a scene right out of the movies, I guess, with RJ driving for all he was worth, passing cars on the two lane bridge, weaving and bobbing, trying to get some distance between them so he could dump the load.

He told me later that his driving experience in Amsterdam had really paid off. He lost them just over the bridge and because of the scanner, he was able to gain enough time to stash the hash and get a little distance away before they nailed him, surrounding him with flashing lights and guns drawn, dragging him out of his truck.

They were livid, especially Wallace. RJ said Wallace was almost in tears, he was so upset. They raked RJ over the coals, but there was nothing they could do but charge him with reckless driving.

Meanwhile I was oblivious to what was happening, still waiting at the restaurant wondering what was taking so long. It was eleven p.m. We had started around nine. By now I knew something was amiss. I left the restaurant and drove out by the auto port and around the city until about one a.m. when I went to RJ's and found him outside of his house. The police had just dropped him off. He was totally freaked out and told me his incredible story. I was blown away and immediately every fibre of my being was vibrating, suspicion peaking. How had they known? There had to be a rat in the woodpile.

He told me where he dropped the hash, but became very upset that I was suspicious of everything. I told him it had to be linked to him and left, making my way to the apartment where I was staying. I altered my appearance, shaving the beard I had at the time, and donning my friend's big hooded raincoat, as it was raining heavily by then.

I drove a safe distance from the area where RJ said he stashed the load and then walked around several blocks looking for anyone or anything out of the ordinary. There was lots of both. There were strange, wired-looking guys lurking in driveways or skulking about, also appearing to be on high alert. There was tension in the air.

The narcs knew the hash was somewhere around and they weren't going to leave the area until they found it. I went to Stan's and told him what had happened. We took his car and headed down to where the stuff was supposed to be, with a daredevil plan. We would scout the area and if it was clear he would pull over and I would grab it and we would take off.

It was just getting light as we were ready to make our move. I jumped out of the car and ran to the spot. Nothing was there. I looked all around. Nothing!

I went back to RJ's to reconfirm the details with him. There was no mistake. It wasn't there.

Later that day he contacted me to tell me that I had missed it, but Ralph had gone by later on and found it and all was safe now.

"Bullshit" was my response. Something was very wrong with this picture and it was obvious that RJ was being used by Ralph. I was certain but RJ protested and wouldn't believe it. I told RJ to tell Ralph to meet us at a certain location with a slab of the hash and then we would figure out a drop-off.

Ralph showed up with a couple of grams and some bullshit story about being too paranoid to carry more. I had never met him before and I didn't trust him at all. I told him we'd meet again the next day and I'd tell him how the transfer would go down.

I then arranged with Stan for six cars, with each of us in a car. We worked out a plan where we could isolate Ralph's car and driver on a nearby but secluded patch of country road and make an easy getaway through the woods, even if it was a setup.

Daring but do-able, with some of the cars blocking the way for the narcs who would obviously be following the drop car.

When Ralph showed up I told him that he was to have the hash in a duffle bag in the back seat and have his driver pull up to a coffee shop near the bridge and wait. My driver would pull in and signal his driver to follow him, and that was all he needed to know.

Well, the next day Ralph informed RJ that the stash was busted overnight and the hash was gone and the following day it was on the news and in the newspaper that several pounds of hash were busted and arrests were to follow.

Some years later I had it confirmed that Ralph was indeed a snitch working with the RCMP at the auto port to do just that sort of thing, set people up so the RCMP could bust them. Ralph was allowed to do whatever he wanted, more or less, with impunity.

It was obvious that the noose was tightening and it would only be a matter of time before I was busted either by set up or fluke.

A couple of months later I was back in Amsterdam for a visit but especially to see Franz and his friend and partner Steve, from New York, the one who had all of the Afghan connections. I wanted to explain to them, face to face, what had happened.

Having already sent them the newspaper article reporting the "non bust" we still needed to havea face to face. That's only normal etiquette.

I had met Steve a few times and had only gotten to know him slightly over the last few years. He lived downstairs from Franz in the same building so stopped by his place on the way, as and I wanted to tell him the story personally, as well.

Steve opened the door and gave me a big hug and a warm greeting and told me not to worry about the hash. As long as I was OK, then all was well. That's the way it was between friends, when a scam went down. The money was secondary.

I went up to Franz's expecting the same kind of greeting, but instead what I got was all this shit about how much money he lost and if it was anyone else he'd beat the shit out of them and all this kind of crap. I couldn't believe my ears.

He was millionaire by now and this shocked the hell out of me, again. I was saddened again by the realization of how money had altered him, just like others I knew who let the money get to their heads...

Money has a seductive power, it can become all important--and there's never enough if you get caught in that web. It can become another form of addiction. Some people begin to think they are brilliant or superior to others. Big Shots, legends in their own minds, you might say. It's quite amazing, I know. I experienced enough to realize and understand just how powerful a drug money can become. I remember how self-important I felt a few years earlier when we were dealing with the most prestigious Toronto lawyers in their skyscraper offices regarding the purchase of a well-known, multi-million-dollar restaurant there. Our egos were on fire. It is intoxicating...but it is all bullshit when the dust settles.

Friendship had definitely taken a back seat to the money as far as Franz was concerned. This change of attitude I had experienced with others I knew well bothered me more and more. The old days and the old ways were dying.

Chapter 38
Near the End

I was living a lifestyle and part of a world that not a lot of people have experienced. It was an education of another kind that I would otherwise never been privy to in a more "regular pursuit." The world truly was my "oyster."

I continued jetting back and forth to the Far East, always stopping in Amsterdam to see my old friends, some of whom had moved to Spain, Portugal, the US or to other parts of the world and would return to Holland periodically to see family and friends or spend the summer months.

My import business was growing and it enabled me and Ginger, to spend our winters in Bali and Thailand, supplemented occasional by my ill gotten gains. Over the years I had less and less involvement in the hash business as I struggled to remove myself altogether but it was always there, beckoning, especially when my funds got low...

I would discuss my feelings with friends who were involved in the hash business and always it was the same response ..."You're not doing anything wrong, it's only hash," "you're not selling to kids." This was the common consensus... "less harmful than booze, tobacco and a lot of pharmaceuticals," and so on.

Ginger thought that the reason I was feeling dissatisfied and troubled was because I had it "too easy." "Easy come, easy go" and therefore I didn't derive the satisfaction I would if I had to work hard and long for the money. Perhaps so. I considered this.

I was feeling disillusioned in many ways. The lies especially were really getting to me. For a long time, I had been living a double life of constant lies to everyone outside the *business*, including close friends and family members, and that bothered me the most.

On occasion I would tell people I loved and cared about that I was going to the country, but instead I would jump on a plane to New York or Montreal and do my thing using my aliases. Then upon my return I would create more bullshit stories for those people, which added to my feelings of estrangement. Lying all the time to people I loved was eating me up inside.

Looking back, I wonder sometimes how I kept it all together. It certainly wasn't like doing business in Amsterdam. Here, in Canada everything was fantasy. I was not the person I appeared to be to many, or maybe my friends and family could see through the lies and just went along with it. Living this duality made me feel uncertain about everything.

During this period Curly, a very dear old friend, from childhood and teen years, "Curly", with whom I rode freight trains, hitch-hiked, drank and chased girls, approached me asking if he could do anything for me to make some money.

We went for a coffee and I explained to him that I really didn't want to get him involved in the hash business based on my past experiences with friends. I explained how twisted things could get and I didn't want to endanger our friendship. He was adamant that nothing would change and he just needed a favor and he was really counting on my help, blah , blah , blah....and so he got involved and after some time when he was making lots of money and drinking too much and doing all the things I had warned him about ...we had a falling out.

We parted company and I sadly watched his world disintegrate over the following years. Money, booze and ego...a bad combination. We had few words after parting but remained friends at a distance, crossing paths now and then, but I carried a heavy burden around that whole thing for many years.

I had become accustomed to *the good life* and I suppose I had that criminal mentality of wanting immediate gratification--not wanting to work too hard for anything if I could get it quick and easy (relatively speaking). I never had a big ego therefore I wasn't into big, impressive houses and flashy cars and all that stuff. Yet I was still seduced by the adventure, intrigue and buzz of living in that state of heightened awareness.

More and more you heard about Kids getting involved with drugs. News stories abounded on radio and TV about schoolyard drug incidents, and not just in high schools. Even grade schools were having drug problems. Knowing that young kids were doing any kind of drugs really bothered me. That idea, "you're either part of the problem or you're part of the solution" resonated deep within me, more and more.

Further discussions with friends outside the "inner circle" about my misgivings mostly got the same response: "You're not doing anything wrong, you're not selling to kids." "It's only hash and, you're not responsible for other people." It's easy to rationalize and extricate yourself from wrong-doing if you embrace that line of thought, but in my heart I knew better. It's all personal, of course, but it's ourselves that we have to live with and no matter how we choose to be, it's our heart that reveals everything in the end. The heart knows...

One Afghani friend I was involved with told me he was supplying medicine to the Mujahideen (Afghan freedom fighters) from the sale of hash but then, later on, I heard through the grapevine that he was dealing in heroin and weapons as well. Another guy who I had done business with in Amsterdam way back, was a member of the IRA. I had to look hard at the fact that I was a link in the chain that bound me to all of these things I didn't believe in.

I'm not sure what sparked the sudden interest in me by the RCMP but one morning I was hungover and went to a local greasy spoon restaurant for a bacon and egg healer breakfast.

Always being aware of my surroundings, I never missed a beat. When you live this kind of lifestyle you either get better or you get busted. As I mentioned before, your senses become heightened...you are always, very "in the moment" and aware of everything that's happening around you; it's a big part of the lure, being on top of your game.

I slid into a booth and ordered and a few minutes later some guy about my age slipped into the next booth with barely a glance at me. I was aware of him, that's all. I just filed his image in my head and thought nothing of it as I stared absently out the window noticing a good looking girl with dark hair leaning against her car in the nearby parking lot.

Finishing my breakfast I left the restaurant to do some errands about town. I had about five kilos of special black hash for a special old friend that I was going to give to his wife, later in the day. Patrick and I had done business from early on, 1971 or so. We never saw each other socially, but had become good and trusted friends over the years since I first started with my monkey business and it was exclusively to him that I gave my best, non-commercial stuff over the years.

He was the only person I ever dealt directly with and we always pre-arranged a time and place where I would meet his wife. I decided to hold on to a half a kilo as it was rare, top quality hash.

Since I was going to meet Patrick's wife, Racheal at a shopping center, I thought I'd make up an innocent looking parcel wrapped in birthday paper in a big shopping bag, just in case something unforeseen happened to her on the way home. I didn't do this kind of hands-on thing very often and I was just concerned that she might get into an accident or something like that. Anything can happen…That old "ounce of prevention"…

I walked along through the shopping center with my big shopping bag assuming the guise and the gait of a shopper until I ran into Racheal coming along in the opposite direction. We stopped, kissed and chatted as nonchalant as could be, for a few moments and then I gave her the bag and we parted company.

It wasn't more than two minutes later when I spotted the girl from the restaurant parking lot earlier that morning.

Immediately I went into "Red Alert" mode. This was no coincidence. Not reacting in any way, I continued shopping, casually watching her following me. Before long who showed up but the guy who had sat near me in the restaurant!

Had they tracked me around all day? I couldn't believe that. If so, they must have lost me somewhere along the way, while I was getting the hash, at least, and then picked me up again on my way to meet Racheal. I had no idea. *This was very bad*.

Now I was concerned for Racheal. I didn't know if they had followed me to the mall or if they had seen the exchange with

Racheal. I waited about half an hour or so for her to arrive home before making a call to Patrick.

All was well! I passed the coded message that there was heat on me and that I would be in touch sometime later on when things settled down.

I thought: How stupid! This is exactly how people get busted. You do all these things, take all the precautions and then for a favor or for a few dollars you stick your neck in the ring and they snag you. Stupid! Careless! There's always an Achilles heel.

Now that I knew everyone was safe I thought I'd have some fun with my "shadows." I drove around pretending they weren't there and taking them on the proverbial "wild goose chase."

The next day, the same couple showed up again as I left my apartment. I didn't want them following me, just because... so I quickly lost them ....And then there were four ...in two cars the following day.

I drove to a big shopping complex downtown which was connected to hotels and other commercial centers by underground passages and overhead walkways--offering many exits and possibilities of escape. I easily evaded them by going into the underground parking lot and quickly making my way through the crowds and hopping a taxi at one of the many entrances.

The next day there were ten...in five cars. When I left my apartment half the street moved with me...this was crazy. It would not be so easy to lose them now. I did my parking routine, but as I got to an exit point one of them already in position waiting for me, I went to another exit, same thing.

They had the place well covered, so eventually I went back to my car and drove up through town. When I had all of the five vehicles pegged, I did a reverse maneuver and shot by a couple of them, waving as I passed, and quickly made my way through side streets to a University parking lot. Ditching my car, I beat it on foot until I was out of the area and able to flag down a cab. Slouching in the back seat and carefully checking all around until we were well on my way, I was certain that I had lost them all.

I was enjoying this cat and mouse stuff. That old adrenaline rush--the thrill of the hunt or being hunted, as the case might be. Cops and robbers...catch me if you can.

After hours visiting friends I didn't know what to expect when the taxi dropped me off at my car later that night. I was a little apprehensive, not sure if they would jump me and get really physical, pull guns or what. Take me down for questioning, perhaps.

It was dark when I started my car and drove out of the campus parking lot, but sure enough, a pair of headlight fell in behind me. I drove around for a few minutes with them on my tail and then I started getting annoyed. Shooting around a couple of corners and into a driveway I quickly backed out and fell in behind them and as they came around the corner, following them for several blocks until I got tired of this and went home.

The next day, armed with my camera and a telephoto lens, I took shots of my entourage at every opportunity although trying to be somewhat discreet as I clicked away.

The following day was more of the same but it took place in Point Pleasant park, a huge wooded park on the edge of the city. Walking through the paths with my dog, didn't I spot my main shadow, the original guy from the restaurant, sporting an identical Nikon camera with a similar telephoto lens!

We spent an hour or so ducking behind trees photographing each other. It was quite humorous actually, as by now I figured they must not have anything solid on me.

Later that day I spotted the girl tailing me as I walked along a downtown street. After awhile I approached her and started chatting with her, asking if she'd like to go for a drink and why she and her friends were following me. She was very friendly but evasive and declined my offer to go for a drink.

After that things died down and they stopped following me but I knew this life was over for me. I had "stepped on the tiger's tail" far too many times and it was inevitable that I was going to get bitten, chewed up and spit into a deep dark hole.

A few nights nights later on, as I sat at home pondering my situation and my life, I consulted my wise old friend the I Ching and the words of wisdom I received changed my life then and there.

The message I got this time basically stated: *We are given so many chances, in life, and then we have our last chance.* If we fail to recognize it for what it is, we are bound for serious consequences. This thought resonated deeply within me.

I had escaped death and eluded capture many times over the years. I had not only stepped on the tiger's tail more than enough, I had jumped on it, bitten it and twisted it in knots. I knew it was time to leave this party, I had for a long time and this just confirmed it.

A few months prior to this, Ben, another very close old friend, who had been released from jail well over a year ago, after being busted with a large quantity of hash was entrapped by a not-so forthright Mountie. He was still on probation, living on the straight and narrow after loosing everything. He had, gone bankrupt and was done with the hash business.

Through a combination of pressure and duress Ben was enticed, against his will, to do a small favor for his pseudo brother-in-law, Walter, who intentionally set him up with an undercover RCMP. Under continued pressure from Walter, who was financially destitute, and who he had been helping out, Ben finally agreed to get Walter a pound of weed to get him off his back, under the condition that it would be the one and only time.

When Ben arrived with the weed, Walter, unbeknownst to him, had a friend there.

Ben was not happy with this, of course but "friend" bought the grass and left. Walter made his hundred dollars or whatever; Ben made nothing. He had only done this because Walter was broke and desperate.

The next evening Ben got a call from the "friend" saying he was down the street and needed to speak to him. Ben told him, just like he had explained to them in the motel room--he was finished with this business and only did it the one time to help Walter out. The "friend" insisted on the meeting so Ben went to tell him to fuck right off.

When he got in "friend's" car, the guy flashed his badge and proceeded to tell Ben that since he was on probation he would be severely dealt with under the law, blah, blah, blah, explaining they weren't really interested in him, but had their sights on me, Mort and a few others. Ben would be sanctioned to deal hash and grass while helping him nail me and others they were interested in. If Ben didn't cooperate with them he would go right back to jail, for a long time.

Of course "friend" warned Ben not to say anything to anybody, but the first thing Ben did was contact me telling of his predicament and what the Mountie was proposing.

As a favor I said I would speak to someone in Montreal whose longtime friend was one of the top criminal lawyers in Canada, specializing in drug cases. I flew to Montreal and took my friend and Andrew, the lawyer, to dinner at a nice restaurant in Old Montreal, to ask his advice and discuss the options.

Over dinner I explained the situation. Andrew said it would cost at least fifty-thousand dollars for him to defend Ben and get him off, but as Ben didn't have the money, he offered Plan B.

The fifty-thousand or so, Andrew explained, would be to pay off a judge. The way it works is that the defense keeps putting off the court date until they have a date with a judge they can work with (pay off). Then they go through the trial motions and the accused walks.

Based on "Plan B" advice from Andrew, the best thing Ben could do was to tell the truth exactly as I had explained it to Andrew, from the heart, in great detail. The set up, the entrapment, the conspiracy and so on. He said that Ben had to convince the judge, just as he had to every day in court. It is about being convincing, after all.

Who is most believable wins the game. Sometimes.

When I got home I relayed this back to Ben. Ben in turn told "friend" to go pound sand at their next meeting. "Friend" freaked out and threatened to have Ben sent away for ten years!

They did bust him that week and when the court date arrived a few months later Ben did exactly as Andrew had suggested, explaining to the judge how he was coerced into getting the grass and how this Mountie(definitely not one of the good ones) had tried to entice him back into dealing and into an ongoing situation where he would set up his friends and have them all busted, along with all of the other juicy details of this would- be conspiracy based on entrapment.

The judge believed Ben and let it be known that he didn't take kindly to this type of behavior by the police. The Mountie "Friend" was severely reprimanded and transferred to some remote outpost in Labrador, while Ben received the minimum sentence.

Actually apologizing to Ben, the judge explained that he had no choice but to convict and sentence him because he did, after all, commit a crime, but under the circumstances, he gave Ben the minimum sentence allowable which was only a couple of months inside.

All of this was going through my mind as the words spilling from the I Ching rang in my head, resonating throughout my whole being. I knew my time was up.

More than anything else, I didn't want to disgrace my family. My father was long dead but my mother and aunts and other family members didn't deserve the disgrace I would bring to them. The disappointment and heartbreak my mother would feel would be unbearable. Over the years I had never been too concerned about being busted, I always felt "protected" in some strange way...except for that time back in Ottawa.

It was getting late in the day. I had a major decision to make. I was on the threshold of a life altering event, perhaps the most important defining moment of my life.

There was a lot to consider.

Was I going to quit this life of excitement, intrigue and fast money entirely and leave behind the friends and contacts I had scattered about the world, many of whom I had grown close to over the years?

Did I have the courage to start anew, without having the safety net of my "personal bank" to fall back on if things didn't work out, or was I going to bury my conscience, ignore all the warning signs and continue screwing around until I got busted?

How would I support myself and the lifestyle I was accustomed to? Who would I become? How would I identify in the world? Would I become a different person?

Chapter 39
Closing In

I had been involved in the international drug underworld for so long and so enjoyed the lifestyle, the intrigue and my friends. I was used to having access to fast cash when I needed it. To work for hours and weeks on end would be challenging to say the least. Was I going to join the world of "drones," those nine to five workers I had pitied for years, thinking they worked so hard for so little, often making in a year what I could make in a day?

I felt like my back was up against the wall. Did I really have so little faith in my abilities that I needed this "backup" to survive? I could pursue a life of photojournalism perhaps, or continue on with the import/wholesale business or a combination of both. These were the thoughts whirling around my head.

I had always scorned those older drug dealers I would read about in the newspapers, people in their forties and fifties and beyond, getting busted for dealing drugs. They were losers, in my opinion. If they were still into dealing drugs of any kind at that age, it didn't speak much for their abilities.

I had always thought of it as a young person's game ...something one did as a kind of lark to have some adventure and make a few bucks. I had only intended to do this business for a short time ...way back when...

Was I really one of *those* guys now? A career criminal, so to speak? This is not how I saw myself. What the hell was I doing...where was I heading?

I had my place in the world, my identity, my path, my sense of security, as it were. All of these thoughts were careening through my mind as I peered over the precipice into the great unknown.

I didn't know what would happen with my friends and contacts. Would I be an outcast of sorts? Some of the people I had dealings with were pretty connected characters. Would there be repercussions? Not likely, but it was a consideration.

It all came down to the basics: I no longer believed in what I was doing and I hadn't for a long time. I had become complacent and perhaps just hadn't had the courage or the confidence to move on. The whole game had changed and I didn't belong in it any longer.

My old friends and I were non-violent, hippie types in the beginning. Now so many things had changed, much of the business taken over by gangsters. The bottom line was... my heart was no longer in it and I had finally reached the point where I just couldn't be part of that world any longer. To continue on would be to "sell my soul." Was that the message in that full moon in Goa..?

My moment of truth had arrived. That was it. Just like that, I made my decision-I was done with it all. I would set out on a new path and see where it took me; Insha Allah (God's will)... as my Muslim friends would say.

I still had that big block of hash, a half Kilo, worth about five thousand at wholesale, but I was finished with the hash business and felt compelled to make a clean, cathartic break.

Selling this last piece and then walking away didn't feel right. I had already walked away in my mind. Come morning I would get rid of it.

It was early spring. Getting up early, I put Sherpa in the car and went to retrieve the hash, suddenly feeling extremely paranoid. (Imagine being pulled over and busted now!)

Driving to Point Pleasant Park with my head on a swivel, I arrived, parked my car and started walking along a path through the trees, looking all around, half expecting the narcs to jump out of the bushes and bust me at the last moment.

Making my way to the edge of the ocean, I stood on the huge granite boulders watching the sun rise on this beautiful morning. Holding the big slab of hash in my hand, I reflected on the life I was leaving behind and the future I was about to embrace.

I had embraced the unknown many times and always made out just fine, why should this be different? I felt exhilarated as I drew a deep breath and heaved my burden as far as I could out into the Atlantic ocean and out of my life. Forever.

EPILOGUE

Everything was changing for me on all levels. Having made the decision to trust my instincts and do what I knew in my heart was right, looking forward was almost as exciting as the old life had been.

I would find that the jewelry business, like the hash business, was based on trust to a large extent,. I did lots of business around the world based on handshakes and strength of character.

My friends reacted differently when I told them of my decision. Some were upset about me tossing that last half kilo away. Their reaction was "Why didn't you give it to me" but they all understood it was the way it had to be.

I invested the last of my money into an old hotel through a Canadian government tourism program that promised much but failed to deliver, resulting in a total loss to me along with many other entrepreneurs like myself, who were sucked in by the empty promise of financial support.

All the while I was contacted by some of my old business associates who offered me large sums of money, in once instance alone—one hundred thousand dollars just for an introduction to some of my international contacts. It was all very tempting but as far as I was concerned, if I arranged the contact I would still be involved, still be "part of the problem" and I couldn't do that in good conscience, so *that was that*. I was done with the hash business.

I kept at the import/wholesale business and continued on in the same vein, seeking out like-minded people with whom felt the same strong bond of trust and who shared the same *joie de vivre*. It was a similar kind of adventure without the hash, as I continued following my passion, documenting people and places of interest around the world *sans* the big money. Life was always about lifestyle for me. Time was always my gold. Fortunately I was still able to travel the world, keeping in touch with my old cronies and still free to do pretty much as I pleased. Most important for me, my time was still my own. I was still "Master of my Fate--Captain of my Soul."

Many years later, I learned from my old friend Curly that Sgt. Wallace had retired from the RCMP and had opened a tavern in another part of the province. As it happened, my old friend, Curly, *who I didn't want to get involved, way back when*, had gotten to know Wallace through their girlfriends, told me, fairly recently, that Wallace had changed his opinion of me over the years.

Back in the day when they first met, Wallace knew that Curly was a friend of mine and was certain he was involved with me in the hash business. After a few drinks at a party not long after they met, Wallace venomously spit out my name in a pass-along threat / warning to Curley; "You tell O'Brian I'm going to bust his ass" or words to that effect.

One day, a year or so after hearing this from Curly, I was up in Wallace's area selling jewelry. I thought it might be interesting to drop into his tavern to see if I recognized him, or him, me.

It was lunch-time as I took a seat in the semi-crowded pub and looked around. The guy behind the bar who I assumed would be the owner, didn't look old enough to be Wallace. The waiter took my order and when he came back with my beer I asked him who owned the pub. He replied, that he did. I asked him his name and he said "Wallace."

Then I asked him if he recognized me. He looked at me a bit quizzically and said "I don't think so." I said "You're sure?" and gave him pause to really look at me… he stared more intently, questioningly…"Jack O'Brian" I said with a smile.

"Jack O'Brian!" he exclaimed with a surprised look and a big grin, sticking out his hand to me "We had some times, didn't we?"

"I don't know, did we?" I replied, also with a big smile, as we shook hands.

He asked me how everything was, what was I up to etc. but the place was quite busy and he had customers waiting, so we couldn't really talk. He said he'd love to sit down and have a yarn with me some day, but that was never going to happen…unfortunately.

I finished my beer and left, feeling good about our encounter. For me there were no hard feelings. It was about "Cops and Robbers" and being on opposite sides of the fence. I felt there was understanding, appreciation and respect on each others part.

He knew from his years of intel and wiretaps that I was not one of the really "bad guys." I never dealt in anything but hash or grass and never involved myself with violence or other criminal activities or associated with anyone who did. I was totally against hard drugs like cocaine, heroin, meth etc. and had often spoken out against them over the years. He knew why I was into it and we all knew it would be legal one day.

AFTERWORD

Many years later I would become close friends with one of the upper echelon of the Halifax Police Department. He told me that over his long service with the police, spanning more than twenty years, at that time, he never had one incident where he was called to a scene because someone was high on marijuana and committing a violent crime.

The police, he told me, looked at marijuana as a low priority item.

Eventually I met a lovely woman from the corporate world, quite different from the one I had known, with whom I was blessed with the most wonderful daughter and I never looked back, that is to say, I never went back.

Reflecting back over the years, it's mostly with a sense of appreciation and immense gratitude for all the wild and amazing experiences I've had and all of the wonderful and weird people I encountered and all of the life lessons that came my way: the Good, the Bad and the Ugly. I embrace them all. I have a few regrets, but not too many and none that keep me up at night.

One of the most important lessons I learned early on was that excessive wealth certainly is not the key to happiness. It's an illusion that many buy into it because we are sold false dreams by those who want us to consume, consume, consume and brainwash us through marketing/media to think that the more we consume the happier we will be. *We need enough, that's all.* Money can be a good or bad thing...as we all know, it all depends on us and how we use it.

Time is life and it's how we spend our time each day what defines our lives. I have always been a seeker--adventure and discovery was my passion. For others it's their career and/or financial "success" and for some, those special ones, it's about the satisfaction they gain from the benefits they provide their communities and the world in general. And so it goes...

Life doesn't have to be a wild ride but what's important is that it is significant to you. It's all about "different strokes".... just not about "punching the time clock of life" as one old friend termed it.

One thing I learned early on my journey is that although we are all different, by culture and circumstance, we are all the same. By this I mean what we feel and desire, in terms of our basic human needs which include:

"Feeling a sense of Love and belonging, security, freedom, fun and personal power." (William Glasser)

≈

The hash farmer in Afghanistan or Morocco wants the same for his children as I do....peace, comfort, security...a chance at a better life... a better world.

It's a small percentage of ISIS fighters who are extreme religious zealots. Most of them are fighting because they lack so much of what we, *the privileged*, take for granted, especially the most important aspect: Security. The majority of these people are desperate and fighting just to feed their families.

Poverty, with its ensuing desperation, from what I've garnered on this sojourn is the main hatred-spawning condition, resulting in all of the unrest and conflict in the world today.

Many things have changed in the world since the days I write about; Indeed, the world has changed dramatically.

Several of the countries I traveled through are now too dangerous to venture into, due in large part to global terrorism, our new reality, corner-stoned on the obscenely unfair and totally unacceptable distribution of global wealth and proxy war.

The drug culture has become epidemic with the evolution of Narco- terrorism, another new term, and another new reality.

The promotion and preservation of basic human values has eroded to the degree that the political will of the world is so much more concerned with economy and the *will of the wealthy* than creating a peaceful secure world for all.

Like the old Sadu said to me back in India in another lifetime… "Heaven is not another place, somewhere out in the clouds. There is no other *"place"*, there's only here, and it is *here* that we create our own Heaven or Hell."

Of one thing I am certain, based on my travels and conversations/ discussions over my lifetime with hundreds or thousands of people across the social strata and around the globe, from super wealthy people to those living in pretty extreme poverty…

Until the extreme, hoarded wealth of the world is shared in a reasonable manner and the starvation and horrors that afflict the most vulnerable and desperate among us are dealt with, there can be no possible chance of world peace. How could there be?

My purpose in writing this story is to share these experiences and perspectives with the hope of contributing something worthwhile to the world.

If this book should do well financially, I pledge a substantial part of my earnings to support the causes I believe in, which are eradicating world poverty through holistic world programs and more pragmatic and fair distribution of wealth and supporting the fight against climate change.

One of the lessons I learned about money along the way, and the irony of it makes me laugh...is that the only thing you can do with it that will give you lasting satisfaction....is to give it away! Ha Ha Ha !
Namaste

ACKNOWLEDGEMENTS

My thanks go out to a number of people who have encouraged and supported me over the years. Special thanks to Kent Baker who always believed in me and encouraged me and whose help with editing and development early on was invaluable. To Syr Ruus for her amazing final editing and suggestions, to Sheri Elwood who believed in me and my project since forever, for her help in rewriting the beginning chapters, cover design, foreword and ongoing support, suggestions and encouragement. To Joel Geyer for his documentarian approach, words of wisdom and encouragement, to my brother Kevin Murphy for his encouragement and steadfast belief. To Anne Campbell for her editing help and suggestions, to Dawn Carson for her editing, encouragement and suggestions. To Tom Hudak for his encouragement, advice and suggestions and Dianne Wheeler for her suggestions and feedback. Judy Lake, for her encouragement and feedback; Dave Erickson for his inspiration for the title and words of encouragement and advice. To my daughter Emma-Leigh for her understanding and acceptance. Special thanks to my wife Hazel Campbel for enduring with me over the years while completing this project and for her idea for the final photo. To Vasanth Kumar for the great photo. And last but not least, to the many people I met during the course of my life who appeared when I most needed them.

Printed in Canada